Instrumentation for Future Parallel Computing Systems

ACM PRESS

Editor-in-Chief:

Peter Wegner, *Brown University*

ACM Press books represent a collaboration between the Association for Computing Machinery (ACM) and Addison-Wesley Publishing Company to develop and publish a broad range of new works. These works generally fall into one of four series.

Frontier Series. Books focused on novel and exploratory material at the leading edge of computer science and practice.

Anthology Series. Collected works of general interest to computer professionals and/or society at large.

Tutorial Series. Introductory books to help nonspecialists quickly grasp either the general concepts or the needed details of some specific topic.

History Series. Books documenting past developments in the field and linking them to the present.

In addition, ACM Press books include selected conference and workshop proceedings.

Instrumentation for Future Parallel Computing Systems

Edited by

Margaret Simmons
Rebecca Koskela
Ingrid Bucher

ACM Press
New York, New York

Addison-Wesley Publishing Company
The Advanced Book Program
Redwood City, California • Menlo Park, California • Reading, Massachusetts
New York • Don Mills, Ontario • Wokingham, United Kingdom • Amsterdam
Bonn • Sydney • Singapore • Tokyo • Madrid • San Juan

ACM Press Frontier Series
Instrumentation for Future Parallel Computer Systems

First printed 1989

Library of Congress Cataloging-in-Publication Data

Instrumentation for future parallel computer systems / [edited by]
  Margaret Simmons, Ingrid Bucher, Rebecca Koskela.
      p.   cm. — (ACM Press frontier series)
  "Based on a Los Alamos National Laboratory workshop conducted in 1988"
—T.p. verso.
   1. Parallel processing (Electronic computers)   2. Electronic digital
computers—Evaluation.   3. Computer software—Evaluation. I. Simmons,
Margaret, II. Bucher, Ingrid. III. Koskela, Rebecca. IV. Los Alamos National
Laboratory.
QA76.5.I4875   1989   004'.35—dc 19   89-302
ISBN 0-201-50390-5

Copyright © 1989 by the ACM Press, A Division of the Association for
Computing Machinery, Inc. (ACM).

All rights reserved. No part of this publication may be reproduced, stored in
a retrieval system, or transmitted in any form or by any means, electronic,
mechanical, photocopying, recording or otherwise, without prior written
permission of the publisher.

ABCDEFGHIJ-AL-89

CONTRIBUTORS

William Bohm
University of Manchester

William C. Brantley
IBM Thomas Watson Research Center

Robert J. Carpenter
National Bureau of Standards

Frederica Darema
IBM Thomas Watson Research Center

Blaine Gaither
Gould Electronics

Harry F. Jordan
University of Colorado

Koji Kinoshita
NEC Corporation

Allen D. Malony
Computer Science Department, University of Illinois

David Mandell
Los Alamos National Laboratory

Kevin P. McAuliffe
IBM Thomas Watson Research Center

James R. McGraw
Lawrence Livermore National Laboratory

Harry Nelson
Lawrence Livermore National Laboratory

Ton A. Ngo
IBM Thomas Watson Research Center

Gregory M. Papadopoulos
Massachusetts Institute of Technology

Daniel A. Reed
Computer Science Department, University of Illinois

Matthew Reilly
Digital Equipment Corporation

Patricia J. Teller
Department of Computer Science, The Courant Institute

Harold Trease
Los Alamos National Laboratory

PREFACE

In May, 1988 a "Workshop on Instrumentation for Future Parallel Computing Systems" was held in Santa Fe, New Mexico. The workshop was organized to exchange ideas among designers of hardware and software for high performance parallel computer systems, users of such systems, and members of the research community. Performance evaluation of parallel computer systems is a complex process; the main challenge in this area is the development of the required performance evaluation methods and tools to keep pace with the explosion of new system designs brought about by rapid technological advances. The next generation of high performance machines will likely all be parallel supercomputers. In order to effectively evaluate the performance of the current and future workloads on these systems, new kinds of measurement techniques and data will be necessary. Performance instrumentation, both hardware and software, on existing parallel systems is inadequate at best, or nonexistent.

The goal of the workshop was to clarify the desirable and feasible features of instrumentation for high performance computer systems, and to determine what should therefore be included in future system designs. The availability of integrated basic hardware and software for the collection of performance data would not only teach us how to program such systems more effectively, but would also lead to the design of more effective systems. To achieve this goal a group of designers, researchers, and users of such systems were invited to two intense days of presentations and discussion sessions.

For the discussions, participants were divided into three working groups: those interested in multiprocessors with common memory, a group concerned with parallel computers with distributed memory, and a group evaluating the special needs of dataflow computers. Each group was asked to consider the following questions during their discussions:

1. What quantities are necessary to characterize the performance of parallel computing systems?
2. If you could choose an ideal list of quantities that you would like to see measured, what would you choose and what priority would you give to each of these choices?
3. Which of the above quantities must be measured simultaneously?
4. Measurement tools usually distort the behavior of the system being measured. How much distortion is tolerable and how can it be minimized or corrected for?

Among the results of the workshop were two lists: a minimum set of measurement tools that are a necessity for future systems, and an additional set of measurement tools that would be highly desirable beyond this minimum set. The interaction between designers and users brought about the realization that many needs are common to both groups. The participants felt that this interaction also further deepened their knowledge of and appreciation for each other's positions and problems. The hardware designers better understood the limitations of software and the software designers felt that they gained insight into the problems presented by hardware. Users and researchers had an opportunity to make their needs and wishes known to both groups.

This volume contains both the papers presented at the general sessions of the workshop and summaries of the working group discussions. The book should be of interest to hardware and software designers of parallel computing systems, to users looking for a deeper understanding of system performance and striving to improve that performance, and to advanced students who wish to gain insight into the performance evaluation of parallel computer systems.

The papers included in the book were selected for their relevance to the questions posed by the workshop. The breadth of interest and expertise represented at the workshop is reflected in the range of papers chosen. The collection as a whole provides a description of the challenges and opportunities facing each of the groups of workshop attendees: designers, researchers, and users. The papers are organized into roughly two groups: those with proposed or existing instrumentation systems, and those relating experiences with such systems.

The first three chapters in the book present are keynote addresses that give details of the two best instrumented research systems in existence today: the Cedar project at the University of Illinois and the RP3 project at IBM. The first chapter relates the approaches taken in the implementation of instrumentation for the multiprocessor Cedar. One of the goals of the Cedar project was to build a prototype of a "performance instrumented computer" that offers the user the ability to observe parallel operation at various levels of detail. The next two chapters are concerned with the IBM multiprocessor project, RP3. Chapter 2 describes the performance monitoring hardware of the RP3. The RP3 system supports both a shared-memory and a message-passing paradigm. Performance monitoring instrumentation was included in the design phase of the machine in order to satisfy the primary goal of understanding parallel hardware and software. A methodology for analyzing the performance of parallel applications is presented in Chapter 3. Performance analysis of parallel applications is considered from two points of view: that of the application programmer and that of the hardware designer.

Chapter 4 discusses the visualization tools and design approach for performance instrumentation in the Cedar project. This chapter addresses the problems posed by the volume of data from performance measurements. These data must be presented in ways that emphasize important events and elide irrelevant data.

Chapter 5 presents an intriguing proposal to those who desire better instrumentation for debugging, program analysis, and performance tuning. Papadopoulos suggests that the perceived need for dynamic and specific instrumentation "is an artifact of the mismatch (and inadequacy) of current parallel programming languages and processor architecture." He proposes that determinate debugging, theoretical performance prediction, and relaxed execution instrumentation can be accomplished through declarative languages and dataflow machines.

In response to the first question posed to the working groups, Chapter 6 lists the minimum set of instrumentation that Gaither finds necessary for shared-memory parallel systems.

Bohm, et. al. state in Chapter 7 that the key problem inhibiting effective use of parallel computer systems is the absence of tools to support the process of mapping an application onto the parallel resources of a machine. They present the "levels of abstraction" view of parallel computer systems that helps to organize and structure an understanding of these systems and to categorize the debugging and monitoring tools needed to visualize program and machine behavior.

Chapter 8 describes the implementation of measurement support for software performance tuning on the 32 processor, shared-memory M31 VAX. It also discusses the problem of distortion posed in the fourth question to the working groups.

Carpenter presents a range of approaches to performance measurements in Chapter 9. This chapter also addresses the problem of the perturbations caused by performance measurements.

The next four chapters discuss performance instrumentation from the users' point of view. Chapter 10 discusses the instrumentation necessary for measuring barrier performance to determine the effect on the performance of a parallel program. Barriers are a convenient synchronization mechanism for parallel programs. In Chapter 11, Nelson describes his experiences with the hardware performance monitors on the CRAY X-MP at Lawrence Livermore National Laboratory. Chapter 12 discusses the problems encountered in parallelizing a large scientific code orginally written for a serial machine. Mandell and Trease list the software tools that would help in the development of large parallel codes. In Chapter 13 Kinoshita describes the ANALYZER/SX, a performance tuning tool available on the NEC series of supercomputers. This tool provides both a static and dynamic analysis of a computer program. He discusses program optimization through vectorization and tuning.

The common memory working group focused their discussions in two areas: measurement and tuning of applications' performance on current and future systems, and the performance analysis of hardware and software to identify bottlenecks in both the computer system and the application. Chapter 14 considers data available from existing instrumentation and the information that is currently not available in these two contexts.

In Chapter 15, Reed begins with a review of distributed-memory systems, including proposed communication paradigms and commercial systems. He then covers the issues relevant to distributed-memory performance instrumentation from the working group's perspective.

Dataflow architectures have major consequences for performance measurement and evaluation. Chapter 16 covers the discussions concerned with performance techniques and tools most appropriate to dataflow computers. McGraw gives some brief background information on dataflow computing and goes on to address the issues raised and to present possible techniques for performance evaluation of dataflow systems.

ACKNOWLEDGMENTS

Many people contributed to the success of the workshop and to the production of this book. We offer our sincere thanks to all of them.

In particular, we thank Ann Hayes, Andy White, and Norm Morse for their support and encouragement, Yvonne Martinez, Debbie Martinez and Sheila Girard, and especially Jan Hull for help with the organization of the workshop. The workshop was sponsored by Los Alamos National Laboratory. We would also like to thank Cray Research, Incorporated and Gould Electronics for their financial support.

A number of people have contributed to the preparation of this book, including Ann Garnett, Kyle Wheeler, Marge Blackwell, Lucille Maestas, and JoAnn Olivas. We are grateful for their help. We thank Pat Teller, Dan Reed, and Jim McGraw for their excellent summaries of the three working group discussions. They each spent many hours with audio tapes and transcripts trying to make sense and order out of confusion and chaos. They have done a superb job.

Finally, Yvonne Martinez has done an outstanding job in her careful and meticulous preparation of the manuscript. For this, we owe her special thanks.

FOREWORD

Time. Where *does* it go? We often ask ourselves this question, partly in the hopes of catching some of the elusive quantity that slips by us and partly to do better in utilizing it the next day. Those of us in the business of supercomputers can justifiably ask the same question and for the same reasons as we try to obtain optimal performance out of the machines and the applications that are executed on them. Where does the time go? Where is it spent?

In an attempt to get a better handle on this process of measuring supercomputer performance, we sponsored a workshop on instrumentation of supercomputers. Experts in hardware and software aspects, as well as major users of supercomputers, were invited to attend. Both the current status of instrumentation monitoring and needs for the future were discussed. This book represents the proceedings of that first workshop, both in the form of presented papers and synopses of workshop discussion groups.

February 1989   Ann H. Hayes

CONTENTS

CHAPTER 1	**Multiprocessor Instrumentation: Approaches for Cedar** *Allen D. Malony*	1
	1.1 Introduction	1
	1.2 The Cedar System	2
	1.3 Cluster Concurrency Instrumentation	4
	1.4 Timing Instrumentation	8
	1.5 Profiling Instrumentation	15
	1.6 Tracing Instrumentation	19
	1.7 Execution Flow Analysis	24
	1.8 Hardware Instrumentation	26
	1.9 Conclusion	31
CHAPTER 2	**RP3 Performance Monitoring Hardware** *William C. Brantley Kevin P. McAuliffe Ton A. Ngo*	35
	2.1 Introduction	35
	2.2 Overview	37
	2.3 Events Monitored	39

	2.4	Sample Data	41
	2.5	Desirable Features not Included	42
CHAPTER 3	**Parallel Applications Performance Methodology** *Frederica Darema*		49
	3.1	Introduction	49
	3.2	Performance Objectives	50
	3.3	Performance Methodology for Parallel Applications	50
	3.4	Tools for Measurement and Analysis	51
	3.5	Scaling Methods for Performance Predictions	53
	3.6	Summary	56
CHAPTER 4	**Visualizing Parallel Computer System Performance** *Allen D. Malony Daniel A. Reed*		59
	4.1	Introduction	59
	4.2	Experimental Performance Analysis	61
	4.3	HyperView: A Hypercube Visualization Tool	64
	4.4	Application Performance Displays	74
	4.5	Current Research	81
CHAPTER 5	**Program Development and Performance Monitoring on the Monsoon Dataflow Multiprocessor** *Gregory M. Papadopoulos*		91
	5.1	Introduction	91
	5.2	Getting the Program Right	94
	5.3	Predicting Performance	95
	5.4	Hardware Support for Idealized Execution	103

	5.5	Instruction Coloring	107
	5.6	Performance Monitoring	108
	5.7	Conclusion	108
CHAPTER 6	**Instrumentation for Future Parallel Systems** *Blaine Gaither*		111
	6.1	Introduction	111
	6.2	Parallel Processing Instrumentation	112
	6.3	Requirements for Instrumentation	113
	6.4	Gould NP1 Instrumentation	113
	6.5	Parallel System Instrumentation	115
	6.6	Implementation	118
	6.7	Conclusion	119
CHAPTER 7	**Monitoring Experimental Parallel Machines** *A.P.W. Bohm J.R. Gurd M.C. Kallstrom*		121
	7.1	Introduction	121
	7.2	The Manchester Dataflow System	123
	7.3	ParSiFal	131
	7.4	Conclusions	137
CHAPTER 8	**Instrumentation for Application Performance Tuning: The M31 System** *Matthew Reilly*		143
	8.1	A Statement of the Problems	143
	8.2	Useful Features for a Measurement System	145
	8.3	An Experimental Implementation	146
	8.4	Some of the Lessons Learned	156

CHAPTER 9	**Performance Measurement Instrumentation at NBS** *Robert J. Carpenter*	159
	9.1 Introduction	159
	9.2 What to measure?	160
	9.3 Cost Considerations in Measurement	160
	9.4 Measuring Execution Duration	161
	9.5 Measuring Resource Utilization	176
	9.6 System Software Aspects	182
	9.7 Summary	182
	9.8 References	183
CHAPTER 10	**Problems in Characterizing Barrier Performance** *Harry F. Jordan*	185
	10.1 Introduction	185
	10.2 Implementation of the Barrier	186
	10.3 Accounting for Barrier Performance	189
	10.4 Instrumentation for Barrier Measurement	191
	10.5 Examples	194
	10.6 Conclusions	197
CHAPTER 11	**Experiences With Performance Monitors** *Harry Nelson*	201
	11.1 Introduction	201
	11.2 What Can be Monitored?	201
	11.3 Results of an Example Run	203
	11.4 Other Uses	205
	11.5 Summary	205

CHAPTER 12	**Parallel Processing a Real Code—A Case History**	209
	David Mandell and Harold Trease	
	12.1 Introduction	209
	12.2 Multitasking POLLY	210
	12.3 Autotasking X3D	211
	12.4 Results	211
	12.5 Lessons Learned and Recommendations	218
CHAPTER 13	**An Experience with the ANALYZER/SX Performance Tuning Tool**	223
	Koji Kinoshita	
	13.1 Introduction	223
	13.2 Outline of the ANALYZER/SX	223
	13.3 Example of Performance Analysis	225
	13.4 Problem	227
	13.5 Conclusion	231
CHAPTER 14	**Common Memory Working Group Summary**	233
	Patricia J. Teller	
	14.1 Introduction	233
	14.2 Algorithm and System Tuning	234
	14.3 Debugging	234
	14.4 Data Collection Tradeoffs	235
	14.5 Instrumentation Techniques	235
	14.6 Conclusions	237

CHAPTER 15	**Distributed Memory Working Group Summary** *Daniel A. Reed*		239
	15.1	Introduction	239
	15.2	Background	241
	15.3	Workshop Discussions	245
	15.4	Conclusions	249
CHAPTER 16	**Dataflow Working Group Summary** *James R. McGraw*		251
	16.1	Introduction	251
	16.2	Background	252
	16.3	Implications of Dataflow Approach for Measurement	254
	16.4	Key Items that Need to Be Measured	255
	16.5	Suggested Techniques for Performance Analysis and Measurement	257
	16.6	Summary	260

Instrumentation for Future Parallel Computing Systems

1

Multiprocessor Instrumentation: Approaches for Cedar

Allen D. Malony[1]

1.1 Introduction

Parallel systems pose a unique challenge to performance measurement and instrumentation. The complexity of these systems manifests itself as an increase in performance complexity as well as programming complexity. The complex interaction of the many architectural, hardware, and software features of these systems results in a significantly larger space of possible performance behavior and potential performance bottlenecks. Programming parallel systems requires that users understand the performance characteristics of the machines and be able to modify their programs and algorithms accordingly. The instrumentation problem, therefore, is to develop tools to aid the user in investigating performance problems and in determining the most effective way of exploiting the high performance capabilities of parallel systems.

This paper gives observations on the parallel system instrumentation problem in the context of the Cedar multiprocessor. The Cedar system integrates several architectural, hardware, and software concepts for parallel operation.

---

[1] This work was supported in part by NSF Grant Numbers NSF MIP–8410110 and NSF DCR 84–06916, DOE Grant Number DOE DE–FG02–85ER25001, the Air Force Office of Scientific Research Grant Number AFOSR–F49620–86–C–0136, and a donation from IBM.

The combination makes Cedar a particularly interesting machine for investigating instrumentation issues and developing prototype tools. The different needs for performance evaluation on the Cedar machine define the instrumentation requirements. The implementation of instrumentation tools, however, involves tradeoffs in design, resolution, and accuracy, and must be weighed against the payoff in better performance evaluation. This discussion of instrumentation tools targeted for Cedar considers these tradeoffs.

The following presentation is somewhat historical in that it describes the tools in the order in which they were developed. It is important to understand that these tools are targeted to an actual machine and therefore might lack certain instrumentation sophistication possible in less restrictive environments, as in the case of simulation. Nevertheless, to develop good instrumentation techniques for generating detailed performance data of parallel system execution, it is instructive to study prototype tools designed within the constraints placed by real parallel machines.

One of the goals of the performance evaluation activities of the Cedar project is to build a prototype of a *performance instrumented computer* [1,2] (see Figure 1.1). The concept is one of a standard computer system that contains additional performance measurement hardware and software. The additional hardware allows easy access to performance-critical information in the machine (e.g., cache misses, memory conflicts); it allows measurements of these points to be easily made in response to various triggers, and it allows easy storage of selected results. The additional software allows a user to specify which measurements to make; it allows the user to observe performance results and store these results in a database of performance information.

1.2 The Cedar System

The Cedar system of the University of Illinois is characterized by the hierarchical organization of both its computational capabilities and memory system [3,4]. It consists of multiple clusters, each of which is a multivector processor comprising eight computational elements (CEs) (see Figure 1.2). Parallelism can be exploited at three levels. Within each CE, operations on vectors can be done in vector mode. Each cluster is a tightly coupled multiprocessor that can exploit fine grained parallelism through loop-level concurrency. Finally, multiple clusters can be used for medium and large grain parallelism, as well as extended forms of fine grain parallelism. Presently, each cluster is a modified Alliant FX/8.

The memory organization is hierarchical as well, with communication increasing in cost at each level. At the lowest level, each CE has a set of private scalar and vector registers. The next two levels, a cache and a cluster memory, are shared by the CEs within the same cluster. Finally, all clusters have access

1.2. The Cedar System   3

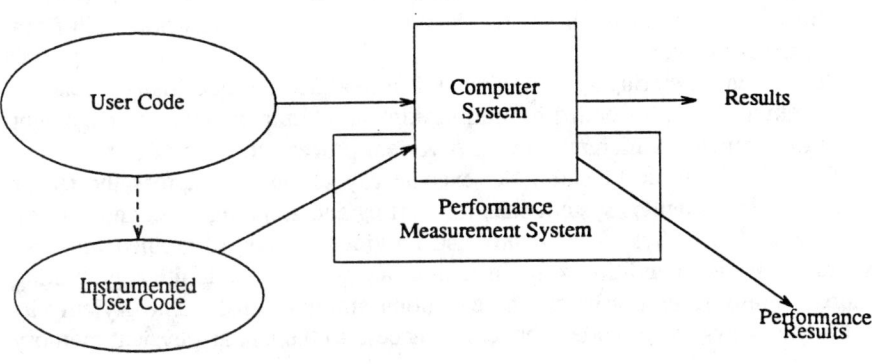

FIGURE 1.1
Performance instrumented computer.

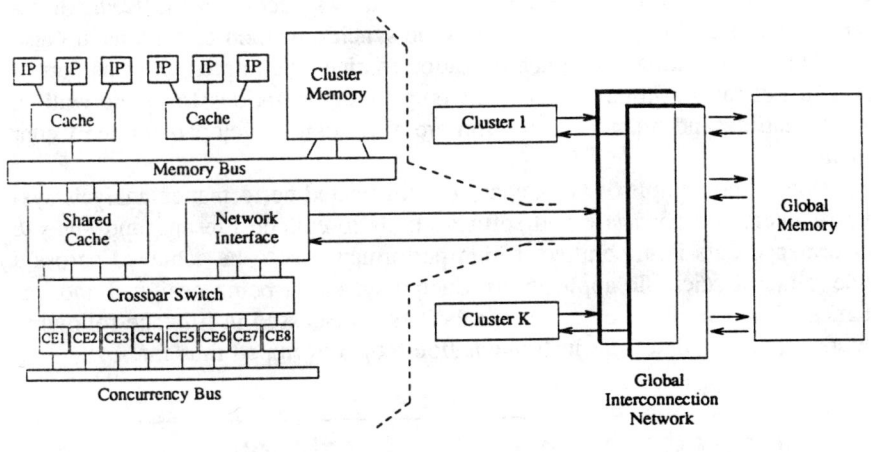

FIGURE 1.2
The Cedar system organization.

to a large global memory. This global memory is accessed through two unidirectional switching networks, one for downloading data from memory, the other for uploading. These switching networks are 2-stage omega networks built from 8 × 8 crossbar switches.

The Cedar operating system, Xylem, is a modification of Alliant's Concentrix operating system extended for multitasking and virtual memory management of the Cedar memory hierarchy [5,6]. A Xylem process consists of one or more *cluster tasks*. Multiple cluster tasks execute asynchronously across the Cedar system. Xylem provides system calls for starting and stopping tasks and waiting for tasks to finish. System calls are also provided for coarse-grained intertask synchronization. In addition to multitasking, Xylem supports multiprogramming whereby multiple processes can be executing simultaneously. The Xylem virtual memory system provides convenient access to the Cedar physical memory hierarchy.

Fortran is the focus of language and compiler development for Cedar. Cedar Fortran is derived from Alliant FX/Fortran with extensions for memory allocation, concurrency control, multitasking, and synchronization [7]. New data type specification statements reflect the Xylem memory access and locality structure. Vector concurrency is available through array section notation, conditional vector statements, and vector reduction functions. DOALL and DOACROSS constructs specify parallel execution of loop iterations on processors within a single cluster task or spread across multiple cluster tasks. Multitasking routines provide an interface between Cedar Fortan and Xylem for task creation and control. A set of synchronization functions allows access to the Cedar hardware synchronization primitives. Cray-style synchronization operations are also provided. Multitasking and synchronization routines are implemented as part of a Cedar Fortran run-time library [8]. Compiler optimizations for vectorization, parallelization, and memory allocation are also being developed for the Cedar machine.

Due to the complexity of Cedar, a sophisticated performance analysis system of integrated hardware and software tools to collect, present, and analyze performance data is imperative if high performance is to be achieved across a wide range of scientific applications. Such a system is being designed and implemented and an overview of its capabilities is discussed in [9]. The following sections give details of the instrumentation tools developed thus far.

1.3 Cluster Concurrency Instrumentation

The first Cedar performance instrumentation tool implemented was a tool to measure the average number of processors physically active during a computation on an Alliant FX/8 cluster [10-12]. To better characterize a parallel program's execution on the FX/8 it was important to determine the degree of physical parallelism actually being achieved. A basic performance efficiency metric, *concurrency efficiency* or CEFF, can be derived from measuring the amount of time i processors are active, where $i = 1, n$ and n is the total number of processors available. CEFF indicates the percentage of available physical parallelism being used by the program. It is an interesting performance metric in that a bound on the maximum speedup possible on a cluster for the measured program run can be obtained.

1.3.1 Concurrent Operation on an FX/8 Cluster

A program that has been compiled for concurrent operation on the FX/8 will be allocated the entire computational complex. All processors are thus available for use by the program during its execution. [1] As the program advances through periods of sequential and concurrent operation, the number of active processors will change. Measurements of how the program's execution time was spent in the different levels of physical parallelism must be made to calculate the CEFF metric.

1.3.2 CEFF Analysis

If T_i is the amount of time a program spends executing with i processors active, where $i = 1, n$ and n is the total number of processors, concurrency efficiency is defined as

$$CEFF = \left(\frac{\sum_{i=1}^{i=n} i * T_i}{n * T} \right) * 100\%$$

$$where\ T = \sum_{i=1}^{i=n} T_i$$

Given the concurrency timing information, T_i, it is simple to derive *concurrency utilization* results, CU_i, as the percentage of time i processors are active:

$$CU_i = \frac{T_i}{T} * 100\%$$

The CEFF metric indicates the average percentage of the available parallel processing resource used by the program. The CU values give a breakdown of execution time spent in each concurrent execution state. [2] The *average concur-*

---

[1] The same is true for a Xylem task that runs concurrently on a cluster.

[2] A concurrent state is defined for each possible number of active processors. Concurrent state i is the state where only i processors are active.

rency, defined as $CAVG = n*CEFF$, gives the average number of processors active as well as an upper bound on program speedup possible for this run. It is an upper bound because active processors may not be directly contributing to the overall program progress; such is the case with synchronization operations. Whereas a low CEFF value implies a low level of concurrent processor activity and, therefore, a poor speedup performance, a high CEFF value is only an indication of high processor concurrency and does not necessarily reflect good parallel performance. CEFF and CU values must be considered with other performance metrics to determine the degree of *effective parallelism* being achieved.

1.3.3 CEFF Implementation

Ideally, changes in the number of active processors should be detected to measure the time spent in the different concurrent states. However, detecting changes in concurrent state is difficult on the FX/8 because it occurs at the instruction level. One alternative considered for the Cedar system was to build a special hardware monitor to look at processor activity signals. This had several drawbacks including signal accessibility, design complexity, and the ability to filter the timing data on a per process basis. The second alternative was to instrument the object code to monitor the instructions that resulted in concurrency state changes and to keep software time measurements. Although exact timing could be maintained by this approach, it was intrusive and its implementation required a more complete tracing facility (see Section 1.4).

A desirable implementation would be easy to design and build, would minimally affect program operation, but would give reasonably accurate CEFF statistics. The approach taken was based on a sampling technique commonly used for profiling. Concentrix was modified to implement the CEFF measurements.

When concurrency efficiency measurements are enabled, the program is interrupted every 10 msec and the state of each processor in the computational complex is sampled. It is possible to determine if a CE is inactive when the program is interrupted by comparing the CE's program counter to a known *idle* value. The total number of active CE's, i, is determined with each interrupt and a counter associated with each concurrent state, N_i, is incremented. The N_is are set to zero at the beginning of the program.

At the end of the program's execution, the time spent in concurrent state i, T_i, is calculated by multiplying the ith concurrency count value, N_i, by 10 msec. The CEFF and CU values can then be easily computed as shown in Section 1.3.2.

From an implementation standpoint, maintaining the information necessary to calculate concurrency efficiency is simple and cheap. Only eight concurrency state counters are needed for the FX/8. These counters can easily be placed in the user's process structure along with the other timing and profiling information.

Determining the active processors and incrementing the appropriate N_i counter is the only real-time processing required.

1.3.4 CEFF Results

CEFF results can be produced for a program's entire execution or for user-selected program sections. The results produced include T_i, CU_i, T, $CAVG$, and $CEFF$. An example of the output is shown in Table 1.1.

There are several things to consider when interpreting the CEFF results. The timing measurements assume that the current process was executing throughout the last 10-msec time interval. Because of the 10-msec sampling procedure, the concurrent state timing data is only a statistical approximation to the actual concurrency timing information. Furthermore, determining CE cluster utilization from a single measurement made every 10 msec is prone to errors because the number of CEs used by the program can change many times during a 10-msec time interval.

It is important also to remember that the concurrency efficiency results only represent measurements of physical processor activity. No analysis is made of what the processors are actually doing when they are active. Thus, the CEFF results should not necessarily be interpreted as effective parallelism.

CEFF results can be used with other measurements to better characterize program performance. For instance, speedups from 1 processor to n processors can help to clarify the effective parallelism. Suppose a program running on eight processors, as opposed to one, achieves a speedup $S = 6$ and a CEFF value of 80% ($CAVG = 6.4$). Although only 80% of the processors are utilized on average, almost all of the average processor concurrency is being used effectively. In this case, the user might conclude that the ability to keep more processors active is the problem. However, $S = 2$ for a program with $CEFF = 80\%$ indicates a low effective parallelism, likely due to synchronization overhead or a large sequential component.

The CU measurements are interesting because they give a histogram of concurrent activity. The CU_i values where $i < n$ are important because they represent periods of reduced parallelism when processors are actually idle. The value CU_1 is most important since it is the percentage of time the program is executing sequentially. The CU_1 value can be plugged directly into Amdahl's equation to get the projected maximum program speedup for p processors.[3] For the results produced by CEFF above:

---

[3] Amdahl's equation is defined as $\lim_{p \to \infty} S_p = \frac{1}{1 - F_p}$ where F_p is the fraction of time all p processors are active. We assume that the percentages of all concurrent activity are summed to get F_p. Thus, the calculated asymptotic speedup is actually optimistic.

TABLE 1.1
CEFF Results

Number of active CEs	Seconds	Concurrency (%)
1	3.37	28.25%
2	0.39	3.27%
3	0.30	2.51%
4	0.51	4.28%
5	0.75	6.29%
6	1.02	8.55%
7	1.49	12.49%
8	4.10	34.37%
avg. active CEs	total seconds	efficiency
5.05	1.93	63.07%

$$\lim_{p \to \infty} S_p = \frac{1}{\frac{CU_1}{100\%}} = \frac{1}{.2825} = 3.54$$

Although $CAVG = 5.05$, the asymptotic speedup is limited by the significant sequential component.

1.4 Timing Instrumentation

After the implementation of the CEFF utility, it was clear that a more extensive overall process timing utility was required for Cedar. There are two main issues in measuring process execution time on a high-performance multiprocessing system: the time measurement accuracy and the timing of concurrent operation. The need for more accurate time measurements increases as system performance increases because of the finer time granularity of events of interest. Measurement techniques based on periodic sampling of the system state are insufficient for a high-performance multiprocessing environment. Strategies to directly measure execution time using a high-resolution real-time clock provide more accurate and detailed execution time measurements. Moreover, tasks can be in various states of execution requiring a more detailed breakdown of execution time measurements [13,14].

A timing utility, called HRTIME, has been implemented for the Cedar system [15]. The goal of the HRTIME utility is to provide high-resolution, detailed timing measurements of parallel operation of multitasked Xylem processes. HRTIME gives a complete timing account of both execution and non-execution task states. In addition, HRTIME provides individual processor timing measurements to give a detailed account of the time spent in various states of sequential and concurrent execution.

1.4.1 HRTIME Motivation

HRTIME addresses several shortcomings of the standard UNIX approach to process timing found on most multiprocessor systems and exemplified by Concentrix. When HRTIME was implemented, Concentrix was using the UNIX sampled execution time technique. More accurate timing can be gained through measured execution time. Briefly, measured execution time is based on determining the elapsed time, spent in a particular process state by recording the value of a high-resolution real-time clock when the state begins and when it ends. The difference between the two recorded time values is the elapsed time which is added to a total execution time kept for that process state. Measured execution time forms the basis for HRTIME and recently has been incorporated by Alliant into Concentrix.

However, Concentrix only records a single USER and SYSTEM time value for each process; for concurrent operation, HRTIME should keep separate time values for each processor used by a program. Additionally, the operating system (OS) instrumentation required to measure execution time allowed the execution state types to be extended as well as nonexecution states to be monitored. These features have been included in the HRTIME design.

Finally, Cedar requires a timing facility that maintains time measurements for a multitasked Xylem process. In particular, there needs to be a way to record a single global process time and to time various levels of task concurrency. HRTIME provides these mechanisms as well.

1.4.2 HRTIME Design

HRTIME is based on measured task timing with all times measured at 10-μsec resolution [13,14]. The Concentrix USER and SYSTEM process states are extended to four task execution states, and the measured times spent in these states are kept on a per-processor basis. Nonexecution states are also defined to track the time a task spends ready, blocked, or idle.

Execution States. Generally, task execution states can be partitioned according to the type of code being executed. Four execution states are defined by HRTIME: USER, SYSTEM, OVERHEAD, and KERNEL. The USER state is active when user code is being executed. Processing of system calls occurs in the SYSTEM state. Interrupt processing that can be attributed to the current task falls into the OVERHEAD state; this includes interrupts for page faults and general exceptions, such as a floating point exception. Interrupts not directly associated with the current task are processed in the KERNEL state; cross-processor interrupts, device interrupts and timer interrupts are considered part of the KERNEL state. Actually, the KERNEL state is not a task execution state at all, but a state in which the operating system itself is executing. For this reason, only the USER, SYSTEM and OVERHEAD states are timed for a task.

In a multiprocessor system such as Cedar, it is possible for a task to be executing sequentially on one processor or concurrently on several processors. To further audit execution time, HRTIME keeps time measurements on a processing resource basis. In Cedar, a sequential task executes on an interactive processor (IP), a detached CE, and/or one CE of a cluster. HRTIME maintains a USER, SYSTEM, and OVERHEAD timer for each of these sequential processing resources as part of the overall task time measurements.

All concurrent tasks execute on the computational complex of the Alliant FX/8. [4] However, it is possible for processors participating in a concurrent computation to be in different states of execution; e.g., CE 0 is in USER mode while CE 3 is in SYSTEM mode and CE 6 is in OVERHEAD mode, and so on (see Table 1.2).

For this reason, the execution states should really be monitored at the processor level. For concurrent tasks, HRTIME measures execution times per processor per state. [5] USER, SYSTEM, and OVERHEAD timers are therefore defined for each of the eight CEs that can participate in a cluster task's execution.

Although the execution state timers defined above give detailed timing information, a complicated calculation must be made to determine total elapsed time, especially in the case of a concurrent task. For this purpose, a VIRTUAL execution state is defined; when any processing resource is executing in USER, SYSTEM, or OVERHEAD state, the task is in a VIRTUAL execution state and a VIRTUAL time value is being updated.

As mentioned before, Xylem supports multitasking of a process for parallel execution across multiple Cedar clusters. Like the VIRTUAL timer for a Xylem task, a Xylem process will also have a process virtual timer, P_VIRTUAL. The motivation for a Xylem process virtual timer is to determine total elapsed execution time for an entire process. The update mechanism is the same as for the task virtual timer except that it is based on when tasks are executing. When any Xylem task is executing in USER, SYSTEM, or OVERHEAD state, the Xylem process is in P_VIRTUAL execution state and a P_VIRTUAL time value is being updated.

---

[4] A task is said to be concurrent if it requires more than one CE during its execution.

[5] This is not done by Concentrix. Whenever Concentrix detects any processor to be in SYSTEM state, the whole process is considered to be in SYSTEM state. USER time accumulates only when all processors are in USER state.

TABLE 1.2
Concurrent Execution States

```
         CE7    CE6    CE5    CE4    CE3    CE2    CE1    CE0
          .      .      .      .      .      .      .      .
          .      .      .      .      .      .      .      .
          .      .      .      .      .      .      .      .
|       +------+------+------+------+------+------+------+------+   UUUUU  single CE
|       |IIIII |IIIII |IIIII |IIIII |IIIII |IIIII |IIIII |UUUUU |   UUUUU  executing,
|       |IIIII |IIIII |IIIII |IIIII |IIIII |IIIII |IIIII |UUUUU |   UUUUU  USER
|       |IIIII |IIIII |IIIII |IIIII |IIIII |IIIII |IIIII |UUUUU |
|       +------+------+------+------+------+------+------+------+   SSSSS  single CE
|       |  u   |  u   |  u   |  u   |  u   |  u   |  u   |  u   |   SSSSS  executing,
  e     |  u   |  u   |  u   |  u   |  u   |  u   |  u   |  u   |   SSSSS  SYSTEM
  x     |  u   |  u   |  u   +------+  u   |  u   |  u   |  u   |
  e     |  u   +------+  u   |  s   |  u   +------+  u   |  u   |   OOOOO  single CE
  c     |  u   |  s   |  u   |  s   |  u   |  o   |  u   |  u   |   OOOOO  executing,
  u     +------+  s   |  u   +------+------+  o   +------+  u   |   OOOOO  OVERHEAD
  t     |  o   |  s   |  u   |  o   |  s   |  o   |IIIII |  u   |
  i     |  o   |  s   +------+------+  s   |  o   |IIIII +------+   IIIII
  o     |  o   |  s   |  s   |  u   |  s   |  o   |IIIII |  s   |   IIIII  idle
  n     +------+------+------+------+------+------+IIIII +------+   IIIII
        |  u   |  u   |IIIII |IIIII |  u   |  u   |IIIII |IIIII |
  t     |  u   +------+IIIII |IIIII |  u   +------+IIIII |IIIII |     u    multiple CEs
  i     |  u   |IIIII |IIIII |IIIII |  u   |IIIII |IIIII |IIIII |     u    executing,
  m     +------+------+------+------+------+------+------+------+     u    USER
  e     |UUUUU |IIIII |IIIII |IIIII |IIIII |IIIII |IIIII |IIIII |
        |UUUUU |IIIII |IIIII |IIIII |IIIII |IIIII |IIIII |IIIII |     s    multiple CEs
|       +------+IIIII |IIIII |IIIII |IIIII |IIIII |IIIII |IIIII |     s    executing,
|       |SSSSS |IIIII |IIIII |IIIII |IIIII |IIIII |IIIII |IIIII |     s    SYSTEM
|       |SSSSS |IIIII |IIIII |IIIII |IIIII |IIIII |IIIII |IIIII |
|       +------+IIIII |IIIII |IIIII |IIIII |IIIII |IIIII |IIIII |     o    multiple CEs
|       |OOOOO |IIIII |IIIII |IIIII |IIIII |IIIII |IIIII |IIIII |     o    executing,
|       +------+IIIII |IIIII |IIIII |IIIII |IIIII |IIIII |IIIII |     o    OVERHEAD
|       |UUUUU |IIIII |IIIII |IIIII |IIIII |IIIII |IIIII |IIIII |
  v     +------+------+------+------+------+------+------+------+
          .      .      .      .      .      .      .      .
          .      .      .      .      .      .      .      .
          .      .      .      .      .      .      .      .
```

Nonexecution States. In addition to the execution states, three nonexecution task states are recognized by HRTIME: READY, BLOCKED, and IDLE. When a task is ready to execute, but not currently running, it is in the READY state. Similarly, a task is in the BLOCKED state when it is blocked from execution. The IDLE state occurs when a task is waiting for some work to do. Because the task is not executing, only one timer is needed for each of these non-execution states.

1.4.3 HRTIME Use

The HRTIME utility is enabled for all processes. Xylem maintains the time measurements as part of each process's state. The state timers are stored as 64-bit integer values indicating the number of 10-μsec time units measured. The timer data structures are allocated as part of a larger process measurement structure in the process's read-only address space. This allocation allows reference to any of the timers directly from the user's program.

The HRTIME utility allows a user to make timing measurements for selected sections of a program as well as for the entire program [15]. The general procedure for making time measurements of a section of a program task is shown below:

1. Read HRTIME measurements for the current task
2. Execute program section
3. Read a second HRTIME measurement sample
4. Calculate the time differences between samples

The time required to execute the program section is the difference between the two HRTIME samples taken before and after the program section. If the time samples are saved, a time-sample trace can be kept during program execution and a post processor used to calculate the desired incremental time values.

In some cases, the user will want to time a program as a whole. The *hrtime* command will time a program and produce HRTIME results for all program tasks. An example of the HRTIME output for one task of a multitasked parallel program running under Xylem is shown in Table 1.3.

1.4.4 Interpreting HRTIME Measurements

HRTIME provides significantly more detailed execution timing information than the standard Concentrix USER and SYSTEM times. Nonexecution times are also generated. Interpreting the time measurements, however, requires some understanding of the program's operation.

TABLE 1.3
HRTIME Results

PROCESS/TASK TIME				
process virtual	:	5.89677		
task virtual	:	5.89677		
not ready	:	0.18924		
ready	:	1.64093		
idle	:	0.10224		

IP, DETACHED CE, and CLUSTER TIME				
		User	System	Overhead
ip	:	0.00000	0.00000	0.00000
dce	:	0.00105	0.05764	0.01262
cluster	:	0.00000	0.00000	0.00000

CE TIME				
		User	System	Overhead
ce [0]	:	5.73250	0.00092	0.00737
ce [1]	:	5.73529	0.00000	0.00335
ce [2]	:	5.73540	0.00000	0.00393
ce [3]	:	5.73318	0.00416	0.00863
ce [4]	:	5.73358	0.00000	0.00436
ce [5]	:	5.73354	0.00000	0.00264
ce [6]	:	5.73285	0.00000	0.00288
ce [7]	:	5.71049	0.02005	0.00373

One aspect of HRTIME that might be curious is the definition of USER, SYSTEM, and OVERHEAD states. Some system processing actually occurs on behalf of the user and, therefore, should be measured separately from the overhead of general OS operations. Separate measurements let the user know how much overhead processing the program really experiences during its execution as well as how much system support the program requires. By monitoring the OVERHEAD times, as well as the USER and SYSTEM times, the user can get a sense of how vulnerable the program's performance is to the overhead processing.

Nonexecution time measurements might be regarded as superfluous. However, these times can reflect interesting task operation behavior. For instance, the READY time is a good indication of the amount of waiting a task experiences in the scheduling queue. The BLOCKED time is more versatile in that it encompasses all dependent waiting time encountered by the task. This time not only includes blocking due to I/O operations but also represents waiting due to intertask synchronization. IDLE time is particularly interesting for Xylem tasks because it can be used to compute a task utilization metric indicating the percentage of time a task executes some portion of the user's program.

For the most part, the execution time measurements are well defined. The complication comes when trying to work back from the measurements to what the program is actually doing. For sequential, single-task programs, the HRTIME measurements are easy to understand. In this case, the breakdown across the different sequential processing resources is interesting because it shows how the process was scheduled during its execution.

The HRTIME measurements for concurrent tasks are more difficult to understand. The goal of the CE execution time measurements is to give some indication of CE resource usage. Ideally, a single global state space is defined where each point describes a different combination of the CE execution states. Time spent in each global state can then be measured. However, the implementation of this measurement model is impractical because of the complex instrumentation needed to detect global state changes.

Using the individual CE measurements, it is difficult to determine the amount of time CE 0 is in USER state when CE 1 is in SYSTEM state, and so on with other CE state combinations. However, it is unclear whether such time measurements have much value. Because the computational complex is assigned to a task as a single resource, it is more important how the individual CEs themselves are utilized. The HRTIME measurements show this as a breakdown between execution states for each CE.

Finally, the Xylem process virtual time, in conjunction with the individual task timings, can be used to give a general impression of the level of parallel task operation. A possible addition to the current HRTIME utility would be the breakdown of the P_VIRTUAL time into values reflecting different levels of simultaneous task execution.

1.5 Profiling Instrumentation

Timing alone is insufficient for characterizing the behavior of parallel programs. Although the HRTIME utility is able to describe how a program spends its time in different execution states on different processing resources, it is unable to correlate the timing data with the code being executed. The approach that has been taken in most multiprocessor systems is to adapt sample-based profiling tools designed for sequential programs. This approach was initially attempted for Cedar but was abandoned because of its fundamental limitations for parallel program performance characterization and its implementation complexity [16,17]. The following describes the conclusions from this investigation that are believed to be generally applicable to other parallel systems.

1.5.1 Standard Sequential Profiling

The goal of program profiling is to provide an accurate characterization of a program's execution behavior and performance. Such information will help the user evaluate alternative implementations and guide program optimization. Two measurements are commonly defined for the profiling of sequential programs: (1) counting the number of times routines are executed and (2) timing the execution of routines. Focusing on routines is reasonable for sequential program profiling. Because only one routine can be executing at any time, the characterization of a routine's execution in terms of call counts and execution times is a direct measure of its individual performance and its relative importance to the overall computation.

The standard profiling tools of the UNIX operating system are *prof* and *gprof* [18]. Two types of profiling output are produced by these tools. The *flat* profile shows all routines called during program execution with the count of the number of times they were called and their *direct* execution time. [6] The *call graph* profile lists each routine, together with information about its parent routines and children routines. The flat profile results are augmented with *cumulative* time for the routine, the number of calls to each descendant, the time inherited from each of its descendants, and the fraction of total routine time represented by the descendant's times. [7] Similar results are shown for the parents of the routine.

Timing in *prof* and *gprof* is based on sampled execution time. When profiling is enabled, a histogram of the location of the profiled program's program

---

[6] The direct execution time for a routine is amount of time spent executing the statements of the routine.

[7] The cumulative routine time is the elapsed time from routine entry to exit.

counter is updated at the end of each interval timer interrupt. [8] Routine execution times are determined from a distribution of program counter samples within the histogram. To determine a routine's direct execution time, the PC histogram counts for that routine are summed and multiplied by the interval timer period. Obviously, such timing measurements are subject to statistical sampling errors and have the potential for giving misleading results.

To determine cumulative execution times, the arc call counts are used to calculate the amount of time that should be propagated from descendants to ancestors in the dynamic call graph. Having determined a descendant's cumulative execution time, each ancestor is propagated a time equal to the fraction of total calls to the descendant made by the ancestor times the descendent's cumulative time. The necessary, but possibly incorrect, assumption is that each call to a routine takes the same amount of time. This assumption, coupled with the statistical approximation of direct execution time, can produce invalid timing measurements.

1.5.2 Parallel Profiling

The goal of traditional profiling tools is to optimize the performance of a program by streamlining routines that are major consumers of execution time. Using the routine call counts and execution times, iterative techniques can be applied to integrate excessively called routines or to streamline routines that are execution time bottlenecks. However, parallel program profiling calls for an extension to the common profiling approaches to include measurements of the dynamic interaction between concurrent execution threads. Unfortunately, there are certain fundamental problems that limit such an approach.

The proposed profiling strategy for Cedar was to extend sequential profiling techniques to gather additional information about parallel program activity. In particular, because parallel program execution implies the potential for more than one routine to be executing concurrently, the standard profiling measurements were to be enhanced to include information about the parallelism present when a routine was executing [16,17].

The first conclusion reached is that sampling is totally inappropriate for generating profile timing information for parallel programs. The reasons for this are the same as for sample-based process timing. Furthermore, the assumptions made about achieving statistical accuracy and propagating time back up the calling tree to determine cumulative execution times are invalid for sample-based parallel program profiling. The main reason for this is the inability of sampling to capture changes in parallel execution state that directly affect how

---

[8] The interval time interrupt usually occurs every $\frac{1}{60}$th of a second. On the Alliant FX/8, it occurs every 10 msec.

1.5. Profiling Instrumentation

time intervals should be classified. Parallel profiling approaches must instead be based on measuring time intervals between successive routine entry/exit events and events reflecting changes in concurrency state.

Unfortunately, many additional execution events are required to capture even basic concurrent activity. These events represent an enumeration of the possible concurrent states that might occur during a program's execution. More importantly, the events do not necessarily occur at routine entry and exit. Thus, a significant amount of additional code instrumentation would be required.

Other timing problems were also identified. In sequential profiling, it is always clear how the current time should be accounted. This is not the case in parallel profiling. Parallel execution necessarily implies that one or more routines are active simultaneously. Several issues arise with respect to accounting execution time to routines in different parallel execution cases:

1. When a routine is executing concurrently with itself, how are direct time and cumulative time for that routine measured?

2. When a routine, B, is called concurrently from the same calling routine, A, how does B's parallel execution time get accounted in A's timing values?

3. When a caller and callee routine are executing concurrently, how are direct and cumulative times being accumulated for the caller and the callee?

4. When there is a concurrent execution overlap of two callee routines (different or the same) from the same caller, how is the overlap time accounted for in the caller's time values?

The root of these issues lies in the definition of execution time. If execution time is to mean *elapsed* time, execution time for a routine A accumulates whenever A is executing, sequentially or concurrently. If, however, execution time means *CPU* time, the time spent on different concurrent execution threads must be accounted for in routine A's execution times. Elapsed execution time measurements are necessary for calculating speedup. On the other hand, CPU time accounts for the amount of computing resources used by the program and is necessary for utilization calculations. Both time values are needed for profiling parallel programs.

The most important conclusion reached concerns profiling as a basis for parallel program optimization. The goal of sequential profiling is to find the routines that take the most time and optimize them. Doing so will directly improve the overall performance of the sequential program. This profile-based optimization strategy is faulty for parallel programs as shown by the simple example in Figure 1.3 for a parallel program running on two processors. The Main routine forks a thread that executes routine A on processor P1 for 10 seconds. The other fork of Main calls routines B, C, D, and E, in that order. Each of these routines executes concurrently with A for 2.5 seconds. The forks then join and the program ends.

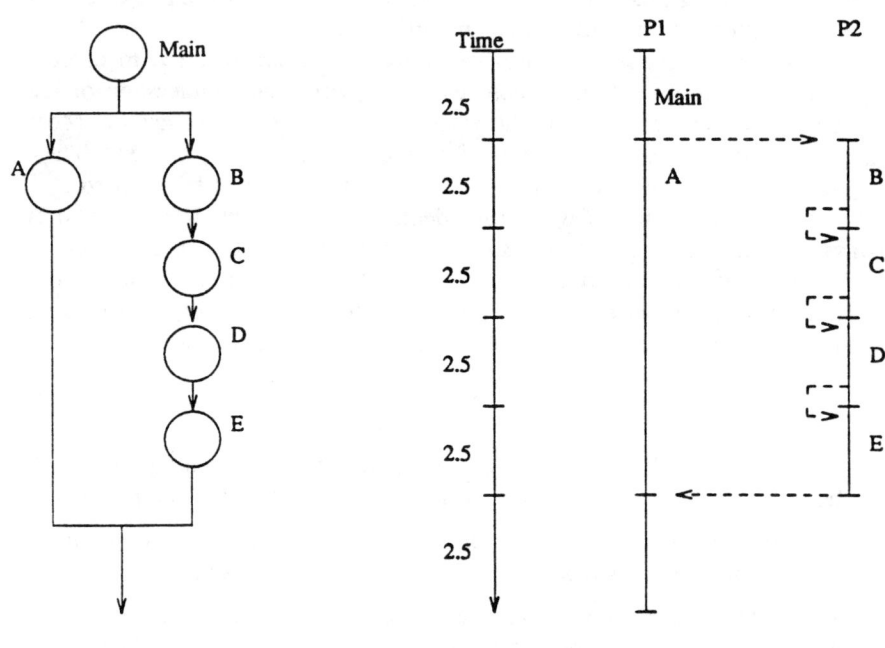

FIGURE 1.3
Parallel program example.

The standard optimization strategy based on profiling results would be to optimize A. However, there are several situations in which this strategy would be incorrect. For instance, suppose there existed dependencies between the routines as shown by the dashed lines. Clearly, A is not the bottleneck since B, C, D, and E have an execution flow dependency. Optimizing A would have little effect on run time of the program. Instead, the programmer should concentrate on improving the performance of the other routines.

The problem is that the profiling data does not make the needed optimization obvious. In order to optimize parallel programs, it is necessary to observe the dynamic interaction of the multiple threads of execution. A parallel profiling approach must describe and measure all the possible parallel execution interaction that might occur as individual events. The instrumentation required to do this would be overly complex to implement.

The instrumentation complexity required for parallel profiling does not pay off in better characterization and optimization. Profiling only summarizes parallel execution information in terms of event counts and times. Unfortunately, it is the dynamic execution information that is required for effective parallel program performance evaluation. Statistical summaries are interesting for some characterization purposes, but parallel program analysis requires the ability to observe and analyze time-ordered concurrent events. A different instrumentation approach is required to achieve this result.

1.6 Tracing Instrumentation

The standard profiling instrumentation approach proved too limited in its ability to measure and characterize parallel execution. Instead, what was needed was a general instrumentation approach simple enough to be efficient but robust enough to capture execution data that could describe complex parallel program behavior. Program event tracing was implemented as an instrumentation technique for performance evaluation of parallel programs written for Cedar [19]. The versatility of tracing comes from the ability to combine low-level primitive event traces to produce information about more complex higher-level events. In the case of parallel program analysis, this is a necessary requirement because of the difficulty of monitoring complex parallel execution states at run time.

1.6.1 The Tracing Approach

The execution of a program can generally be described as a time-ordered sequence of events. The events can be defined to be any logical or physical consequence of program execution. The goal of program performance evaluation is to capture information about these events in meaningful ways that can be used to guide performance optimization.

Three operations can be identified in this process: (1) event detection, (2) event measurement, and (3) event analysis. For an event to be observed, its occurrence must first be detected. The complexity of event detection depends on the scope of the event. For instance, if the event is the entry to a routine, monitoring the routine for an entry event is sufficient. If, however, the event is defined to be a certain number of processors being active, the detection mechanism must continually be testing all processors simultaneously. The scope is broader and, thus, the detection is more difficult.

Event measurement records information about event occurrence and event analysis uses the data to derive various performance results. If event analysis is done at the same time as event detection, all measurement information that describes an event must be known at a central point. Not only does the detection have to be centralized in this case, but so does the measurement. This requirements makes it difficult to define very complex events about program execution. Unfortunately, the scope of many parallel program events is broad. That is, interesting parallel program events tend to be defined with respect to some global parallel execution state, such as the level of parallelism.

The profiling instrumentation discussed in the previous section suffered from a requirement to perform event detection, measurement, and analysis at the same time during program execution. Each event had to be completely described in the profiling instrumentation, including the complex events regarding global parallel execution state. This severely limited the range of events that could be realistically profiled.

The functions of event detection, measurement, and analysis must be separated if practical performance tools are to be realized. Furthermore, complex events must be defined hierarchically as combinations of more primitive events which are monitored during program execution.

Event tracing is an instrumentation technique whereby data about an event are saved in a buffer whenever the event occurs during program execution. Part of the data is a timestamp indicating the actual time the event took place. The subtle power of timestamped event tracing is that all information required for analysis is saved. The analysis function, therefore, can take place independently of the event detection. Furthermore, detection and measurement of complex events can often be derived from the data saved for the low-level events. Thus, only primitive event measurement is necessary during execution.

The benefit of tracing as an instrumentation technique for parallel program performance evaluation is that very detailed information about a program's execution can be recorded in a trace from which complex queries about performance behavior are answered. The tracing operations are simple to implement and the instrumentation efficiency issues are localized to the management of the trace buffers. Indeed, the functional partitioning allowed by tracing can be seen in the highly modular and parallel approaches to its implementation.

1.6.2 CTRACE – A Tracing Facility for Cedar

CTRACE is a tracing utility developed for the performance evaluation of the parallel programs written for Cedar [19,20]. CTRACE has three components as shown in Figure 1.4. The event specification component defines the events that will be traced during program execution. The measurement component is responsible for enabling program and operating system instrumentation that will monitor the events of interest and generate the program trace. The CTRACE analysis component processes the trace data to produce various performance results. Together, the three components of the CTRACE utility form an integrated performance evaluation environment.

1.6. Tracing Instrumentation   21

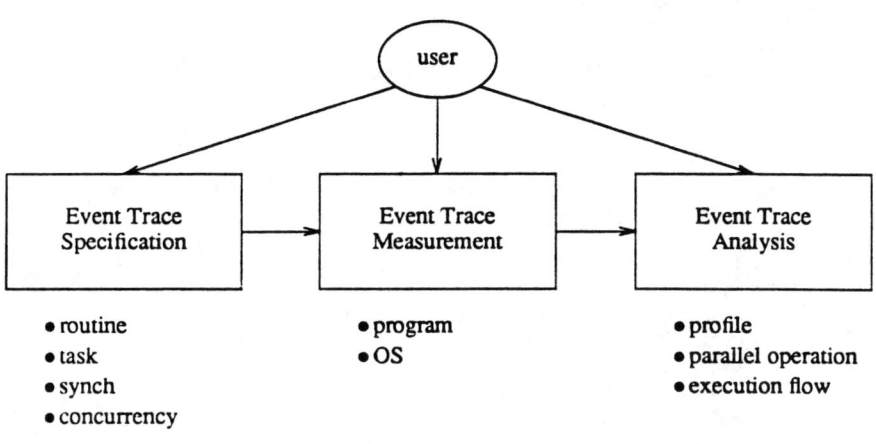

FIGURE 1.4
The CTRACE environment.

Event Specification.   Software event specification in CTRACE serves two functions. First, it informs the measurement phase about the nature of the event: what the event is, when it occurs, and what data are needed to describe the event in the trace. Second, the specification serves as the basis for event trace interpretation in the analysis phase by providing information about how the various events are associated.

Two general types of events can be specified: standard and user-defined events. Standard events are defined with respect to common actions in the execution environment and are always available to the user. The set of standard events in the current version of CTRACE is shown below:

```
Program
      routine entry, exit
      basic block entry, exit

Cedar Fortran: Cluster Loop Parallelism
      CDOACROSS entry, exit
      CDOALL entry, exit

Cedar Fortran: Spread Loop Parallelism
      SDOACROSS entry, exit
      SDOALL entry, exit
```

```
Cedar Fortran: CDOACROSS Synchronization
    advance synchronization
    wait synchronization entry, exit

Cedar Fortran: Simple Synchronization
    fetch and op

Cedar Fortran: Cray-XMP Synchronization
    lock on, off
    event post, clear
    event wait entry, exit

Xylem: Multitasking
    create task, delete task
    queue task, resume task
    start task, stop task
    suspend task
    wait task entry, exit

Xylem: Synchronization
    set lock
    clear lock
    wait lock entry, exit
    dawdle entry, exit

Xylem: Task States
    running
    ready
    block
    idle
```

If the programmer desires an event not included in the standard set, the event must be described by the user. CTRACE currently provides for three general types of user-defined software events: MARK, ENTRY, and EXIT. MARK events simply indicate the occurrence of an event during execution. ENTRY and EXIT events indicate the entry into a block of computation and the associated exit, respectively. An ENTRY event must always be paired with an EXIT event.

In general, software event tracing allows any data that the user wants to associate with an event to be recorded in the trace. These data must be defined in the specification phase. The standard event data are predefined. A minimal amount of data will be automatically recorded by CTRACE. These data include an event identifier and a high-resolution global timestamp.

Event Trace Measurement. Currently, CTRACE performs all tracing in software. The approach taken is to provide a separate trace buffer per processor per task. This supports efficient concurrent tracing operations because there is no trace buffer contention.

The approach of separate trace buffers requires that event timestamps be generated from a global clock. The high-resolution timestamps for CTRACE are obtained from a 10-μsec real-time clock maintained by each Alliant FX/8 cluster and directly readable by each CE. The time value is stored as a 64-bit quantity. Because Cedar has one central hardware clock source, all individual FX/8 real-time clocks are synchronized. Thus, global time is distributed across the Cedar machine.

One artifact of using a real-time clock for timestamps is that periods when a task is not running must be identified in order to make execution time measurements. The beauty of tracing is that context switch events can be traced as well as other program events [21]. This makes it possible to have low-overhead timestamp generations as well as accurate execution time measurements. The context switch events are also useful for showing task scheduling behavior.

Support for event measurement takes several forms. A library of tracing routines is provided for initializing the tracing facility, recording events in trace buffers, and writing events to a trace output file. Trace-instrumented standard libraries are also available and can be compiled with a program. These include trace-instrumented run-time libraries for Cedar Fortran. Compiler preprocessor support is provided to insert instrumentation for events defined with respect to Cedar Fortran language statements. Event instrumentation can be enabled either through compile-line arguments or compiler directives. Finally, events external to the program, such as context switch events, require instrumentation in the operating system for their measurement.

Event Trace Analysis. The idea of event trace analysis is simple. Using the event specification and measurement information, the program traces are scanned to determine certain performance results. Two general event trace analysis tools are provided in CTRACE. The *execution profile analysis* tool produces statistical summary results of the program's execution. The statistics are similar to, but more extended than, the common sequential profiling results produced by *prof* and *gprof*. The *execution flow analysis* tool allows the programmer to observe the time-sequenced flow of events as they occurred during program execution. This tool is able to isolate certain periods of execution to identify particular characteristics of program behavior.

In general, the program traces should be viewed as a database of time-related information from which queries can be made regarding parallel program execution. A highly interactive analysis environment can be imagined that interfaces with the user through some query language and displays responses in various statistical and graphical representations.

Execution Profile Analysis. The execution profile analysis tools generate statistical information regarding program execution from the program traces. For instance, given only standard routine and task event data, all of the following common profiling measurements can be produced:

- routine call counts
- descendant routine call counts
- direct execution time
- cumulative execution time
- average cumulative time per call
- descendant cumulative execution time

In addition to the above measurements, the following concurrency statistics can be generated without the need for defining additional events:

- sequential and concurrent routine call counts
- sequential and concurrent routine execution time
- number of tasks created
- average task execution time
- execution time histogram of task concurrency
- average task concurrency

Data from the other events only increase the database from which execution profile statistics can be drawn. Of particular interest is the execution time of parallel loops and synchronization operations. The following represents the types of statistics provided:

- CDOACROSS and CDOALL execution time
- SDOACROSS and SDOALL execution time
- task wait synchronization counts and times
- event wait synchronization counts and times
- lock wait synchronization counts and times

1.7 Execution Flow Analysis

The ability to observe the program events in a time-ordered sequence of occurrence differentiates tracing from profiling tools. Statistical summaries give a global picture of program execution but lack historical perspective. Execution flow analysis provides the programmer with a window into the program traces at various levels of detail. The concept of *replaying* the program's execution with respect to the traced events forms the basis of execution flow analysis tools.

In general, execution flow analysis is used as a means to explore the program's execution for evidence of good, bad, or strange behavior. Sometimes the programmer just wants to see general characteristics, such as the sequence of routine execution. At other times, the programmer will use execution flow analysis in combination with highly specialized event traces for "search and destroy" missions to pinpoint some anomalous behavior or dissect a poorly performing section of code. The execution flow analysis toolset provides an environment for the programmer to intelligently search and analyze the program trace database.

A basic set of execution flow analysis functions is currently provided in CTRACE. The function of moving around in the program trace and displaying events is called *event trace browsing*. In addition to enabling forward and backward movement in program event history, event trace browsing provides different ways of searching through the event trace. Textual and graphical presentation capabilities also exist for showing the events that occur in certain regions of the trace.

One such graphical representation is the *dynamic call graph* display. The display shows the active calling arcs of the static *subroutine interconnection graph* with the nodes being drawn dynamically as the routines are encountered in the program trace. Figure 1.5 gives an example of the state of a task's execution on an FX/8 Cedar cluster in the form of a dynamic call graph. The path through the static call graph is shown for each execution thread with the leaf node representing the currently executing routine. The global dynamic call graph of the task shows a merge of the individual calling branches with all currently active routines drawn as square nodes.

The key feature of the event trace browser is that it is interactive. It takes the event specification and the program trace and provides a front-end for general inquiries about program execution. Basic searching and event presentation are be handled by the browser. More sophisticated analysis is the responsibility of execution flow generalization.

The basic idea behind execution flow generalization is to provide the programmer with a way of observing higher-level execution behavior not represented directly by some traced event. Execution flow generalization builds high-level events from combinations of traced events. As an example, task concurrency events reflect the number of active tasks during a program's execution. Each level of task concurrency represents a separate event. Although the occurrence of events of this type is difficult to detect at run time, it is easy to derive from analysis of the individual task traces. From the task state event data, the beginning and ending times for the high-level task concurrency events can be determined. A task concurrency event "trace" can be generated from this analysis and a graph of task concurrency produced. An example task activity graph and the accompanying task concurrency graph are shown in Figure 1.6.

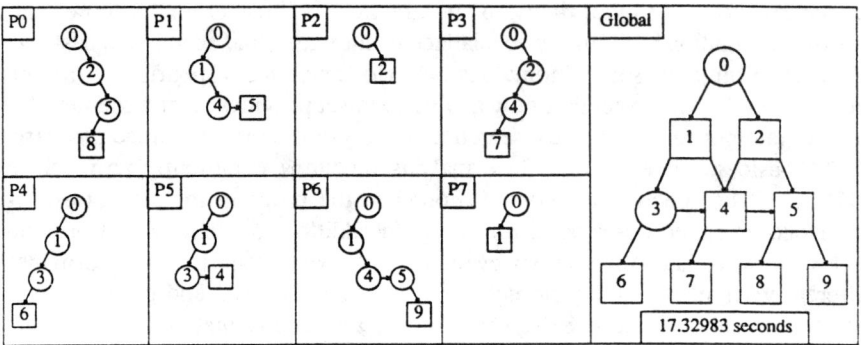

FIGURE 1.5
Dynamic call graph.

Notice the period of time during which none of the program tasks are active. In multiprogrammed multiprocessing systems such as Cedar, this can occur because all tasks within the system are sharing processing resources. Although this is a simple example of execution flow generalization, it illustrates the basic idea upon which more complicated generalizers can be designed.

As the range and details of events increase, so does the complexity of trace analysis. Additional tools will be developed that allow the user to more easily browse through the trace at various levels of detail and query the analysis system about program behavior. These tools will require new techniques for interpreting the trace data as well as reducing the data into meaningful representations for presentation to the user.

1.8 Hardware Instrumentation

In addition to software instrumentation, several hardware instrumentation approaches are being pursued for Cedar. Hardware measurements focus on the physical events taking place within various Cedar machine components. These measurements include Alliant FX/8 cluster, global interface, global network, and global memory measurements (see Table 1.4) [22]. A flexible hardware perfor-

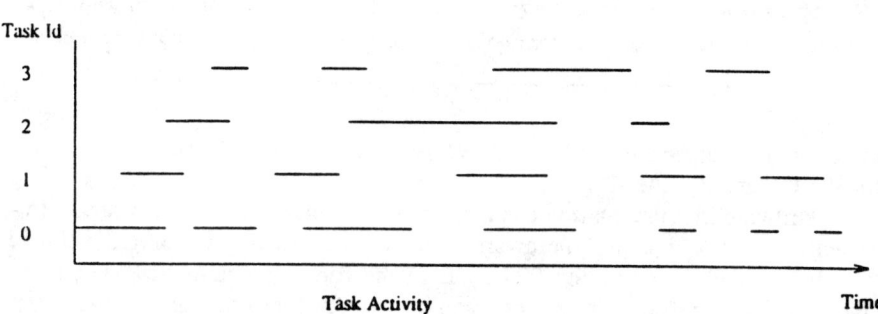
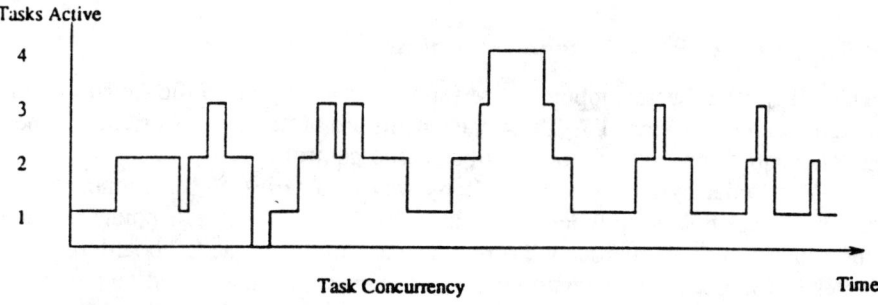

FIGURE 1.6
Task concurrency graphs.

TABLE 1.4
Hardware Measurements

Alliant FX/8 Cluster	Global Interface	Global Network	Global Memory
instructions	reference type	input port utilization	reference type
vector operation	prefetch operation	network contention	reference distribution
concurrent operation	data buffer usage	bandwidth utilization	utilization
cache operations	interface delay	network delay	reference delay
memory references	data transfer rate	output contention	memory contention

mance monitoring system is being developed that will make these measurements for the Cedar machine [9].

Hardware instrumentation can also be used to make certain software instrumentation more efficient. A hardware trace buffering facility is being developed that will provide support for CTRACE in the form of automatic event timestamping, trace buffer management, and a fast path for generating events.

1.8.1 Hardware Performance Monitor

The integral hardware support for performance monitoring in the Cedar system is represented in Figure 1.7. The key elements are buffered on-board test points, a data acquisition system, and multibus-based control.

The Cedar system is observable by way of a series of performance-measurement test points provided on each circuit board. These test points provide information such as microcode instruction and address on the CE boards, control states and important counters on the network interface boards, and other signals specific to the global network and global memory boards. The signals provide important information on the activities of each board.

The signals are monitored by a general purpose high-resolution data acquisition system, called the black box. A black box card cage can hold up to 32 modules. Several different types of modules have been developed including signal conditioning, counting, timing, and data-logging. The hardware monitoring system is generally configurable to the type of measurement experiment desired. For example, one module can be configured as an interval timer and another as a counter to count the number of floating-point operations. Using this configuration, MFLOPS (million floating-point operations per second) can be easily obtained.

The black boxes are connected to a controller card resident in one of the multibus backplanes used by the IPs in a Cedar cluster. Each controller can

1.8. Hardware Instrumentation

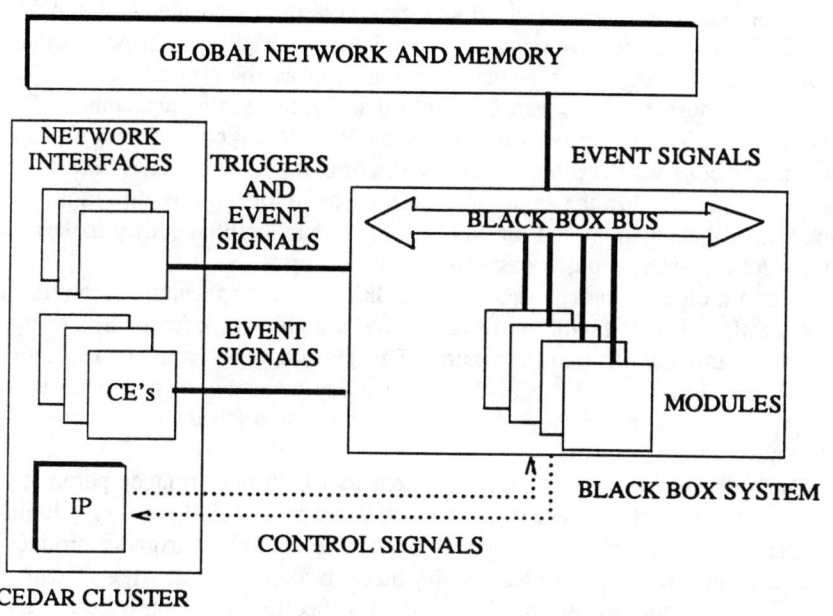

FIGURE 1.7
Cedar hardware monitoring system.

handle as many as 16 black box systems. Multiple controllers can be installed in one multibus, for centralized control by one IP, or in multiple multibuses, for distributed control by several IPs within one cluster or across multiple clusters.

The IP directly controls each black box and can read the contents of the black box registers and memory to obtain the collected data. Since an IP is also responsible for providing disk I/O to the cluster, it is possible for run-time performance data to be logged to disk as they are collected. Real-time analysis by the IP critically depends on the volume of data received and the amount of processing to be performed.

One advantage of using such a hardware monitoring system is that it is highly modular. Each module in a black box system has an identical standard interface that makes the system easily expandable. Special types of performance modules can be designed as needed, and as long as their interfaces stay the same, all of these modules can be controlled by the same mechanism. This allows different types of modules to work together to collect different kinds of data simultaneously. It is often necessary to correlate data collected in different parts of a system within the same time frame. The ability to mix different types of modules together to collect different types of data simultaneously makes the post collection analysis much easier and more accurate.

Within a cluster, under the proper conditions, the performance monitoring can be tightly correlated with events produced by a given task (software), or by a given computational element (hardware). This software and hardware resolution degrades as measurements are made farther away from the cluster, e.g., in the global memory, where it is very difficult to know which CE instruction required the memory access.

The software resolution (i.e., the extent to which performance parameters measured throughout the system can be correlated with specific tasks) is highly dependent on the number and type of explicit and implicit triggers produced by the task that can be detected by the black boxes. Explicit triggers can be generated by special instructions in a task specifically for the purpose of starting, stopping, or signaling the black boxes. The global interface for each CE was designed such that certain instructions issued by the CE would generate special external trigger signals. The trigger instructions can be embedded in a user's program or in the operating system to precisely start and stop hardware measurements in the software. Implicit triggers are sets of circumstances that can be identified as characteristic of the task under analysis (such as certain "unique" sequences of operations that can be correlated with the execution of the task). Recognition of implicit triggers depends either on an accurate program flow model or on a detailed understanding of the task under investigation.

1.8.2 Hardware Trace Buffering System

A hardware trace buffering utility is being developed for Cedar that will support CTRACE program event tracing by providing the means for low-overhead event generation and trace buffer storage. The hardware tracer consists of an interface to the hardware performance monitor, a trace buffer memory, a timestamp clock, and an interface to disk. Each CE in the Cedar system will have its own tracer module.

The hardware performance monitor will provide access to the software trigger signals that will indicate the occurrence of an event. Event data indicated by the triggers will be captured by the monitor and passed to the tracer. The tracer will timestamp the event and store it in a trace buffer specific to the CE producing the event. The tracer is designed to accept events as fast as the CE can produce them.

In addition to providing fast paths for writing event data, the tracer relieves CTRACE of the need to manage trace buffers in software. The automatic time-stamping of events also reduces the cost of generating software events. Hopefully, the tracer will help reduce the impact that trace instrumentation has on parallel program execution. It should also improve the resolution at which events can be observed.

1.8.3 Real-Time Performance Analysis

The hardware trace buffering utility together with the hardware performance monitor will provide the basis in the future for a real-time performance analysis system. The researcher's intent is to design a system that processes in real time the performance data produced by Xylem and parallel programs running on Cedar and shows system and program performance through various forms of graphical performance displays. It is hoped that the system will provide immediate feedback of current performance as well as summary information of past performance that will be useful for tuning the overall performance of Cedar.

1.9 Conclusion

Instrumentation for parallel systems must offer the user ways of observing parallel operation at various levels of detail. However, the hardware and software constraints imposed by real systems make it difficult to implement instrumentation mechanisms that do not somehow perturb the parallel behavior. The challenge is to design instrumentation techniques that integrate well with parallel architectures and parallel execution environments. In the future, these techniques should be included as part of the overall parallel system design and be provided as standard components on all parallel machines.

The instrumentation tools developed for the Cedar multiprocessor are prototypes used to explore various tradeoffs in design and implementation. The set of tools is continually being improved as more instrumentation is being placed in the hardware and software to gather additional data about the system. Many of the basic instrumentation approaches, however, are considered general enough in scope to serve as a performance instrumentation framework for other machines.

References

1. D. J. Kuck, A. H. Sameh, A Supercomputing Performance Evaluation Plan, *Proceedings 1987 Supercomputing Conference*, Greece, June, 1987.

2. D. J. Kuck, D. H. Lawrie, W. Jalby, P. Yew, A. Malony, and A. Sameh, Methodology for Performance Evaluation for High Performance Computer Systems, CSRD Report No. 725, Center for Supercomputing Res. & Dev., Univ. of Illinois at Urbana-Champaign, Dec. 1987.

3. D. Gajski, D. L. Kuck, D. Lawrie, and A. Sameh, Cedar – A Large Scale Multiprocessor, *Proceedings 1983 International Conference on Parallel Processing*, Belaire, MI, 1983.

4. D. J. Kuck, E. S. Davidson, D. H. Lawrie, and A. H. Sameh, Parallel Supercomputing Today and the Cedar Approach, *Science*, Vol. 231, Feb. 28, 1986, pp. 967–974.

5. P. Emrath, An Operating System for the Cedar Multiprocessor, *IEEE Software*, Vol. 2, No. 4, 1985, pp. 30–37.

6. R.E. McGrath and P. Emrath, Using Memory in the Cedar System, *1987 International Conference on Supercomputing*, 1987.

7. M. Guzzi, Cedar Fortran Reference Manual, CSRD Report No. 601, Center for Supercomputing Res. and Dev., Univ. of Illinois at Urbana-Champaign, 1987.

8. M. Guzzi, Multitasking Runtime Systems for the Cedar Multiprocessor, CSRD Report No. 604, Center for Supercomputing Res. and Dev., Univ. of Illinois at Urbana-Champaign, 1986.

9. K. Gallivan, W. Jalby, A. Malony, and P. Yew, Performance Analysis on the Cedar System, to appear as a chapter in *Performance Evaluation of Supercomputers*, J.L. Martin, Ed., North-Holland, 1988.

10. A. D. Malony, Cedar Performance Evaluation Tools: A Status Report, CSRD Report No. 582, Center for Supercomputing Res. and Dev., Univ. of Illinois at Urbana-Champaign, July 1986.

11. A. D. Malony, Proposal for Concurrency Efficiency Measurements, Internal memo, Center for Supercomputing Res. and Dev., Univ. of Illinois at Urbana-Champaign, August 1986.

12. A. D. Malony, Concurrency Efficiency User's Manual, Univ. of Illinois at Urbana-Champaign, Center for Supercomputing Res. and Dev., CSRD Report No. 675, June 1987.

13. A. D. Malony, Virtual High-Resolution Process Timing, CSRD Report No. 616, Center for Supercomputing Res. and Dev., Univ. of Illinois at Urbana-Champaign, Oct. 1986.

14. R. Barton, P. Emrath, D. Lawrie, A. Malony, and R. McGrath, New Approaches to Measuring Process Execution Time in the Cedar Multiprocessor System, CSRD Report No. 744, Center for Supercomputing Res. and Dev., Univ. of Illinois at Urbana-Champaign, Jan. 1987.

15. A. D. Malony, High Resolution Process Timing User's Manual, Univ. of Illinois at Urbana-Champaign, Center for Supercomputing Res. and Dev., CSRD Report No. 676, June 1987.

16. A. D. Malony, Ideas on Profiling Parallel Programs, Internal memo, Center for Supercomputing Res. and Dev., Univ. of Illinois at Urbana-Champaign, August 1986.

17. A. D. Malony, Program Profiling in Cedar, CSRD Report No. 654, Center for Supercomputing Res. and Dev., Univ. of Illinois at Urbana-Champaign, March 1987.

18. S. L. Graham, P. B. Kessler, and M. K. McKusik, An Execution Profiler for Modular Programs, *Software – Practice and Experience*, Vol. 13. pp. 671–85, 1983.

19. A. D. Malony, Program Tracing in Cedar, CSRD Report No. 660, Center for Supercomputing Res. and Dev., Univ. of Illinois at Urbana-Champaign, April 1987.

20. A. D. Malony, CTRACE User's Manual, CSRD Report No. 710, Center for Supercomputing Res. and Dev., Univ. of Illinois at Urbana-Champaign, Nov. 1987.

21. A. D. Malony, Process Context Switch Tracing, Univ. of Illinois at Urbana-Champaign, Center for Supercomputing Res. & Dev., CSRD Report No. 688, Oct. 1987.

22. A. D. Malony, Cedar Performance Measurements, CSRD Report No. 579, Center for Supercomputing Res. and Dev., Univ. of Illinois at Urbana-Champaign, June 1986.

2

RP3 Performance Monitoring Hardware

William C. Brantley
Kevin P. McAuliffe
Ton A. Ngo

2.1 Introduction

The Research Parallel Processor Prototype (RP3) is a parallel processor developed at the IBM T. J. Watson Research Center [1,2]. Its architecture provides support for both message passing and shared memory programming paradigms. The RP3 system, shown in Figure 2.1, consists of an interconnection network and up to 512 Processor-Memory Elements (PMEs). Each PME contains an equal part of RP3's memory, a Romp processor [3], floating-point unit (FPU), I/O interface device, Memory Management Unit (MMU), cache, and an interface to the interconnection network. In addition, each PME contains a Performance Monitor Chip (PMC).

Early in the RP3 project, hardware performance monitoring capabilities were included in the machine design. It was felt that an experimental machine must include performance monitoring to satisfy the primary goal of understanding parallel hardware and software. Whereas software monitoring (e.g., [4]) is useful for applications and, to a lesser degree, for operating systems, hardware monitoring is necessary for the analysis of hardware devices (e.g. cache miss rate) and to determine the source of bottlenecks. Such detailed monitoring is also useful to the programmers as it provides a means for discovering software bottlenecks and evaluating aspects of the system architecture.

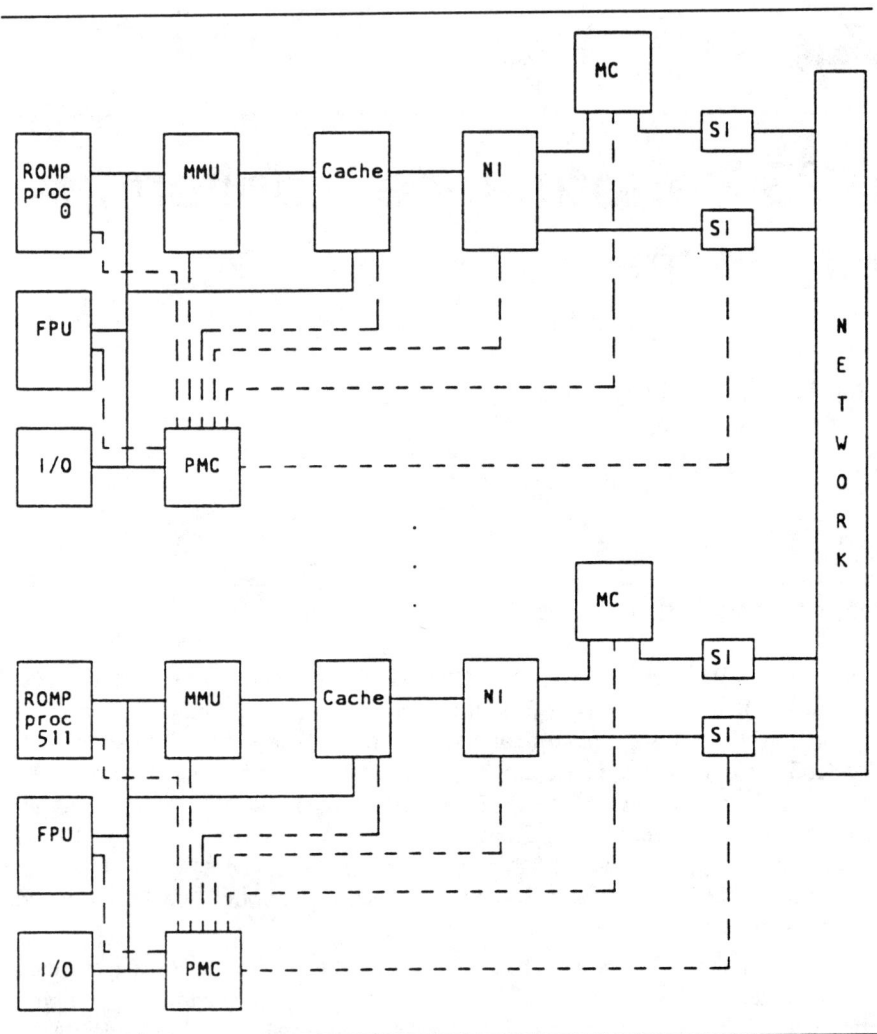

FIGURE 2.1
RP3 dataflow.

Although convinced of the value of performance monitoring, there were numerous constraints on the design: cost, chip area, chip I/O, board space, and development time. Due to these restrictions, RP3's performance monitoring hardware was distributed throughout the devices making up a PME. Each hardware device decodes its own events and signals their occurrence through special I/O pins. A separate device, the PMC, counts these event signals. The PMC also samples memory reference information. The sources of the dashed lines in Figure 2.1 indicate the devices that generate event signals. Distributing the monitoring functions allowed the detailed design of the PMC to be deferred until the other PME devices were functional. In fact, the detailed design of the PMC did not begin until after a two-PME multiprocessor was operational.

In designing the PMC, two forms of control were provided: PME mode and transparent mode. PME mode implies that an application or operating system running on the PME's processor is directly controlling the PMC (e.g. starting, stopping and reading the counters). In transparent mode, the I/O subsystem controls the PMC. In this mode, an application on the processor is unaware of the monitoring activity. Since the PMC is accessed through the processor bus, some small (200 bytes per second) perturbation of the processor activity will occur when the I/O system reads the contents of the PMC.

After a brief overview of the RP3 hardware, this paper describes the events monitored, the data sampled, and the organization of the PMC. The paper also describes some additional features are desirable monitoring features that were not included in the current monitoring hardware. A companion paper [5] describes a methodology for analyzing the performance of parallel applications. An appendix provides detailed information about controlling the PMC and lists the events counted and data sampled.

2.2 Overview

As mentioned in the previous section, the RP3 system can support both a shared-memory and a message-passing programming paradigm. This is possible because of the flexible memory management capabilities and the storage hierarchy of the RP3 system. The RP3 address translation is performed in two levels: a segment/page mapping and an interleave transformation. The segment/page translation maps a virtual address into a real address with interleave, cacheability, and temporarily-cacheable attributes. These attributes can be specified on a page basis. The real address and the interleave attribute are inputs to the interleave transformation. The result of this transformation is called the absolute address; the upper nine bits specify which memory will service a request. Functionally, the interleave attribute specifies how consecutive addresses in a page are distributed in memory. An interleave amount of zero indicates that all addresses in a page are sequential in one memory. An interleave of n indicates that addresses, on a double-word basis, are distributed across 2^n memories.

The cacheable attribute specifies whether the reference data can reside in cache (some data must be marked as non-cacheable to ensure correct execution of a program). The temporarily-cacheable attribute indicates that the referenced data can be put into the cache for a period of time, but can be invalidated independently of normal cacheable data. In general, the interleave and cacheability attributes specify where data reside in the memory hierarchy, i.e. in remote memory, physically local memory, or in cache.

Read and write requests are generated by the Romp processor, FPU and I/O interface device. The other PME devices service these requests. A read or write request can be done within either the I/O address space or the memory address space (similar to the Intel 8086). The I/O address space is used to address PME control registers (for example, the counters maintained by the PMC). All memory is addressed via the memory address space. When a device places a request on the processor bus, a tag is associated with the request. After the request is serviced, the tag is used to associate the reply with the requesting device. This tagging allows multiple requests to be outstanding.

Requests in the memory address space can be either non-translated or translated requests. In either case, the MMU initiates service of the request and passes the request to the cache. For non-translated requests, the MMU associates an interleave attribute of non-interleave and a cacheable attribute of non-cacheable with the request. For translated requests the MMU performs the segment/page translation.

The action of the cache will depend, in part, on the cacheable attribute. If the request is a cacheable read and the data are resident in the cache, the cache completes service of the request. If the request is a store, a non-cacheable or a cache miss, the request must be serviced by one of the memories. The cache forwards the memory request to the network interface (NI). The NI performs the interleave transformation, generating the absolute address. It then checks the upper bits of the absolute address to determine if the request is to be serviced by the physically local memory or by a remote memory.

To support the multiple requesting devices and to reduce the effects of memory latency, the RP3 cache is lockup-free [6], i.e. the cache will continue operation even though it has outstanding misses. In order to support such a feature, NI maintains a list of all outstanding PME requests. For each request in the list the NI retains: the cache-line address, the cacheability, the processor-bus tag, the target memory number, the memory operation, and a time stamp indicating when the request was sent to memory. The former three items are used to complete read requests. The latter three items are used for monitoring purposes.

When a request returns from memory service, if the request is a read, the NI forwards the read data to the cache with some of the retained information (for example, the processor-bus tag). If the request is a store or a read, the NI removes the request from the list, indicating completion. In either case, the NI moves the retained information about the completed request to the Latency Register. The NI also adds to the Latency Register a time stamp when the request returned and the number of outstanding requests at the time the request returned.

2.3 Events Monitored

The event signals used for monitoring are generated by various PME devices and are counted by the PMC. Since chip area and chip I/O pins were limited, each device could signal only a few events. Because effective use of the storage hierarchy is vital in obtaining good performance on the RP3 system, event signals that can be used to analyze the utilization of various levels of the storage hierarchy were given priority during the design of the system.

Figure 2.2 depicts the categories in which a storage request can be a member. The categories that are capitalized are those that are monitored by the hardware. The device listed above one of these categories generates an event signal if the device services a request that is a member of the category. Refinements to some categories can be made (e.g. instruction cache-hits). Multiple runs of a benchmark may be necessary to collect all the desired information about a category that can be refined. These refinements are indicated in Figure 2.2 by the arrowed lines at the bottom of the figure.

PMC counters count the occurrence of events signalled by other PME devices. A master counter, which is incremented each processor cycle, is provided as a time reference for the other counters. To ensure correlation between the counters, the PMC stops all counting whenever one of the counters overflows. Since the number of PMC counters was restricted by hardware constraints, there are more event signals than counters. Thus, multiple runs of a benchmark are necessary to count all event signals.

Although the number of monitored events and the number of PMC counters is relatively small, a substantial amount of information about the utilization of the RP3 memory hierarchy is provided. For example, the cache miss ratio can be determined by dividing the cache-miss count by the cacheable count. However, this does not give the real utilization of the cache since some data can be non-cacheable. To determine the utilization of the cache, one is interested in the percentage of cacheables as well as the miss rate. The percentage of cacheables is found by dividing the cacheable count by the sum of the number of translated and non-translated requests serviced by the MMU (this sum gives the total number of requests serviced and is used as a divisor for several calculations).

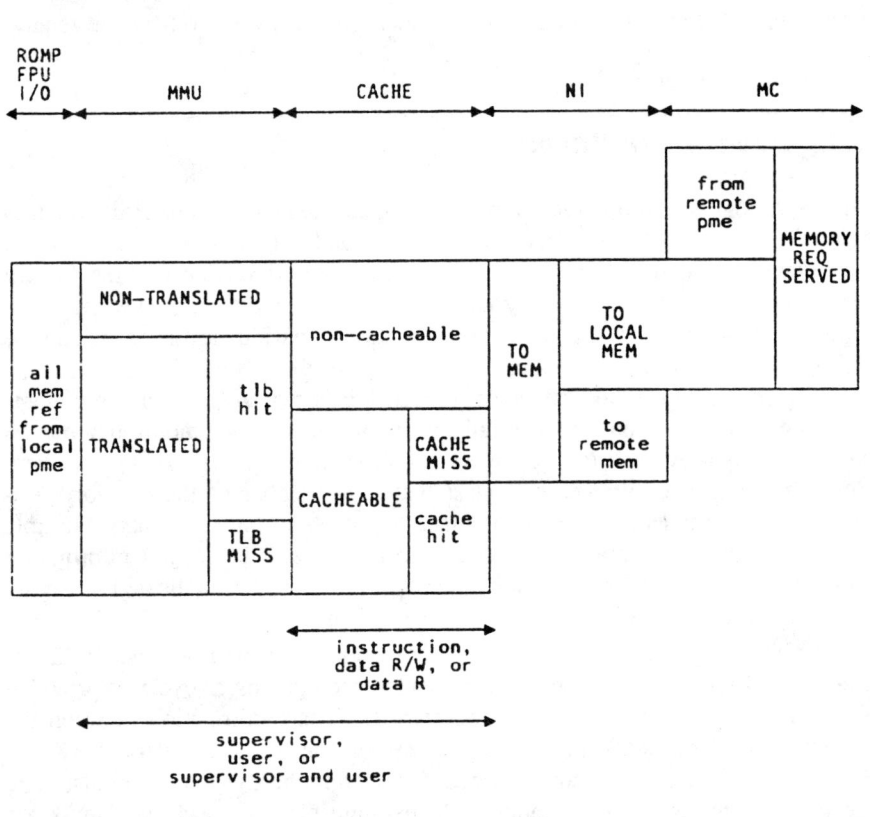

FIGURE 2.2
Categories of memory references measured in PME: those in capital letters are counted by the PMC; those in lower case letter may be derived.

If an application programmer observes that the percentage of cacheables is low, they can try to reorganize their data to more effectively use the cache, and by doing so, increase performance.

Since access time to the physical local memory of a PME is less than to a remote memory, effective use of local memory is also important for performance. The percentage of requests serviced by the local memory is calculated by dividing the local-request count by the count of requests serviced by the NI.

Another important event to monitor is the occurrence of hot spots [7], i.e. a single memory location that has high frequency of references over a short time period. The RP3 monitoring functions do not provide a direct way of detecting a hot spot. However, information is provided that can help an application programmer discover the presence of a hot spot. Using the counters recording the number of memory references made by the local NI and the number of operations performed by the memory, the number of references made by remote processors can be calculated. To estimate the average memory service time, a count of the number of cycles the memory is busy is maintained by the PMC. If a memory has a high utilization and the remote count is high, the memory may be a hot memory or contain a hot spot. Correlating the sample information (described below) from various processors may indicate where the hot spot is located.

2.4 Sample Data

In addition to the various counters that track memory references, the PMC also samples two types of data: virtual addresses and absolute addresses. Due to the limit storage capacity of the PMC, only one type of sampled data can be collected at a time. The sample frequency can be set to either every 2K, 8K, 32K or 128K processor cycles. The last sixteen samples are maintained in the PMC memory.

The PMC samples virtual addresses by observing the processor bus. When a sample is to be taken, the PMC stores into its sample memory the last virtual address accepted on the processor bus. A sample includes the double word address, whether the reference was a read or write and whether the reference was made in supervisor or user mode.

Absolute addresses are sampled using the NI Latency Register. When a sample is to be taken, the PMC signals the NI to start a serial shift-out of the Latency Register into a PMC register. Once all the data are received, the PMC register contents are stored into the PMC sample memory. As indicated earlier, the NI Latency Register contains information about requests that have been serviced by memory. This information consists of the memory address, the operation, and the time the request was sent by the NI and the time the reply was received by the NI. These times allow network latency to be estimated.

2.5 Desirable Features not Included

Although the RP3 performance monitoring functions provide a substantial amount of information about program and hardware performance, they do not have all the features that are desirable. Chip area and I/O pin constraints limited the monitoring functions that could be provided. Desirable enhancements to the monitoring functions fall into two categories: refinements and new features. A trivial example of a refinement is larger counters and more space for sample data. A new feature would be a hot-spot detector.

Larger counters and more sample space would allow longer monitoring runs or finer sampling rates for more precise analysis. A greater number of counters would eliminate the need to multiplex event signals thereby eliminating the need to run a benchmark multiple times. Providing the capability to record all memory references satisfying a set of criteria (e.g., all references to a page, word, or in a set of pages) would also be very beneficial. In fact, such a feature would enable the support of parallel debugging techniques [8,9].

A more sophisticated refinement is the ability to distinguish the memory references generated by the various requesting devices (i.e. Romp, FPU, I/O interface). Such a capability would provide a means of determining the utilization of the system by each requesting device. Such a scheme is possible in the current RP3 system because each device uses a unique set of processor-bus tags.

Another area for improvement would be a separate bus for passive readout of the PMC. Even though the PMC provides the I/O interface the ability to read its contents without logically interfering with the processor, this read-out steals bus cycles from the processor. A separate bus between the I/O device and the PMC would eliminate any perturbation of data.

As indicated above, the PMC provides only indirect means of detecting "hot memories" and "hot spots". Repeated experiments may be necessary to isolate a hot spot. A more effective means would require special hardware in the memory controller. This logic could maintain a list of the most active location in a memory. These locations could be read by the monitoring hardware on a sample basis.

Acknowledgments

The following engineers included instrumentation logic within the devices they designed: J. Anthony, M. Cassera, W. Groh, R. Jackson, M. Salamian, S. Wakefield, and J. Weiss. Discussions with R. La Maire, A. Norton, D. Rathi, J. Stone, and W. White have been useful.

This work was sponsored in part by Defense Advanced Research Projects Agency under contract #N00039–87–C–0122.

References

1. W. C. Brantley, K. P. McAuliffe, and J. Weiss, RP3 Processor-Memory Element, *Proceedings of the 1985 International Conference on Parallel Processing*, pages 782–789, 1985.
2. G. F. Pfister, W. C. Brantley, D. A. George, S. L. Harvey, W. J. Kleinfelder, K. P. McAuliffe, E. A. Melton, V. A. Norton, and J. Weiss, The IBM Research Parallel Processor Prototype (RP3): Introduction and Architecture, *Proceedings of the 1985 International Conference on Parallel Processing*, pages 764–771, 1985.
3. IBM publication SA23-1057, IBM RT Personal Computer Technology, 1986.
4. D. Ferrari, *Computer System Performance Evaluation*, Prentice-Hall, 1978.
5. F. Darema, Parallel Application Performance Methodology, in *Instrumentation for Parallel Computer Systems*, M. L. Simmons, R. J. Koskela, and I. Y. Bucher, Eds. (Addison-Wesley, 1989).
6. D. Kroft, Lockup-free Instruction Fetch/Prefetch Cache Organization, *Proceedings of the Eighth Symposium on Computer Architecture*, pages 81–88, 1981.
7. G. F. Pfister and V. A. Norton, "Hot Spot" Contention and Combining in Multistage Interconnection Networks Introduction and Architecture. *Proceedings of the 1985 International Conference on Parallel Processing*, pages 790–795, 1985.
8. T. J. LeBlanc and J. M. Mellor-Crummey, Debugging Parallel Programs with Instant Replay, *IEEE Transactions on Computers*, C–36(4):471–482, April 1987.
9. B. P. Miller and Y. Cui-Qing, *IPS: an Interactive and Automatic Performance Measurement Tool for Parallel and Distributed Programs*, University of Wisconsin, Report TR 613, 1987.

APPENDIX A

The PMC

The PMC consists of a status register, a mutual exclusion facility, a collection of counters, and a small memory for sampled data. The status register is used to control the types of data to be collected and the frequency of collection as well as providing status about the data collection. The mutual exclusion facility is used to coordinate the potential controllers of the PMC (the processor and the I/O system).

The PMC provides several features that facilitate acquiring measurement over an extended period. First, acquisition stops whenever any counter overflows. Second, the PMC may be configured to interrupt the processor whenever a counter overflows thereby allowing the interrupt service routine to save the PMC contents and then restart PMC acquistion. Last, the PMC provides several registers that may be written during acquisition to identify the epoch in which the measurements were made.

The following sections describe in detail the control functions and status information provided by the PMC. A list of the PMC counters and data sampled is also given.

Mutual Exclusion Functions

To insure correct operation, only one of the two potential users of the PMC (I/O device or processor) can control the PMC at a given time. Two coordination functions are provided for implementing the mutual exclusion protocol.

Reserve PMC: returns the current value of the status register, then sets the busy bit.

Release PMC: returns the current value of the status register, then clears the busy bit.

Before using the PMC, a potential user (the I/O device or processor) must reserve the PMC using the Reserve PMC function. After the user is finished with the PMC, the Release PMC function is used to release the PMC making it available to the other potential user.

PMC Control Functions

The following bits in the status register are used to control the activity of the PMC. The bits are set/cleared by writing the appropriate bit pattern into the PMC status register.

Enable PMC: when set, enables the PMC to count events and take data sample.

Clear PMC: when set, causes the valid bits in the counters of the sample data and the indicator bits in the status register to be cleared.

Delay Enable: when set, causes the Master Timer to increment from its current value until it overflows and wraps around to zero; then the PMC starts to count and sample. This feature allows a program to delay the start of monitoring; the length of the delay is dependent on the value loaded into the master counter by the program.

Enable Interrupt: when set, causes an interrupt to be generated from the PMC to the processor when one of the PMC counters overflows. The program can then unload the measurement data, reset, and restart the PMC.

Monitor Supervisor: when set, causes the PMC to count and sample all supervisor requests.

Monitor User: when set, causes the PMC to count and sample all user requests.

Sampling Rate: set to select one of the several data sampling rates provided internally by the PMC.

Reset PMC: clears all PMC counters, sample memory and registers.

Cache event: used to select the events to be signalled by the cache: all cache requests, instruction requests only, data requests only, data read requests only.

PMC Indicator Bits

The following is a list of bits that indicate the status of the PMC. These bits are obtained by reading the PMC status register.

Overflow: when set, indicates that one of the counters has overflowed, and the PMC has stopped counting and sampling. If the Interrupt is enabled, it will generate an interrupt to the processor. When a counter overflows, no information is lost in any counter.

Wrap: when set, indicates that the sample RAMs have overflowed and old samples have been written over; therefore, the data represents the latest samples taken.

Bus error: when set, indicates that the PMC has detected an error condition on the processor bus.

Busy: set by the Reserve PMC, cleared by the Release PMC operation, used for processor coordination.

PMC Events Counted

The following is the list of events that are accumulated in counters by the PMC. Counters vary in size from 19 to 22 bits, depending on the maximum event frequency.

- Master timer (number of processor cycles)
- Number of instructions completed by the processor
- Number of times the processor executes a specific instruction
- Number of times the processor references a specific memory address
- Number of instructions completed by the Floating Point Unit
- Number of translated requests
- Number of non-translated requests
- Number of Translation Look-aside Buffer (TLB) misses
- Number of cacheable requests (based on the value of cache event in the status register)
- Number of cache misses (based on the value of cache event in the status register)

2.5. Desirable Features not Included

- Number of requests to the Network Interface (including requests to local and remote memory)
- Number of requests to local memory (node's own memory)
- Number of requests to the Memory Controller (including requests from local and remote processor)
- Total number of cycles the Memory Controller is busy servicing requests (including memory access time and refresh)
- Total number of cycles the Switch Interface is waiting to send requests into the network

PMC Sample Date

The following is the list of items that can be sampled. The rate of sampling is controlled via the status register. The sample rates are 2K, 8K, 32K, and 128K processor cycles.

- Virtual addresses
- Absolute addresses
    - Latency of request
    - Memory address
    - Memory operation code
    - Number of outstanding requests at time of reply

3

Parallel Applications Performance Methodology

Frederica Darema

3.1 Introduction

The advent of parallel systems as a means of obtaining higher computational power, has opened new domains of investigation into how to use such systems to perform computations efficiently and to understand the characteristics that the parallel systems must have to facilitate this task. Much effort is presently expended in software-related areas such as parallel applications/algorithms, computational models, parallelizing compilers, operating systems (OS), cost program development tools, debugging, and performance.

In this paper we concentrate on performance. There exists an interplay between algorithm design, hardware, OS, compiler, and computational model that affect the execution efficiency of a program. Here we will discuss the issues and objectives of performance studies, the approach we take for performance measurement and analysis of parallel applications, and the methods and tools that are needed to achieve that performance.

3.2 Performance Objectives

Performance measurements and analysis have two aspects: one is from the applications' (or the user's) perspective, the other is from the hardware designer's perspective. However, these two aspects share common ground.

The performance analysis effort of the application may be focused either specifically on the performance of a given application or may have a broader scope and be aimed at determining the potential of parallelism in compute-intensive applications. In the more focused sense one would analyze a given application to fine-tune the application in order to obtain maximum efficiency on a given system, or one would analyze the performance of the application across a multitude of parallel systems to determine a suitable system. On the broader perspective, the analysis has the objective to enable understanding the effect of the underlying parallel architecture or machine characteristics on the applications' performance, and to investigate the effect on efficiency of the underlying computational model, the compiler, and the operating system.

The hardware performance analysis effort is aimed at determining the requirements on parallel architectures to support compute-intensive applications. Currently, parallel architectures range from systems where the parallel processors can have access to the entire memory (*shared memory systems*) to systems where each processor has immediate access to only a portion of the memory (*distributed or message-passing systems*), with many variants in between. It is not certain, currently, which class of architectures is more general, that is, suitable for the majority of applications. Further understanding must also be acquired on specific design characteristics within a given architectural framework. To study system performance, one would consider a number of applications and examine the performance of specific hardware components or architectural characteristics such as the memory organization, in order to design or improve hardware.

Both perspectives have a common ground in that they both aim to understanding the interplay of algorithm design and hardware features, and as we will discuss, also share common tools that may be used to understand this interaction.

3.3 Performance Methodology for Parallel Applications

The study and understanding of parallel application performance analysis can be separated into several levels, depending on the depth of analysis desired. Understanding at each particular level requires different types of hardware and software tools as discussed in the next section.

The most basic information one would like to have is how fast the problem runs. This is displayed by quantities such the speedup over a one processor run, and the millions of instructions processed (MIP) and floating-point operation (FLOP) rates. These measures indicate how efficiently the underlying parallel hardware is being utilized.

On a more detailed level, the user would like to understand why a given efficiency is obtained. Therefore it is also desirable to know the percentage and the degree of parallelism in the problem and the synchronization overhead. Knowledge of these quantities can be desirable for the entire program but also for each section in the program, in order to identify possible bottlenecks. Sources of inefficiencies may be due either to the parallel algorithm used or the result of other software aspects such as the computational model, the compiler, the operating system, or the hardware system itself.

Typically the applications designer will address the algorithmic inefficiencies. A layer below that would be to understand the performance effect due to the other software components or the hardware system. It might also be desirable to study the effect of specific architecture features on performance. For example, accessing the shared memory in a shared memory system or communication in a distributed system can be costly and users might want to understand the effect of these features on performance.

The applications designer might also wish to be able to predict the performance achievable on large problems. Typically applications developers experiment with a small problem but performance predictions are useful for larger problems that may take many CPU hours. We discuss below a methodology that allows extrapolation of measurements made on small problems to predict performance on bigger problems.

3.4 Tools for Measurement and Analysis

In this section we describe tools for performance measurement and analysis that we feel would be useful to the applications developers. We will discuss tools that we have used, developed by ourselves or others, as well as tools that we feel would be desirable. Such tools can be divided into three categories: pre-run, run-time and post-run tools; they may be implemented either by software or hardware assists.

Several kinds of pre-run tools can be useful. Tools that identify compute-intensive parts of the program may identify areas for the applications developers to focus attention and optimize for maximum efficiency. Other tools that can be useful are those that allow one to study the algorithmic behavior of a parallel application. Tools in this category, such as [1,2], can be used to study the expected speedup of an entire program, or sections of it, for a range of processors and a given problem size. Again, such tools can aid the applications designers in focusing and improving the parallel performance of the most significant sections of a program. Tools that allow users to study the impact of a machine's architectural characteristics on algorithm performance are useful in helping users to understand the advantage of exploiting these features. For example, users who prepare a parallel program for a system with shared memory, local memory, and cache, could improve performance by exploiting the local memory or cache. Tools such as PSIMUL [3] may be used to understand the effect of algorithm restructuring on reducing traffic to the shared memory. If adequate modeling is incorporated in these tools, they may also be used to understand trade-offs between different hardware configurations. In the pre-run stage, it is also useful for users to have at their disposal modeling tools to predict expected performance for a range of problem sizes. The methodology we describe in the next section is intended to assist in this regard.

At run-time one would like to collect measurements that can either be analyzed on line or that can be accumulated and analyzed after the run, with the objective of predicting and/or improving performance of future runs. The most elementary measurements are timings of the entire run or of sections of the program. We assume that the hardware system provides a global clock and that the operating system provides the capability to query the elapsed time, as well as the computational time spent, by each of the running processes. Timing measurements, combined with measurements of the number of instructions or the number of floating point operations, can give the MIP and FLOP rates during the computation. Systems such as RP3, [4], provide hardware monitoring [5] capabilities that allow measurements of the MIP or FLOP rates directly. Hardware monitors may also provide many measurements that can provide insights to the applications and hardware designers; such measurements are discussed in [5].

In addition to hardware assists, valuable run-time information can be collected via software-directed event recording and time-stamping [6-8]. In these environments, libraries are provided that have built-in capability to record multi-processing events such as locks, synchronization variables, selected application shared variables, and creation and completion of tasks, and record the time of their occurrence. Typically such environments are accompanied by graphics capabilities to visualize the parallel computation sequence in terms of the computation graph and the associated events.

The post-run performance analysis environment provides modeling tools to display the measured data and/or use such data to predict or improve the parallel algorithm. Here again, visualization of the performance measurements or the modeling of such measurements is an integral and essential part of the development of useful tools.

3.5 Scaling Methods for Performance Predictions

The philosophy behind this methodology is to use measurements made on small problems to predict the expected performance of bigger problems.

The basis for the proposed method is the algorithmic performance methodology used in the SPAN [2] tool, currently used to analyze the performance of parallel programs. In this method, the program is considered as a sequence of tasks, some of which can be executed concurrently. The parallel system is represented by a set of self-scheduling processes. The parallel execution entails mapping the sequence of tasks onto the parallel system. To simulate this procedure, the tasks are *marked* and a task trace is collected by running the program on a single processor. The task trace is a sequence of markers marking (the beginning and end of) various sections of the program, together with the execution cost (either in CPU time or instruction count) for each task. For example, a group of concurrent tasks might be independent iterations in a parallel loop. Markers are also used to mark sub-tasks of each task. An example is the overhead cost to acquire a loop iteration and the execution cost for each iteration being recorded in the task trace. The trace is then used to predict the speedup for a range of processors for that problem size by simulating the self-scheduling procedure. A limitation of this method is that it is impractical to run a large problem through the simulator and predictions are limited to the problem size measured.

In the proposed methodology we provide the capability to extend the measured results and to make performance predictions for other problem sizes as follows: in addition to the markers introduced to capture the parallelism overhead or the execution length of each iteration, additional markers are introduced within the body of a section to capture the execution length of subsections in that section. For example, one may wish to collect such information on each iteration of a parallel loop. These markers are user-directed, and their place is dependent on the algorithm analyzed. The tool will also allow the user to introduce scaling factors to the various subsections of the trace. The implementation of such a tool is, in effect, an extension of the current SPAN tool. Markers are provided in the form of macros, such as @MARK, that a preprocessor will convert to distinct markers and for which scaling factors are calculated in the post-processing stage by appropriate user-provided subroutine or function calls.

An example of the capabilities provided by such a tool is given using a Monte Carlo program [9]. The problem solved is the placement and optimal wiring of chips on a board. Each Monte Carlo history consists of the pair-wise exchange of chips (*a move*). Each history is composed of three distinct stages: the selection of a pair, the computation of the effect of the proposed move and the acceptance or rejection of the move. The techniques for the parallel execution of this algorithm are discussed in [9]. According to the methods discussed in [9], the process of selecting a pair is a function of the problem size, the chip interconnection topology, and the number of parallel processors executing the problem. The computation of each move is dependent on the chip interconnection topology. A move rejection is independent of the chip layout, but the acceptance computation depends on the chip interconnectivity. The computational loop is shown in Figure 3.1, with the appropriate markers in place. The @DO, the @ENDO, and @MARK macros are converted by a preprocessor to appropriate markers for the overhead sections, the end-of-iteration, and subsection markers. A trace is generated for the N iterations.

Applying this technique to the small (81-chip) problem we obtain a speedup curve that agrees fairly closely with results obtained experimentally. Next we extrapolate to compute speedup curves for a larger (900-chip) problem. In the example problem considered here, we assume a simple case where the chip interconnection remains the same as the problem size increases. This amounts to simply computing the factor needed in the first stage: the pair selection. Let $\beta * N$ be the scaling factor for the number of iterations needed for a problem β-times larger. Let α_1 be the scaling factor for subsection 1. The post-processor will read randomly each history from the original trace and will recycle that trace β times. In even simpler cases, where each iteration in the loop is the

---

@DO I = 1, N

...

(code for subsection$_1$)

...

@MARK

...

(code for subsection$_2$)

...

@MARK

...

(code for subsection$_3$)

...

@ENDO

FIGURE 3.1
Computation loop with user inserted markers.

3.5. Scaling Methods for Performance Predictions

same as any other, only one iteration needs to be sampled. Each iteration will be scaled by α_1 and the bin-packing method emulating the parallel processor self-scheduling algorithm is used until $\beta * N$ iterations are processed. Thus speedups, efficiencies, and other characteristics for the entire problem or problem section can be defined as is done in the SPAN tool. In Figure 3.2 the speedup curves are presented for the 81- and 900-chip problem sizes.

This methodology may be applied not only for traces collected by simulators but similar techniques may be used for compiler generated information or run-time event traces.

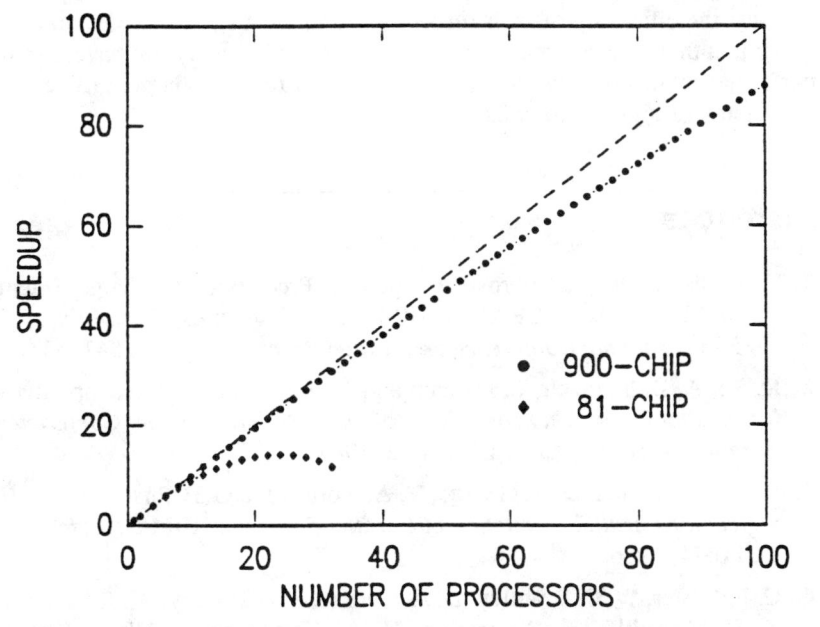

FIGURE 3.2
Speedups for a 81 and a 900-chip placement problem. The 900-chip problem size predictions are based on measurements of the 81-chip problem.

3.6 Summary

We have presented the objectives of parallel applications performance analysis. Our thesis is that the parallel applications performance is affected not only by the numerical techniques and algorithms used, but also by the computing systems environment: programming model, compiler, operating system, and hardware. We feel that applications developers need to understand the influence of such factors and need to have tools for probing their effects. On the other hand, the applications can be the vehicle used by systems software and hardware developers to test the efficiency of their respective components. We have elaborated on the fact that there are common tools that can be used. Finally, we have discussed a performance methodology that allows scaling of results to larger problem sizes and systems of higher parallelism.

References

1. E. Williams and F. Bobrowicz, Speedup Predictions for Large Scientific Parallel Programs on CRAY X-MP-Like Architectures, *Proceedings of the 1985 International Conference on Parallel Processing*, pages 541–543, 1985.

2. K. So, A. Bolmarcich, F. Darema and V. A. Norton, A Speedup Analyser for Parallel Programs, *Proceedings of the 1987 International Conference on Parallel Processing*, pages 653–662, 1987.

3. K. So, F. Darema, D. A. George, V. A. Norton and G. F. Pfister, *PSIMUL: A System for Parallel Simulation of Parallel Programs*, IBM Research Report RC11674, 1986.

4. G. F. Pfister, W. C. Brantley, D. A. George, S. L. Harvey, W. J. Kleinfelder, K. P. McAuliffe, E. A. Melton, V. A. Norton and J. Weiss, The IBM Research Parallel Processor Prototype (RP3): Introduction and Architecture, *Proceedings of the 1985 International Conference on Parallel Processing*, pages 764–771, 1985.

5. W. Brantley, K. P. McAuliffe and T. A. Ngo, RP3 Performance Monitoring Hardware, in *Instrumentation for Parallel Computing Systems*, Addison-Wesley, Reading, MA, in press.

6. J. J. Dongarra, D. C. Sorensen, K. Connolly and J. Patterson, Program Methodology and Performance for Advanced Computer Architectures, *Parallel Computing*, Vol 8, Oct. 1988.

7. M. Seager, S. Campbell, S. Sikora, R. Strout and M. Zosel, *Graphical Multiprocessing Analysis Tool (GMAT)*, Lawrence Livermore National Laboratory Technical Report UCD–21348, 1988.
8. A. D. Malony and D. A. Reed, Visualizing Parallel Computer Systems Performance, in *Instrumentation for Parallel Computing Systems*, Addison-Wesley, Reading, MA, 1989.
9. F. Darema, S. Kirkpatrick and V. A. Norton, Simulated Annealing on Shared Memory Parallel Systems, *IBM Journal of Research and Development*, May 1987.

4

Visualizing Parallel Computer System Performance

Allen D. Malony[1]
Daniel A. Reed[2]

The purpose of computing is insight, not numbers.

Richard Hamming

4.1 Introduction

The appearance of any new computer system raises many questions about its performance, both in absolute terms and in comparison to other machines of its class; parallel computer systems are no exception. Unfortunately, parallel computer systems are among the most complex of man's creations, making satisfactory performance characterization difficult. Despite this complexity, there are

---

[1] Supported in part by the National Science Foundation under grants NSF MIP–8410110 and NSF DCR 84–06916, by the Department of Energy under grant DOE DE–FG02–85ER25001, and by the Air Force Office of Scientific Research under grant AFOSR-F49620–86–C–0136 (URI).

[2] Supported in part by the National Science Foundation under grants NSF DCR 84–17948 and NSF CCR86–57696, by the National Aeronautics and Space Administration under NASA Contract Number NAG–1–613, and by the Air Force Office of Scientific Research under grant AFOSR–F49620–86–C–0136 (URI).

strong, indeed almost irresistible, incentives to quantify parallel system performance using a single metric. The fallacy lies in succumbing to such temptations. Just as it is now widely recognized that human intelligence is not subsumed by the spatial and verbal abilities measured by standard intelligence tests, complete characterization of parallel computer system performance encompasses more than operations executed per second.

Peak performance ratings in MIPS (millions of instructions per second) or MFLOPS (millions of floating point operations per second) obscure the importance of interacting *performance levels* and *dynamic equilibrium*. Repeated studies have shown that a system's performance is maximized when the components are balanced (i.e., there is no single system bottleneck) [1]. As an example, optimizing the performance of message-passing systems [2] requires a judicious combination of node computation speed, message-transmission latency, and operating-system software. High-speed processors connected by high-latency communication links restrict the classes of algorithms that can be supported efficiently.

A complete performance characterization requires not only an analysis of the system's constituent levels, it also requires both *static* and *dynamic* characterizations. Static or average behavior analysis may mask transients that dramatically alter system performance. By analogy, biological researchers have long recognized the importance of both *in vitro* and *in vivo* measurements. Laboratory measurements of isolated cells or biological molecules often differ from similar measurements in natural environments.

The history of virtual memory research offers a classic example of transient behavior and its importance. The slow drift model [3] predicted that program reference locality changed slowly. Later, more detailed measurements showed that reference localities change swiftly and catastrophically. Most page faults and associated overhead occur in small time intervals, and a phase-transition model more accurately reflects observed behavior.

Performance measurements of high-speed computing systems can quickly generate vast quantities of numerical data. Indeed, recognition of the importance of virtual memory phase transitions was hampered by the volume of data generated during simulation and measurement; post-measurement data compression yielded page-fault rates, a static performance measure. However, phases and transitions can be seen only by examining significant portions of the reference trace; this is best done via dynamic graphic displays.

Although the human visual system is remarkably adept at interpreting and identifying anomalies in false color data, the importance of visual scientific data presentation has only recently been recognized [4]. Large, complex parallel systems pose equally vexing *performance interpretation* problems. Data from hardware and software performance monitors must be presented in ways that emphasize important events while eliding irrelevant details.

In collaboration with the Center for Supercomputing Research and Development at the University of Illinois, we are developing a suite of performance visualization tools. These tools and our design approach are the subject of this paper. In §4.2 we examine the importance of performance levels and formalize the empirical performance evaluation process. In §4.3 we discuss HyperView, a prototype that dynamically displays performance data obtained from hardware measurement and simulation of message-passing systems. Techniques for visualizing application performance are the subject of §4.4; linear programming [5],[6] is used as a test problem. Finally, §4.5 summarizes our experience and development plans.

4.2 Experimental Performance Analysis

As Figure 4.1 illustrates, there are four levels in the hierarchy of performance measurements. The answer to the oft-asked question, "How fast is it?" depends on the intended use of the performance data. At the lowest level lies the performance of the hardware design.

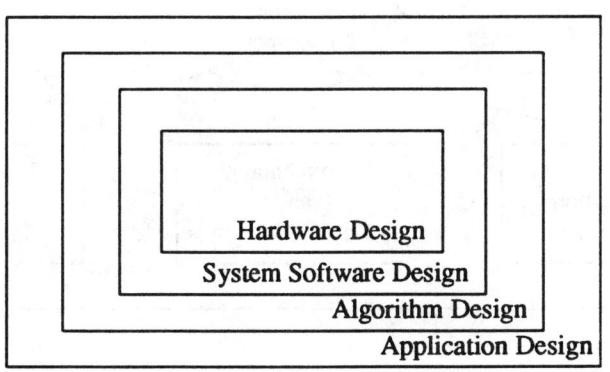

FIGURE 4.1
Performance levels.

Determining this performance provides both a design validation and directives for system software design. Only by understanding the strengths and weaknesses of the hardware can system software designers develop an implementation and user interface that maximizes the fraction of the raw hardware performance available to the end user. As an example, consider a hypothetical hypercube operating system that provides dynamic task migration to balance workloads. Here, meeting these goals, refers to dynamically migrating tasks to balance workload; it must be possible to rapidly transmit small status messages. It is fruitless to design such a system if the underlying hardware provides only high-latency message transmission. Given some characterization of the balance between processing power and interprocessor communication resulting from the system software, users can develop algorithms that are best suited to the parallel system. Finally, the best mix of key algorithms will maximize the performance of user applications.

Regardless of the system level, performance characterization requires specification of the desired measurements, instrumentation and data collection mechanisms, and data reduction and display; see Figure 4.2.[1]

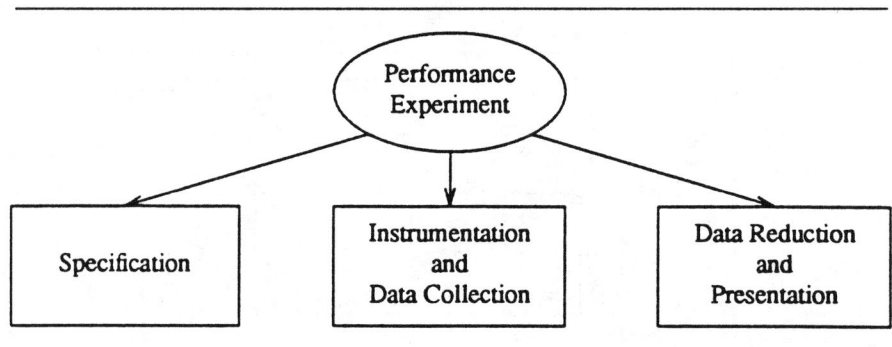

FIGURE 4.2
Performance analysis phases.

---

[1] By analogy with news reporting, "What do I want?" "How do I get it?" and "How can I see it?"

Although it is clear that a parallel computer system is a *gestalt* whose performance is inextricably tied to the performance of its constituent hardware and software levels, it is less clear that performance instrumentation and data collection techniques for one level, or even one system, are applicable to other systems or other levels. As an example, Table 4.1 shows a subset of the important performance measurements for three levels—hardware, system software, and algorithm—and three systems—the CRAY X-MP, the University of Illinois Cedar system [7], and the Intel iPSC hypercube [8].

The diversity of underlying technology and system architecture makes it impossible to develop a single set of performance instrumentation techniques. Memory bank conflicts on the CRAY X-MP have no analog on the distributed memory Intel iPSC. Moreover, the event time scales differ by six orders of magnitude. Similarly, the shared memory access patterns of Cedar application algorithms may cause interconnection network conflicts, but these patterns are not predictors of performance degradation due to network contention. Although it is impossible to develop a single performance instrumentation mechanism applicable to all levels, *mechanisms* for specification of noteworthy performance events and their presentation are largely system independent.[2]

TABLE 4.1
Performance Level Comparison

Level	Cray X/MP	Illinois Cedar	Intel iPSC
Hardware	vector startup memory conflicts	network contention vector/cache interaction	processor speed communication latency and bandwidth
Software Algorithm	compiler vectorization	compiler shared memory access	OS support communication pattern

---

[2]The *events* vary but the specification and display *mechanism* need not.

At all performance levels there exists a minimal set of required events (e.g., counts and times). Capture of these events should be enabled by signals to a hardware monitor, operating system calls, or flags to a compiler preprocessor. In addition to standard events, certain others must be enabled selectively, either to minimize the performance perturbations of instrumentation or to reduce the data volume to tractable levels. Ideally, a standard user interface should permit event specification regardless of the event type or the performance level.

Despite the diverse instrumentation events of differing levels and systems, the performance measures can be presented using a small number of display types (e.g., bar and strip charts, three-dimensional plots, and state transition diagrams). These graphical displays are the subject of the remainder of this paper.

4.3 HyperView: A Hypercube Visualization Tool

In collaboration with the Center for Supercomputing Research and Development, we have designed and implemented `HyperView`, a prototype performance visualization tool for distributed memory parallel processors configured as hypercubes. `HyperView` dynamically displays architectural and system activity via a multiplicity of system views. Detailed performance measurements also are provided via standard statistical displays.

`HyperView` was inspired by *Seecube* [9], a hypercube visualization system built for the SunView[3] window environment. Although many of the `HyperView` displays were borrowed from *Seecube*, the implementation is based on the X window environment [10] and the user interface libraries provided by the Faust parallel programming environment being developed at the University of Illinois Center for Supercomputing Research and Development [11-13]. The portability provided by X permits use of `HyperView` in a variety of workstation environments. Because X supports a client-server paradigm, the data analysis and display portions of `HyperView` are decoupled, potentially executing on different systems. This decoupling not only makes the visualization portions independent of message passing hardware and system software, it also is crucial if real-time performance display and dynamic system reconfiguration are to be supported. Thus, `HyperView` contains three cooperating modules: data capture, state analysis, and visualization.

---

[3] SunView is a trademark of Sun Microsystems.

4.3.1 Data Capture

The `HyperView` visualization component accepts event traces generated by the processors of a message-passing system. Because the data capture is decoupled from visualization, the event trace can be generated via simulation, (permitting study of new message-passing architectures), or from program execution. At present, the `HyperView` visualization is driven by data obtained from simulation of communication hardware for different message-passing paradigms [14], including store-and-forward message switching, circuit switching, staged circuit switching, and wormhole circuit switching. Our experience has shown that visual comparison of system dynamics quickly reveals differences in communication paradigms.

When an event is detected by the performance instrumentation, an event identifier, a timestamp, and any additional event data are written to a trace buffer. For our message passing simulations, we instrumented the simulator to record the following information about message events at each hypercube node. The following events suffice to display message-passing activity for fixed-path and adaptive variants of both circuit and store-and-forward message switching.

```
i <time> <nodes> <string>                    Initial message
m <time> <msg id> <from> <to> <size>         Create message
q <time> <msg id> <at>                       Enqueue message
Q <time> <msg id> <at>                       Dequeue message
e <time> <msg id> <at>                       Circuit establishment
v <time> <msg id> <from> <to> <link>         Visit node via link
t <time> <msg id>                            Begin message transmission
T <time> <msg id>                            End message transmission
V <time> <msg id> <from> <to> <link>         Delete link between nodes
E <time> <msg id> <from> <to>                Circuit termination
M <time> <msg id>                            Message delivery
```

For both circuit- and packet-switching, messages may require several transmissions and may cross multiple communication links to reach their final destination. Hence, the events recorded by a single hypercube node are insufficient to reconstruct the history of a message. Thus, the *from* and *to* arguments in the message creation event represent the point of message origination and the final destination. Because we are studying routing paradigms that can choose one of many paths to the destination node, *link* traversal information must be saved to reconstruct the routing path.

Although the instrumentation events just described suffice to display communication traffic and queueing delays, other events are needed to display system software and application behavior. Thus, we are developing software and hardware instrumentation for an Intel iPSC/2 hypercube that will permit near real-time data capture of user, system, and hardware events, including support for local event buffering, global timestamp synchronization, and trace processing. See §4.5 for additional details.

4.3.2 State Analysis

In a distributed-memory parallel system such as a hypercube, each node must record events based only on local knowledge; the absence of global memory precludes data sharing with the granularity necessary to dynamically maintain a consistent, global state. Moreover, the nodes of many distributed memory systems are individually clocked, the clocks often are not synchronized, and the clocks may tick at different rates. Thus, the event trace at best defines a partial time order, and the timestamps may be logically inconsistent with the logical order of events.

To recover global state during trace analysis, the trace timestamps must be reconciled and enough event data must be saved to correlate distributed events. The analysis requires interpreting each event in sequence and incrementally modifying the current system state; for complete details see [9].

4.3.3 Performance Visualization

The HyperView user interface permits simultaneous display of the dynamic system state via a variety of differing *views*. Each view emphasizes certain system aspects (e.g., the network topology, the multiplicity of partially overlapping paths from a source to a destination node, or queues of waiting messages). Each view provides a different insight; collectively they convey system dynamics.

Although Hamming's dictum applies, numbers are often necessary and important. In addition to graphical displays, HyperView provides statistical displays at both macroscopic levels (e.g., number of messages transmitted) and microscopic levels (e.g., link utilization). Finally, HyperView permits *selective* display of message traffic and statistics, permitting the performance analyst to isolate anomalous behavior for further study.

Because HyperView is a *dynamic* performance visualization system, much is lost in description of static, monochrome images. Despite these limitations, we discuss HyperView as a performance analyst might encounter it, beginning with the top-level user interface shown in Figure 4.3.

User menus are shown at the top of the screen. Pulling down the **Trace** menu lists the *Description, Execution Control,* and *Statistics* items shown in Figure 4.4.

Trace Description. In the *Trace Description* window, a performance analyst can select, by clicking the mouse on the *Trace File* item, a trace file that contains the event information captured during system execution. A dialogue box (not shown) will pop up requesting the user to enter the trace file name. After reading the trace file, HyperView begins the state analysis needed to recover the time-varying global state of the message-passing system. During state analysis, HyperView computes the number of events, messages and bytes

4.3. HyperView: A Hypercube Visualization Tool 67

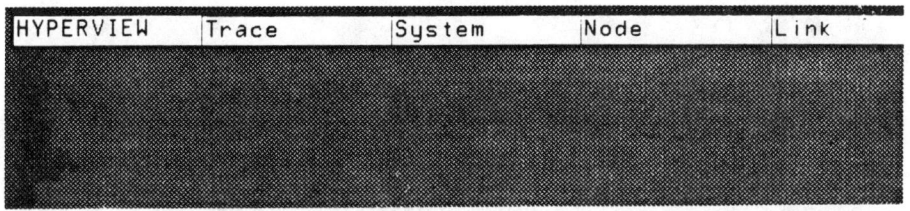

FIGURE 4.3
HyperView top-level display.

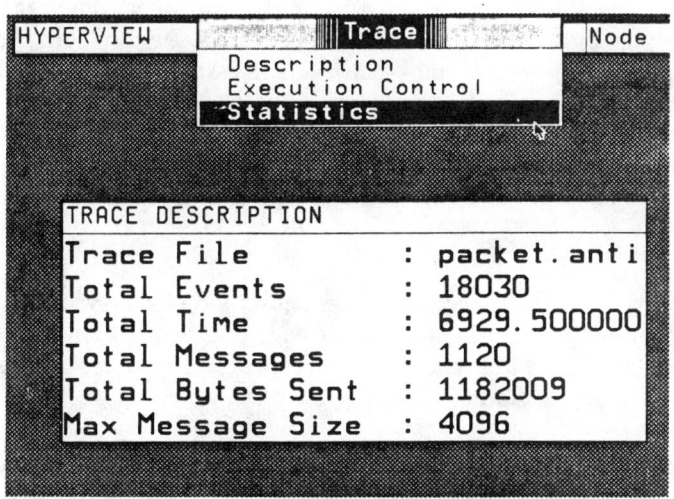

FIGURE 4.4
HyperView trace window.

transmitted. Throughout the visualization session, these statistics can be viewed by selecting the *Trace Description* menu.

Execution Control. As the name suggests, the *Execution Control* window controls updates to the graphical and statistical displays. During state analysis, HyperView identifies a series of globally consistent display points. During updates of the trace display, HyperView moves between these display points. The current point can be marked by a position in time and/or location in the event trace. Thus, the performance analyst can select a current display time either by clicking the mouse on *Current Frame Time* and entering a time, or by clicking the mouse somewhere within the *Frame Time* slider bar. Event trace positions are selected similarly. When a new time or event is selected, HyperView moves to the next consistent system state and its corresponding display. Because the event trace is processed *a posteriori*, the performance analyst can move both forward and backward in time.[4]

A *Frame* in HyperView corresponds to a displayed system state. The user can change three aspects of frame display: mode, rate, and state differential. Frames can be displayed either in single-step mode or continuously. If the mouse is clicked on the *SINGLE STEP* button, the user must explicitly request display of the next frame. Conversely, *CONTINUOUS* mode automatically advances to the next frame according to the specified frame rate and differential controls.

Via the *Frame Rate* control, the performance analyst can adjust the interval between display of new frames. The third aspect of frame display is the change in system state—in events or time—between successive, displayed frames. This state difference is the minimum of the specified number of *Events per Frame* and the number of *Clock Ticks per Frame*. By adjusting the display mode, frame rate, and state differential, the performance analyst can study gross behavior, examining a small subset of all states, or examine the trace event by event.

Global Statistics. The *Statistics* window shows the global system state, both cumulative message statistics and *current* node and link activity. Because the performance analyst can browse the trace, cumulative statistics are not monotonic — they reflect performance data relative to the current trace state.

System Displays. Figure 4.5 shows the menu of dynamic system views provided by HyperView.

Figures 4.6 and 4.7 show the *CUBE, FFT, PASCAL,* and *QUEUE* views. Each display gives a different view of the hypercube that shows current system activity as highlighted nodes and links. Each view emphasizes certain system

---

[4] §4.5 discusses both the advantages and disadvantages of time independent browsing.

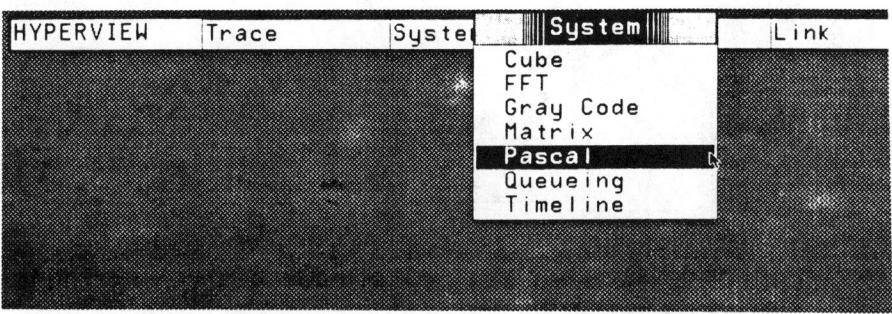

FIGURE 4.5
HyperView system menu.

aspects (e.g., the network topology, the multiplicity of partially overlapping paths from a source to a destination node, or queues of waiting messages). For example, the *CUBE* view is the "natural" multidimensional representation of a hypercube. In contrast, the *FFT* view emphasizes message routing paths. The *GRAY CODE* view, not shown, emphasizes subcube communication— communication links connecting the two $(D-1)$-dimensional subcubes of a D-dimensional hypercube appear as parallel lines [9]. The *PASCAL* view reflects the logarithmic combining (e.g., global minimization) when logical trees are embedded in the hypercube topology [6]. The *QUEUE* view in Figure 4.7 shows the instantaneous state of the message queues at each node. Each message awaiting transmission is shown as a small box. Communication transients appear as bursts of enqueued messages. Similarly, the effects of differing communication paradigms (e.g., store-and-forward message switching and circuit switching) appear as differences in mean queue size.

In all views, colors emphasize activity—links change color when messages are sent, nodes flash when processing messages.

Moreover, each system view supports pull-down menus for inquiries about nodes, links, messages, and circuits. In each topological view (i.e., *CUBE*, *FFT*, and *PASCAL*), unwanted detail can be elided via the *Node* and *Link* menus. For example, display of any combination of transmitting, active, or receiving nodes and links can be disabled. Figure 4.8 shows the *Link* menu; the *Node* menu is similar. *All*, *Active*, and *Transmitting* select the displayed link states.

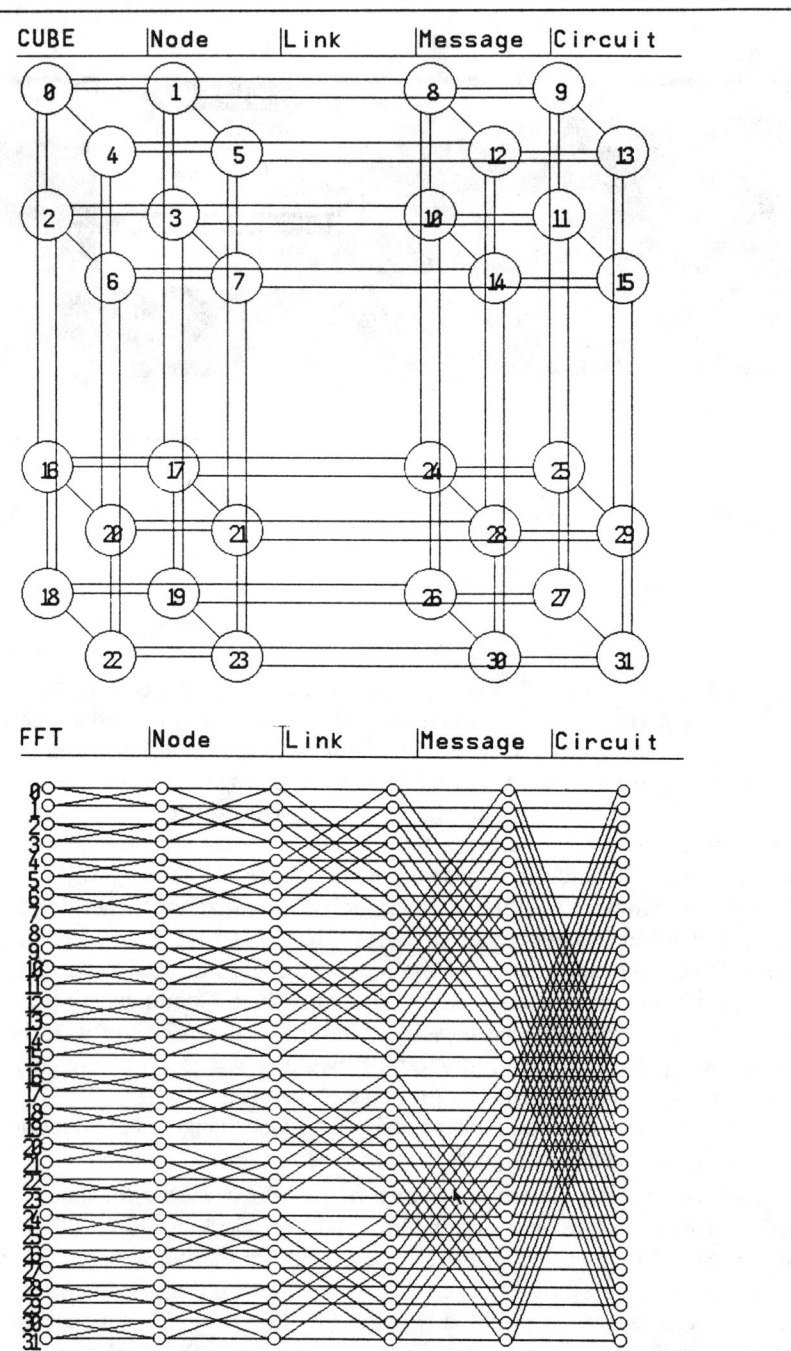

FIGURE 4.6
CUBE and *FFT* displays.

4.3. HyperView: A Hypercube Visualization Tool   71

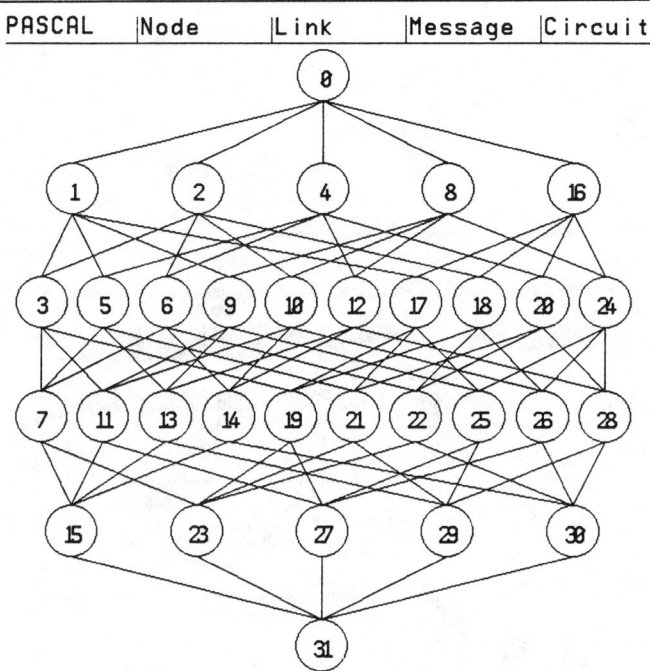

FIGURE 4.7
PASCAL and *QUEUE* displays.

72   Chapter 4. Visualizing Parallel Computer System Performance

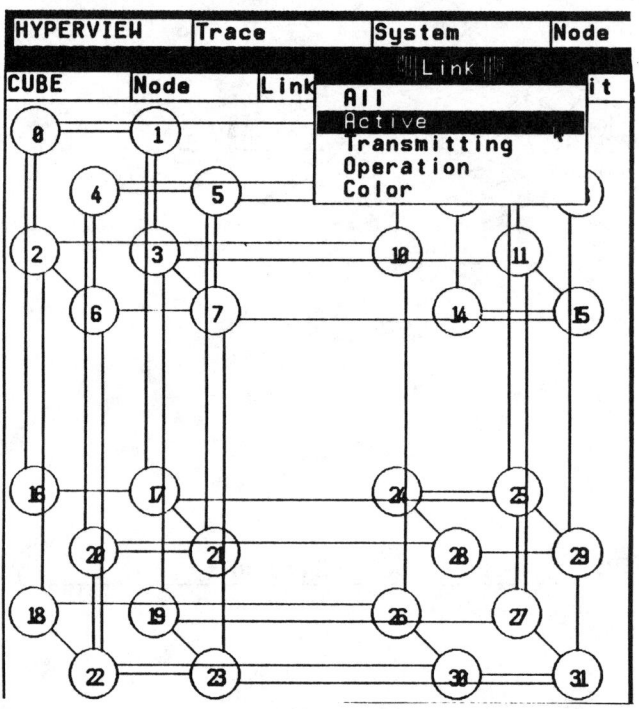

FIGURE 4.8
Link menu.

Message and Circuit Tracking. In addition to the elision of unwanted node and link details, `HyperView` supports *message tracking* and *circuit tracking*.[5] After identifying source and destination nodes, *only* those messages in transit between the specified nodes are displayed. Figure 4.9 illustrates message- and circuit-tracking in a system with circuit switched communication. In the figure, nodes 0 and 20 have been selected for circuit-tracking and message-tracking, respectively. Node 0 is transmitting a message to node 15 along the path shown. The intermediate nodes on the path are not active because only circuit connections have been established there. Concurrently, node 0 is sending a message to node 20, and node 20 is sending a message to node 29.

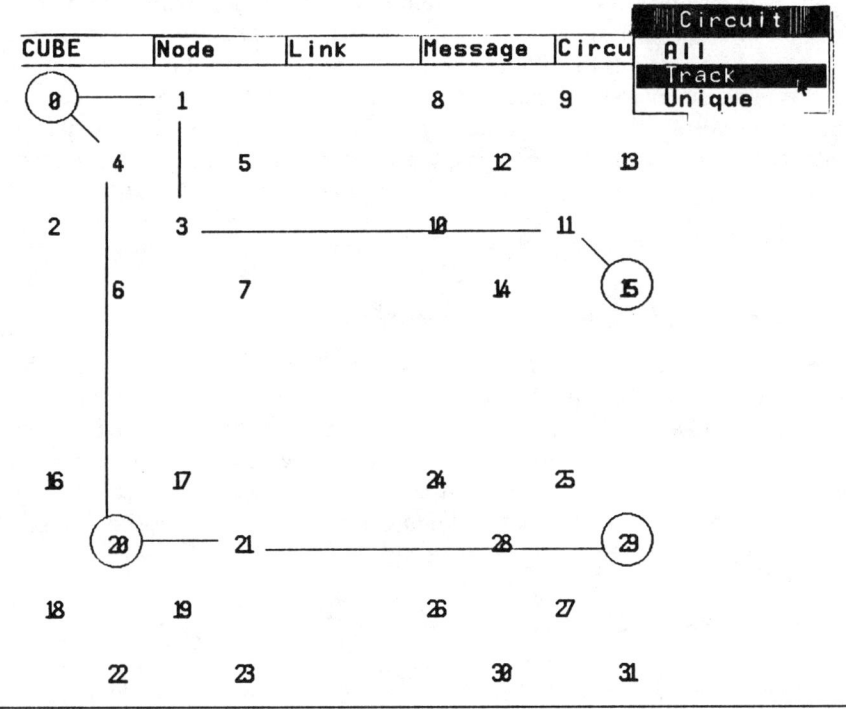

FIGURE 4.9
Message and circuit tracking.

---

[5]The choice and semantics depend on the underlying hardware communication paradigm.

Message- and circuit-tracking have proven invaluable when comparing communication paradigms. By eliding extraneous detail, the dynamics of circuit establishment in both fixed and adaptive routing paradigms can be easily compared.

4.4 Application Performance Displays

Performance visualization at both the hardware and system software levels provides important insight for *system* design and analysis. And because system performance is manifest in the application software executed during performance analysis, system-level performance visualization indirectly provides application performance insight. However, insight from visualization of system performance must be coupled with insight from application performance visualization to understand the interactions of different performance levels. To illustrate these interactions and the importance of integrated visualization tools, we use a parallel implementation of the simplex linear optimization algorithm [5,6], as an example. Like many parallel algorithms, the performance of the simplex method varies greatly with input data, and these variations are intimately related to both the algorithm and its interaction with the hardware and system software.

4.4.1 Linear Optimization: An Example

Large, sparse, linear systems of equations arise frequently when constructing mathematical models of natural phenomena. Most often, these linear systems are fully constrained and can be solved via a variety of direct or iterative techniques.

However, one important problem class requires solutions to *underconstrained* linear systems that minimize some objective function. These linear optimization problems often contain hundreds of equations with thousands of variables. Mathematically, this can be stated as:

$$\begin{aligned} Maximized: \quad & c^T x \\ Subject\ to: \quad & Ax = b \\ & b \geq 0 \\ & x \geq 0 \end{aligned}$$

Here, c^T is an n vector of variable coefficients that defines the objective function (i.e., the function being maximized). For a maximization problem, the negative of the objective function can be minimized. The objective function can thus be viewed as a cost function, where the goal is to minimize total cost.

The $m \times n$ linear system $Ax = b$ defines the linear constraints on the objective function x. Each of the m rows of the matrix A defines a constraint on the n variables of the objective function.

The optimization problem arises because the linear system $Ax = b$ is underconstrained—i.e., m is smaller than n, and the matrix A contains many more columns (variables) than rows (constraints).[6]

Consequently, there are many possible x vectors that satisfy the system $Ax = b$. A fundamental theorem of linear programming states that an optimal solution, if it exists, occurs when $n - m$ elements of x are zero (i.e., when there are precisely m nonzero elements of x.) This theorem corresponds to the solution of an $m \times m$ linear system, the *basis*, obtained by selecting m of the n columns of the matrix A.

Clearly, exhaustive solution of the possible linear systems is not feasible. The simplex method is a search algorithm that decreases the value of the objective function at each iteration by selecting a nonzero element of x, a so-called *basic* variable, and replacing the corresponding column of A with another column. The simplex method provides a systematic way of moving from one basic feasible solution (i.e., one satisfying the constraints) to another. This systematic movement, called *pivoting*, must

- identify a new basis column that decreases the objective (cost) function value,
- identify the column which if removed from the basis, will maximize the decrease in the objective function value while still satisfying the constraints, and
- remove the old basis column and replace it with the new one.

These transformations are realized by standard techniques from numerical linear algebra (i.e., Gauss-Jordan elimination).

4.4.2 Parallel Simplex Variants

In message-passing architectures, interprocessor communication is much more expensive than local memory access. Hence, many algorithm implementation details are constrained given the mapping of data to processors. The simplex algorithm shares similar characteristics with solutions of linear systems, matrix multiplication, and other common matrix operations. Previous work on distributed matrix algorithms has advocated row or column partitioning of matrices [15-17]. We have considered similar schemes for distributing the matrix of constraints across the nodes of a hypercube [6].

---

[6] See Figure 4.11 for an example.

In the column-partitioned method, shown in Figure 4.10, complete columns are divided equally among the processors.

To identify the column to enter the basis, each hypercube node must first find the local minimum of the objective values for those columns in its local memory, then cooperate with other nodes to identify and distribute the identity of the column containing the minimum objective value. Conversely, the *single node* containing the pivot column must identify the column to leave the basis. Thus, partitioning the matrix by columns creates both parallel and sequential computation phases.

In the row-partitioned strategy, complete rows of the matrix are divided equally among the processors. As Table 4.2 shows, this approach also creates both parallel and sequential computation phases.[7] Despite the similarities suggested by Table 4.2, the performance of simplex algorithms based on row- and column data partitions can be strikingly different. Why? Distributed linear systems solvers process $n \times n$ matrices. The constraint matrices processed by the simplex method contain many fewer rows than columns. Moreover, the ratio of the number of rows to columns can vary dramatically. This variance, coupled with the differences in matrix sparsity, is manifest in the relative costs of communication, sequential computation, and parallel computation. Hence, neither

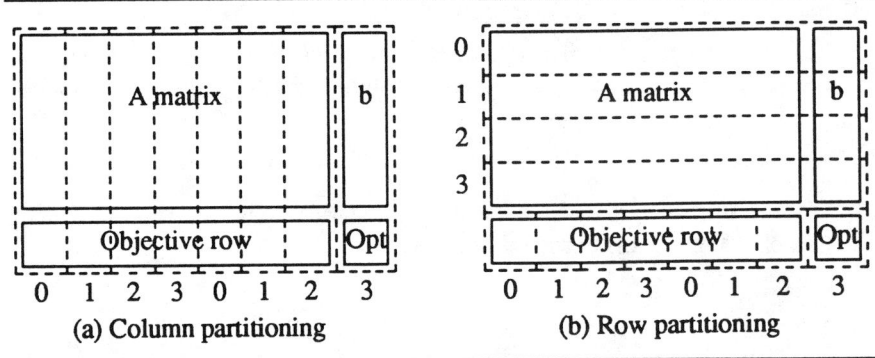

FIGURE 4.10
Data Placement for simplex row and column partitions.

---

[7] In reality, there are many subvariations of both row- and column-partitioning, and each has differing performance; see [6] for complete details.

TABLE 4.2
Hypercube Simplex Variations

Partition	Entering Basis Column	Departing Basis Column	Gauss-Jordan Elimination
Column	Parallel computation Global minimization	Sequential computation	Column global send Parallel computation
Row	Parallel computation Global minimization	Parallel computation Global minimization	Row global send Parallel computation

row nor column partitioning is uniformly superior. To understand the dynamics of algorithm interaction with matrix structure, application visualization tools are necessary.

4.4.3 Simplex Performance Visualization

An earlier study [6] suggested that despite variations in matrix structure, row-partitioned simplex implementations often yielded better performance. However, counterexamples exist; Figure 4.11 shows the nonzero matrix structure of one such problem. Although the 7:1 ratio of columns to rows suggests the reason that column partitioning is preferable, the details are best grasped via visualization.

Figures 4.12 and 4.13 show four views of the number of messages sent between tasks of the row-partitioned simplex algorithm on a 16-node Intel iPSC/2 hypercube. Recall that in a D-dimensional hypercube, a node with address n is directly connected only to those other nodes with addresses whose binary expansions differ from n in exactly one bit. Although messages must cross multiple communication links to reach some nodes, the maximum distance between any two nodes is D. When exploring performance at the hardware and system software levels, understanding node connectivity is crucial. However, at the application level, messages are exchanged by tasks, not hypercube nodes. Hence, Figure 4.12[8] and subsequent figures show the *logical* interaction of tasks, not the physical transfer of data. We emphasize that complete understanding requires performance visualization at all levels: hardware, system software, algorithm, and application. By separating the levels, the performance contributions of each level are manifest.

In Figure 4.12 the peaks represent the logarithmic combining necessary to identify global minima. In Figure 4.13 the logarithmic combining appears as lightly shaded regions in the density view and as clustered contour lines in the

---

[8] In the three-dimensional displays, counts greater than thirty were clipped, hence the uniformity.

78   Chapter 4. Visualizing Parallel Computer System Performance

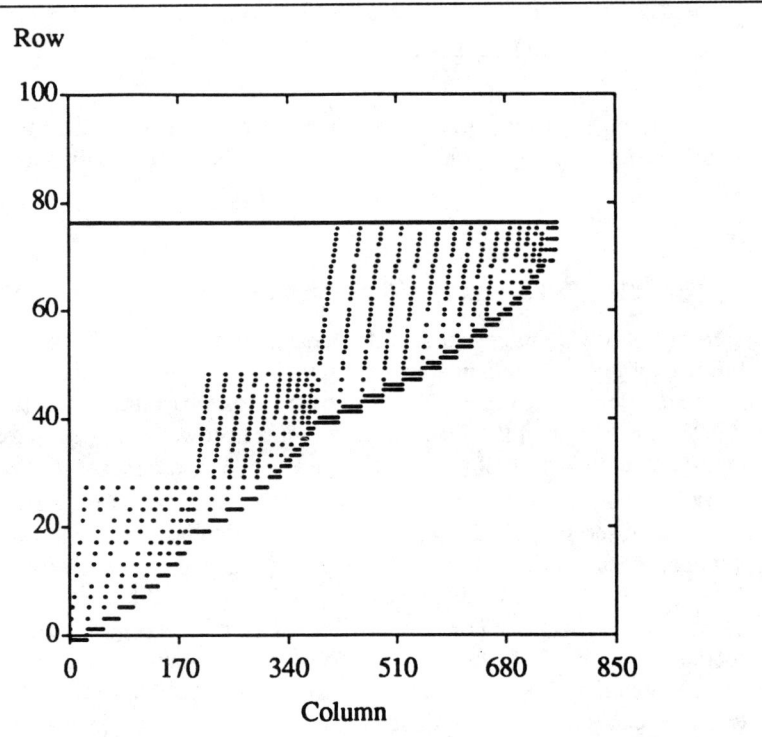

FIGURE 4.11
Simplex benchmark SCSD1.

4.4. Application Performance Displays   79

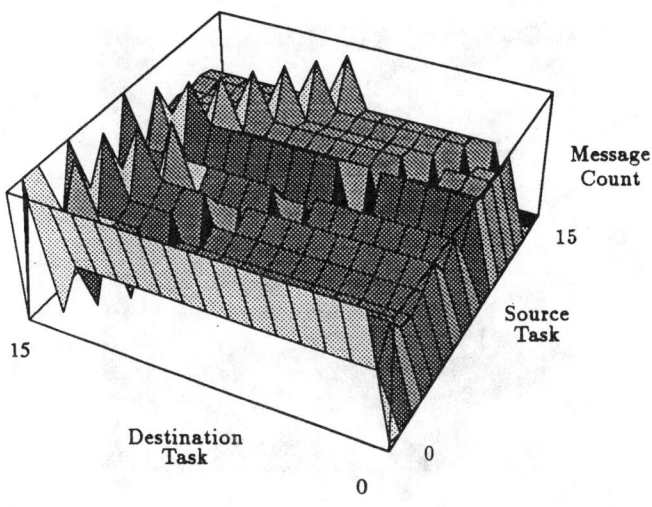

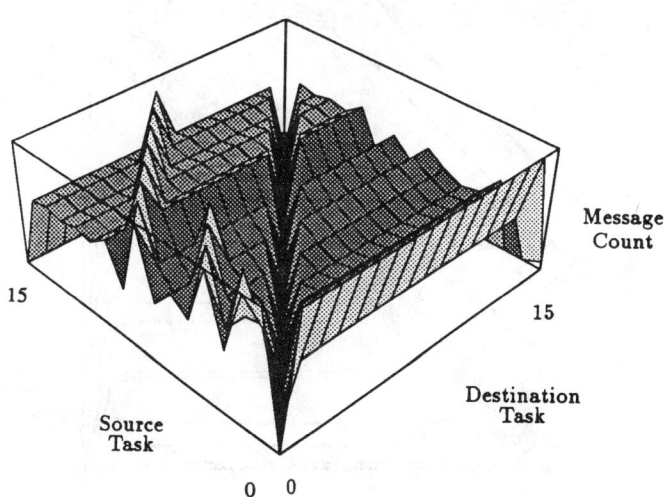

FIGURE 4.12
Perspective view of message counts (row partitioning).

80   Chapter 4. Visualizing Parallel Computer System Performance

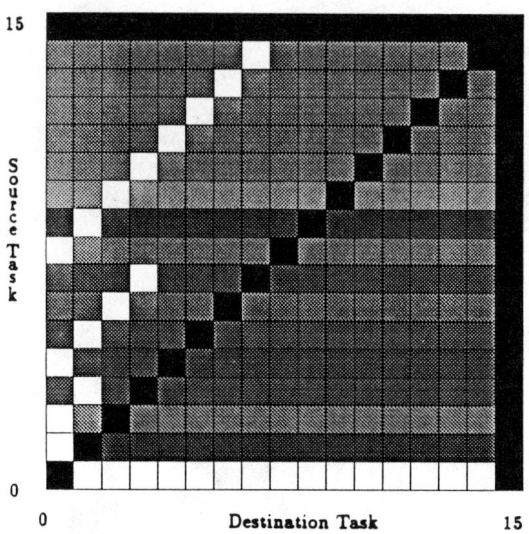

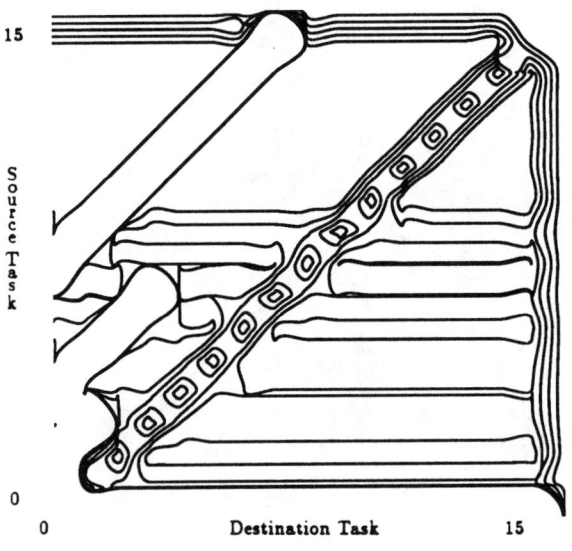

FIGURE 4.13
Density and contour view of message counts (row partitioning).

contour view. Because task 0 is the root of the combining tree, during each simplex iteration it must broadcast the identity of the task containing the global minimum. The identified task then broadcasts the needed row to all other tasks. If the workload were perfectly distributed, each task would broadcast an equal number of times. Excluding messages due to the logarithmic combining, all other variations in communication traffic are attributable to this load imbalance. The multiplicity of views reflects our belief that an integrated performance visualization system should permit the performance analyst to select those views that correspond to his or her personal preference and needs.

Figure 4.14 shows the *volume* of data exchanged between tasks. A comparison of Figure 4.14 with Figure 4.12 shows that tasks exchanging many messages do *not* exchange a large volume of data. Why? The many messages necessary to realize the combining tree are small; the row broadcasts require fewer, larger messages. The performance ramifications of this bimodal distribution of message sizes can be understood only by examining hardware and system software performance displays. These displays show that message-passing systems like the Intel iPSC/2 have large message preparation times relative to communication link bandwidth, thus penalizing small messages. Hence, message count is the important performance metric, not message volume.

Finally, Figures 4.15 and 4.16 show the message count and volume for the column-partitioned simplex algorithm. As before, a combining tree is used to identify global minima. However, as Table 4.2 shows, this global minimization is used only when finding an entering basis column. Because each task contains columns, a sequential computation is used to identify the departing basis column. This reduces the number of small message transmissions at the expense of sequential parallelism. More importantly, however, broadcasting matrix columns is *much* less expensive than the row broadcasts of the row-partitioned algorithm. The scales for Figures 4.14 and 4.16 differ significantly; this is the reason the column-partitioned variant is superior for the matrix of Figure 4.11.

4.5 Current Research

The hardware and application performance visualizations just described are *ad hoc* and are not integrated. First, HyperView was designed primarily to display hardware performance. As such, it is not easily extensible to display of application performance, nor should it be—display techniques for system and application performance differ. Second, the simplex application visualizations required manual instrumentation of the simplex code and extensive preprocessing before they could be displayed using *Mathematica*, a symbolic manipulation system and mathematician's assistant not intended for this use. HyperView and the simplex application visualization are *facsimiles* or rapid prototypes of

82   Chapter 4. Visualizing Parallel Computer System Performance

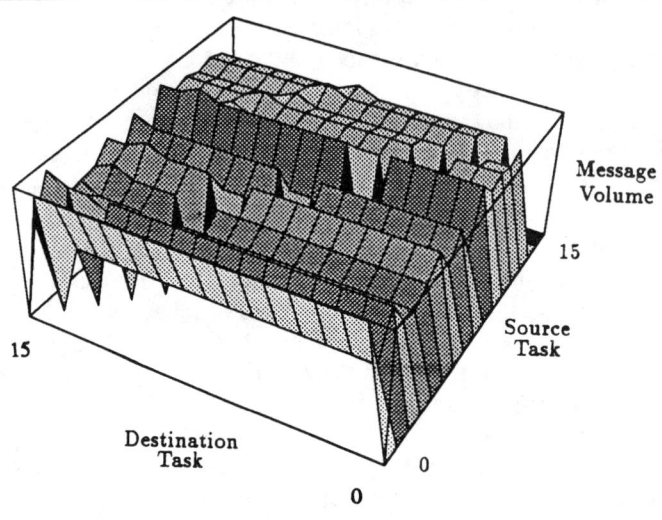

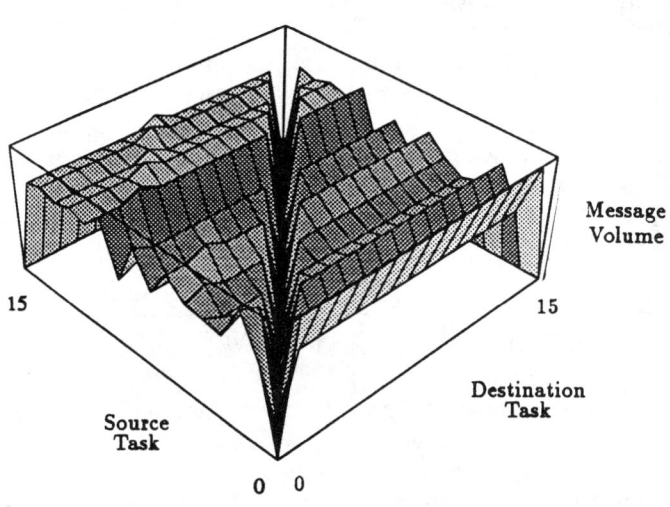

FIGURE 4.14
Perspective views of message volume (row partitioning).

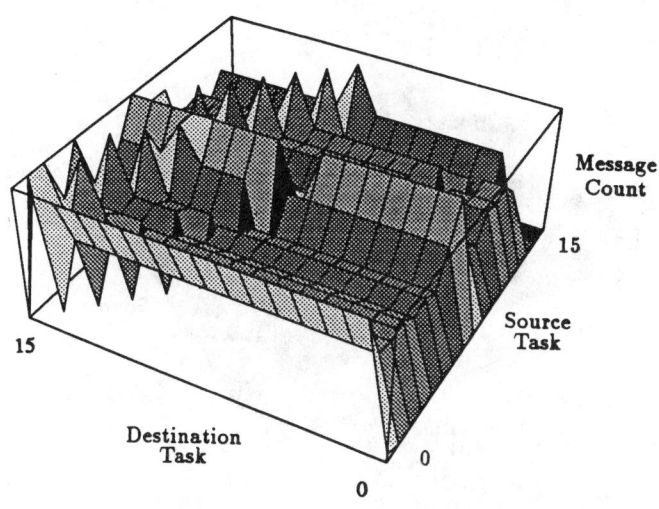

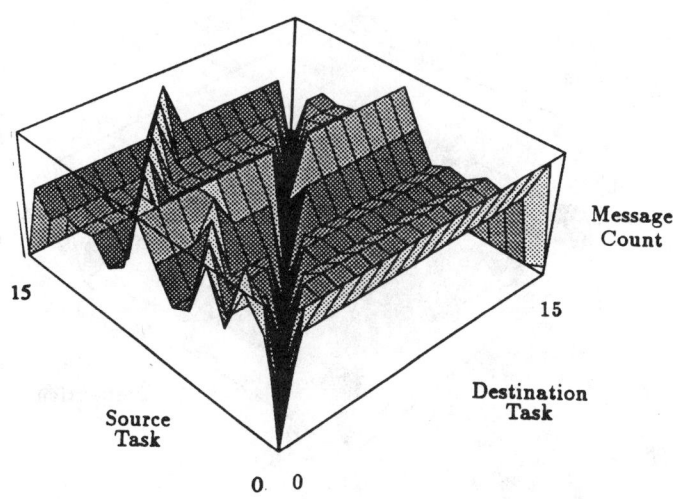

FIGURE 4.15
Perspective view of message counts (column partitioning).

84 Chapter 4. Visualizing Parallel Computer System Performance

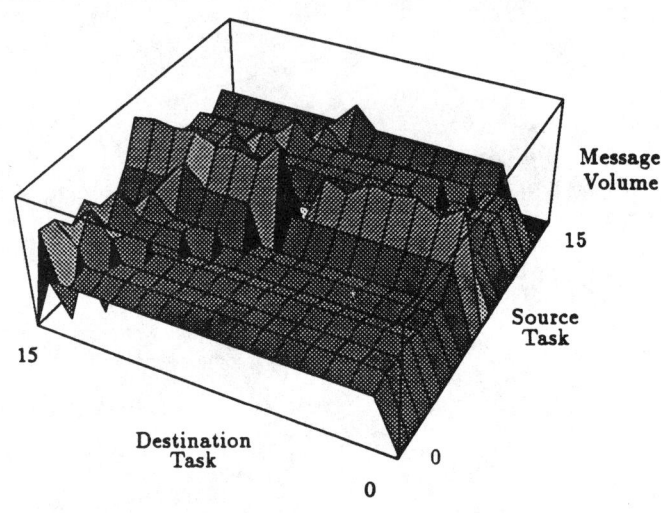

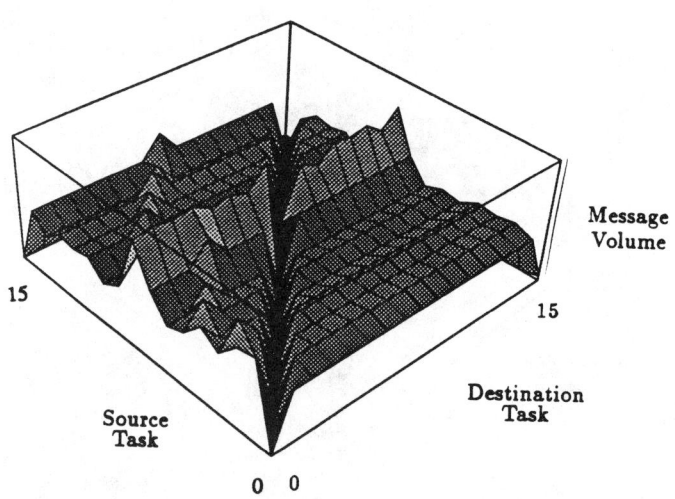

FIGURE 4.16
Perspective views of message volume (column partitioning).

what is desired—an integrated performance specification, instrumentation, and visualization system for message-passing systems.

Figure 4.17 illustrates the ideal system. This hypothetical system, called Tapestry would weave together elements of the hardware, system software, and application levels. The hardware and system levels, shown at the top of the figure would, like HyperView and *Seecube*, dynamically display internode communication traffic [9] using multiple colors. Dynamic displays would include current messages, cumulative traffic (either counts or volume), and link utilization. Via a mouse, the performance analyst also could choose from an extended menu that would include the following performance displays for each node and link:

- external input/output (i.e., file accesses),
- processor utilization,
- context switches,
- system calls,
- memory utilization,
- memory reference patterns (i.e., reference localities),
- virtual memory paging activity, and
- message counts and volume by destination.

Each of these could be displayed in a variety of formats (e.g., perspective, histogram, strip chart, contour, or density).

The application performance level, illustrated at the bottom of Figure 4.17, would display the *logical* graph of the intertask communication pattern, not the physical graph of the underlying interconnection network. By dragging graph nodes and edges with a mouse, the topological orientation of the graph could be modified to reflect the performance analyst's preferences. The application performance level, like the hardware level, would include dynamic displays of message traffic on the parallel program graph via perspective, density, and contour plots. In addition, pull-down menus for tasks would include:

- message counts and volume by destination,
- delays for message transmission or receipt,
- dynamic procedure call graphs, and
- execution profiles.

Finally, the visualization system would permit correlation of system and application performance.

---

[9] Although the figure shows a four-dimensional hypercube, other views, such as the Pascal triangle, Gray code, or FFT, would be supported also.

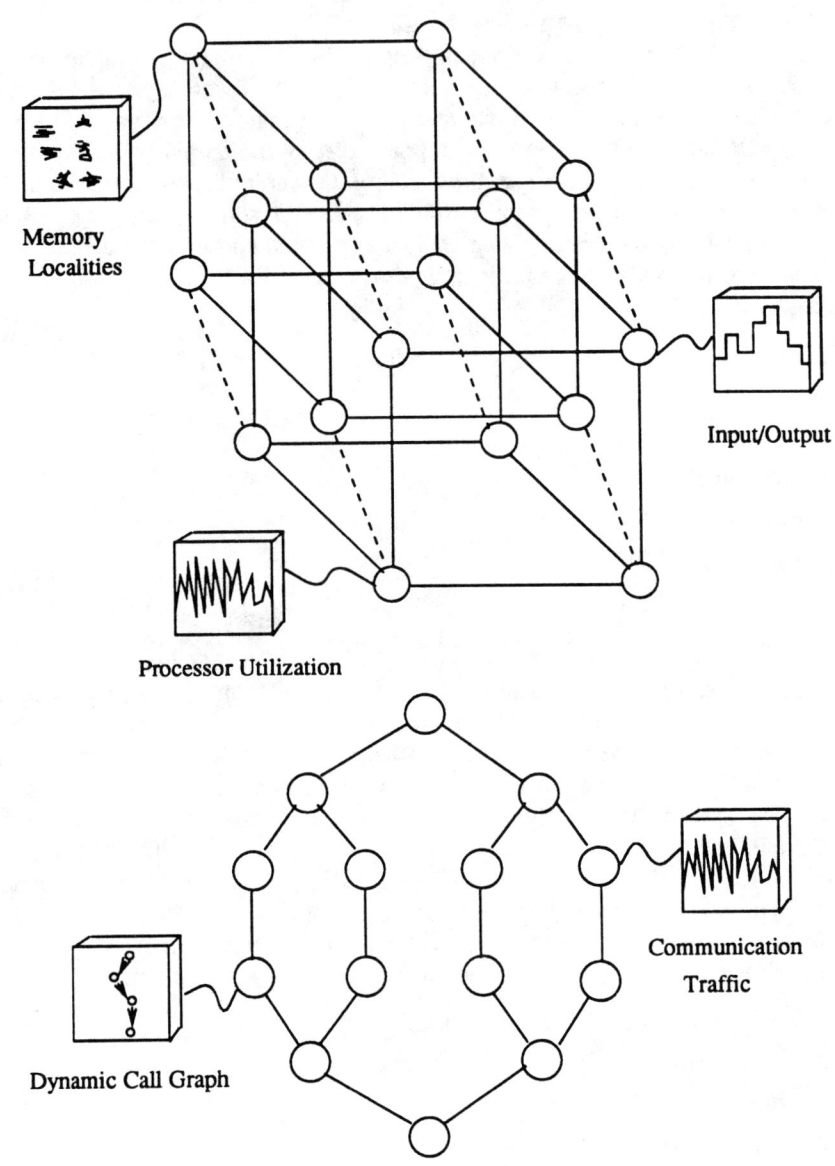

FIGURE 4.17
Tapestry performance visualization system.

The astute reader will have realized that near real-time processing and display of such detailed performance data (e.g., memory reference patterns) implies prodigious, indeed unrealistic, computing, storage, and display requirements. Below, we discuss those features we believe are necessary to achieve the goal of an integrated performance visualization system.

4.5.1 Instrumentation and Visualization

The major limitation of `HyperView`, *Seecube*, and the simplex application visualization is the absence of near real-time behavior. A *posteriori* examination of performance data means that *all* data of potential interest must be captured *a priori*. Despite the consequent increase in storage requirements, this is sometimes desirable — it permits performance data browsing across the entire interval of execution, and it permits data capture at a level of detail incompatible with near real-time processing. However, *a posteriori* examination also precludes dynamic system or application reconfiguration based on observed performance. Real-time display of even a portion of the captured data would permit the performance analyst to selectively enable and disable performance instrumentation based on observed behavior, reducing the storage requirements.

Despite the manifest advantages of interactive performance instrumentation and display, on most message-passing systems including the Intel iPSC/2 hypercube, *a posteriori* data display is unavoidable because there is insufficient communication bandwidth to transmit performance data to an external host without distorting the performance being measured. Moreover, the limited memory at each node constrains the volume of performance data that can be buffered for subsequent transmission. Clearly, hardware support for performance data recording is crucial, and we assume its existence. However, detailed discussion of hardware designs for performance instrumentation is beyond the scope of this paper. See [18] for a discussion of the hardware requirements for performance instrumentation.

A visualization system must be evolutionary, adapting to the changing demands of hardware, system software, applications, and users. Thus, the implementation must be extensible, permitting addition of new display formats and performance metrics, and portable, permitting use with a variety of systems. These twin goals, extensibility and portability, suggest a modular, object-oriented design that separates interface from implementation. Using the X client-server paradigm [10] would provide portability and ensure future extensibility based on an emerging standard for window systems. However, X alone provides neither the necessary abstractions (e.g., hierarchical performance displays) nor the rapid prototyping support; object-oriented window libraries such as `InterViews` [19] are needed.

4.5.2 Current Status

Based on the lessons learned with `HyperView`, we are implementing an initial version of `Tapestry` for the Intel iPSC/2 using X and `InterViews`. Initially, software instrumentation of NX/2, the iPSC/2 operating system, will provide data on system performance; a hardware monitor will be added later. Application performance data are captured by instrumenting application and system libraries, by modifying a compiler to automatically instrument application code, and by manually inserting instrumentation directives in application code.

Acknowledgments

Craig Stunkel designed the simplex code and conducted the experiments that motivated the application performance displays. Steven Wolfram's *Mathematica* [20] was used to generate Figures 4.12-4.16. We are grateful for use of prototype versions of this software; the ability to generate many data views quickly has been immensely useful. Finally, *Seecube* [9] provided the inspiration for `HyperView`; many of the ideas and displays were borrowed from this pioneering work.

References

1. P. J. Denning and J. P. Buzen, The Operational Analysis of Queueing Network Models, in *ACM Computing Surveys* 10,3 (September 1978), 225–261.
2. D. A. Reed and R. M. Fujimoto, *Multicomputer Networks: Message-Based Parallel Processing*, The MIT Press, 1987.
3. P. J. Denning, Working Sets Past and Present, in *IEEE Transaction on Software Engineering*, SE–6, 1 (January 1980), 64–84.
4. K. A. Frenkel, The Art and Science of Visualizing Data, in *Communications of the ACM* 21, 2 (February 1988), 110–121.
5. L. R. Foulds, *Optimization Techniques: An Introduction*, Springer-Verlag, New York, NY, 1981.

6. C. B. Stunkel and D. A. Reed, Hypercube Implementation of the Simplex Algorithm, in *Proceedings of the Third Conference on Hypercube Computers and Concurrent Applications*, (Pasadena, CA, January 1988).

7. D. J. Kuck, E. S. Davidson, D. H. Lawrie and A. H. Sameh, Parallel Supercomputing Today and the Cedar Approach, in *Science* 231 (February 1986).

8. J. Rattner, Concurrent Processing: A New Direction in Scientific Computing, in *Conference Proceedings of the 1985 National Computer Conference*, AFIPS Press, pp. 157–166.

9. A. L. Couch, Graphical Representations of Program Performance on Hypercube Message-Passing Multiprocessors, PhD thesis, Tufts University, Department of Computer Science, April 1988.

10. R. W. Scheifler and J. Gettys, The X Window System, in *ACM Transactions on Graphics* 5, 2 (April 1986), 79–109.

11. V. Guarna, D. Gannon, Y. Gaur and D. Jablonowski, An Environment for Programming Scientific Applications, in *Proceedings of Supercomputing '88*, (Orlando, Florida, November 1988).

12. V. Guarna and Y. Gaur, A Portable User Interface for a Scientific Programming Environment, in *Proceedings of the Siggraph Symposium on User Interface Software*, (Banff, Alberta, Canada, October 1988).

13. D. Jablonowski and V. Guarna, A Dynamic Graph Tool and Its Use in an Integrated Programming Environment, CSRD Report No. 746, University of Illinois at Urbana-Champaign, Center for Supercomputing Research and Development, June 1988.

14. D. C. Grunwald and D. A. Reed, Networks for Parallel Processors: Measurements and Prognostications, in *Proceedings of the Third Conference on Hypercube Computers and Concurrent Applications*, (Pasadena, CA, January 1988).

15. C. Aykanat and F. Ozguner, Large Grain Parallel Conjugate Gradient Algorithms on a Hypercube Multiprocessor, in *Proceedings of the 1987 International Conference on Parallel Processing*, (St. Charles, IL, August 1987), pp. 641–644.

16. G. A. Geist and M. T. Heath, Matrix Factorization on a Hypercube Multiprocessor, in *Proceedings of the First Conference on Hypercube Computers and Concurrent Applications*, (Knoxville, TN, August 1985), pp. 161–180.

17. C. Moler, Matrix Computation on Distributed Memory Multiprocessors, in *Proceedings of the First Conference on Hypercube Computers and Concurrent Applications*, (Knoxville, TN, August 1985), pp. 181–195.

18. D. A. Reed, Distributed Memory Working Group Summary, in *Instrumentation for Parallel Computing Systems*, Addison-Wesley, Reading, MA, 1989.
19. M. A. Linton and P. R. Calder, The Design and Implementation of InterViews, in *Proceedings of the USENIX C++ Workshop*, (Santa Fe, NM, November 1987), pp. 256–267.
20. S. Wolfram, *Mathematica: A System for Doing Mathematics by Computer*, Addison-Wesley, July 1988.

5

Program Development and Performance Monitoring on the Monsoon Dataflow Multiprocessor

Gregory M. Papadopoulos[1]

5.1 Introduction

Developers of parallel applications often feel like they are living in a Heisenbergian purgatory; instrumenting a program can radically change its run-time behavior, even causing it to produce different answers! Such experiences lead to the natural conclusion that we should fundamentally improve the way real-time data are collected on multiprocessors and expand the kinds of measurements being taken. But perhaps we should first understand *why* the need for quality multiprocessor instrumentation is so much more acute than the historical demands placed on uniprocessors. Is getting a parallel program to run well (or at all) somehow inherently more difficult than doing the same thing on a sequential processor? Can better instrumentation really abate our frustration and accelerate the effective use of parallel machines? It seems that the requirements of three development activities are confounded under the desire for better instrumentation:

---

[1] The author is funded in part by the Advanced Research Projects Agency of the Department of Defense under Office of Naval Research contract N00014–84–K–0099.

- **Debugging.** Getting the program right.

- **Program Analysis.** Understanding the inherent properties of a program (*e.g.*, its average concurrency).

- **Performance Tuning.** Making the program run well on a particular implementation.

Our investigation of dataflow architectures [1] and associated declarative languages has led us to believe that each of these activities can and should be approached independently of the others, and that much of the perceived need for highly dynamic and specific instrumentation is an artifact of the mismatch (and inadequacy) of current parallel programming languages and processor architecture.

To start, a program should be able to be developed and debugged without regard to the target architecture. There should be no "surprises"—the exposing of latent bugs—when changing the machine configuration. A declarative (or functional) programming language (*e.g.*, fp [2], SISAL [3], Id [4]) guarantees *determinate* execution, even in the presence of program bugs; re-execution of a program on the same set of data will always yield the same results and set of errors, independent of the number of processors or relative execution timings.

But determinacy does not guarantee good *performance* on a given problem; different mappings of a computation onto a machine will always yield the same answers (and errors) but may result in dramatically different execution times. And it can also be the case that *no* mapping yields acceptable performance—meaning the problem (inherently) has insufficient parallelism for the given machine configuration. But when observing a poorly running program, how are we to know if the mapping is bad or if there is simply too little parallelism for the problem size?

Ideally, it would be nice to perform an experiment that would tell us the inherent parallelism and thus *predict* the best performance that we could ever hope to get on a machine with a given number of processors. Then, we could compare our prediction with the actual measured performance and determine if further improvement is possible.

To these ends, we unabashedly propose a *scientific method* for the development of parallel applications. As shown in Figure 5.1, a debugged program can be analyzed to expose its inherent parallel characteristics and the expected performance on a given machine configuration can be predicted theoretically. Measurements from the actual program execution can then be compared against the predicted performance; a mismatch would point to either inadequate analysis or a deficiency in the machine implementation.

The utility of *instrumentation* in a multiprocessor should be gauged by its contribution to facilitating program development under this paradigm. The experimental *Monsoon dataflow multiprocessor* [5] now under construction at

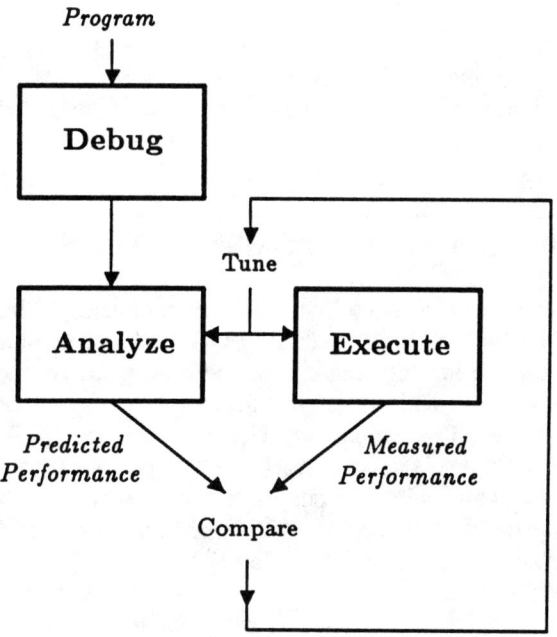

FIGURE 5.1
A scientific method for developing parallel applications.

M.I.T. incorporates a number of features to aid in program debugging, analysis, and performance tuning. We present two novel features in this discussion:

1. Hardware support for machine-independent program analysis. Using a pair of "ping-pong" token queues we can efficiently simulate an infinite processor array on a finite collection of processors.

2. An instruction coloring technique that allows instruction mix statistics to be focused on programmer-selected subsets of procedures, allowing the rapid determination of the contribution from a given procedure to the overall program.

Our ultimate goal is to replace the *ad hoc* development of parallel applications with a rational methodology based on analysis and measurement where the processes of debugging, program analysis and performance tuning are distinct, well-defined tasks.

5.2 Getting the Program Right

Parallel machines seem to have induced a regression in programming. A programmer is often concerned with the reflection of implementation details onto the structure of the program (*e.g.*, number of processors, interconnection topology, synchronization costs). This is usually accomplished by annotating programs written in conventional sequential languages (*e.g.*, FORTRAN, C and Lisp) to indicate that certain things should be performed in parallel [6]. At a high level it may be evident that an application possesses ample parallelism, but the complexity of exposing the parallelism through annotations may introduce new errors that did not exist in the sequential version [7,8].

For example, matrix multiplication is a determinate computation, but if the the programmer accidently uses the same variable to accumulate the parallel inner products, the program is likely to show indeterminate behavior. The indeterminate behavior is often difficult to reproduce when debugging because it depends upon the relative execution *timings* and the debugging instrumentation itself alters these relationships. Moreover, the explicit parallel task model of these computations leads to execution traces that comprise collections of independent processes competing for machine resources. Pragmatically, it is hard to name and "talk about" a specific process and relate it back to the program text, as the processes are apt to move around from run to run.

For these reasons, debugging places the greatest demands on instrumentation; it must be non-invasive and it must deal with the *timing of events* rather than the statistical abstraction (the number of events) of execution performance. In fact, we believe that the instrumentation problem for debugging timing-dependent phenomena is so hard that trying to identify the sources of nondeterminism through measurement is fundamentally impractical. While there appears to be significant progress in the development of automatic dependence analysis tools (*e.g., Ptool* [9]) to assist in detecting incorrect parallelization, we question whether these techniques can ever really uncover the truly insidious bugs in programs that employ sophisticated data structures and/or attempt to manage their own storage.

We believe the best approach to developing robust parallel codes is to provide a programming environment that guarantees determinate execution *even in the presence of program bugs*. Declarative languages can offer such a guarantee:

> Independent of the relative timing of concurrent processes and the distribution of data and processes across processors, a program will always yield the same result and the same set of errors (given the same input data, of course).

This property, known as the *Church-Rosser property* [10] is not without its costs, and the implementation efficiency of declarative languages is the subject of much research—and beyond the scope of this discussion.

It is encouraging to note, however, that scientific programs expressed in the declarative language *Id* [4,11] for our dataflow processor yield dynamic instruction mixes within a factor of two of the same applications written in FORTRAN and executed on contemporary von Neumann uniprocessors [12,13]. In addition, the FORTRAN codes generally experience a measurable increase in execution overhead when they are executed in parallel (after suitable annotations) while the number of instructions executed for the Id program is independent of the number of processors.

Thus, one option for the parallel programmer is to debug the application in the familiar development environment of a single processor. The Church-Rosser property guarantees that the program will behave identically (in terms of results produced) when executed on a multiprocessor configuration[1].

5.3 Predicting Performance

Amdahl's law for vector processing provides a simple machine-*independent* characterization of the performance limitations of vectorization. Given an application that is, say, 90% vectorizable, Amdahl's law limits the *best case* speedup to about a factor of ten—even given an infinitely fast vector unit. When we

---

[1] We gloss over the obvious requirements that the machines all have the same arithmetic behavior. Not to mention the fact that some applications simply exhaust the resources (like memory, or the patience of the programmer) of a single processor, in which case debugging would have to take place on a multiprocessor. We will address the problem of debugging on a parallel machine in a moment.

execute the program on an actual vector processor we are able to roughly predict its expected performance. If the experienced performance and the predicted performance agree, then we know the only way to further decrease execution time is to adjust the code to increase the amount of vectorization. If experience and analysis substantially *disagree* then we turn to performance measurements to diagnose the cause of the problem, *e.g.*, bank conflicts, short vectors, poor compilation, *etc.*

Amdahl's law applies to parallel execution as well—the maximum expected performance gain from processing things in parallel is ultimately limited by that portion of the computation that is inherently sequential. We can all understand this rule in the abstract sense and can sometimes apply it in practice. However, its utility is limited by the ability to precisely distinguish that fraction of the computation that is truly sequential.

Fundamentally, the sources of parallelism in a program are manifold[2] and trying to predict what fraction of the parallelism can be exploited by a particular machine organization can be exceedingly complex. Moreover, the language in which the application is coded may unintentionally obscure certain kinds of parallelism. It appears that there is no substitute for actually running the program on a real set of input data and then, somehow, analyzing real-time measurements in an effort to determine both the available parallelism and how much of it is effectively exploited.

Our approach is try to determine the *potential parallelism in programs* by considering only the essential data dependences involved in computing the result. Then we try to predict how the potential parallelism is attenuated during execution. Armed with these predictions, we have a better chance of understanding actual real-time measurements of the program on a particular machine configuration.

We believe that fine-grained dataflow graphs offer one of the cleanest formulations of parallel computation. Dataflow graphs *avoid overspecifying* the instruction execution sequence by dictating only the essential data dependences. An actual execution of the program may impose additional ordering, but all such orders obey the data dependences. Thus these graphs capture all sorts of parallelism—vector, inner loop, outer loop, producer-consumer, *etc.*

The first step is to interpret the dataflow graph in an *ideal* environment that imposes no additional ordering and thus reveals an amalgam of the potential program parallelism. Then, we refine our estimations by selectively accounting for finite processor resources and non-zero communication latency. At the center of this analysis is a time-independent formulation of computational progress.

---

[2]Indeed, vector processing is a restricted form of parallel processing.

5.3.1 Idealized Execution

The dataflow graphs produced by the Id compiler are based on a fixed set of schema and rules for composition that ensure deterministic behavior on all execution orders [14]. One such execution order of interest is the so-called *infinite-processor* or *ideal execution order* that follows the simple execution rule:

> At step j execute all instructions that have their operands, then proceed to step $j + 1$.

We term each step a *parallel computation step*. While we do not specify the order in which instructions should be executed within a step, the set of instructions executed by step j is completely determinate. The *parallelism profile* of the computation is defined as a plot of the number of instructions executed in each parallel computation step versus the step number. By definition, all of the instructions in a step are completely independent of each other (they all have their required operands and don't need to intercommunicate). So the parallelism profile graphically reveals inherent parallelism in the program.

Figure 5.2 shows the parallelism profile of the SIMPLE code, a hydrodynamics and heat code that has been studied extensively both analytically and by experimentation[3]. This profile shows three iterations on a 20×20 mesh, while a typical production run performs 100,000 iterations on a 100×100 mesh. We can interpret the parallelism profile as the trace obtained from measuring an *ideal machine* with the following properties:

- Unit time per operation,
- Unbounded number of processors,
- Zero communication delay,

In the SIMPLE example, almost one and a half million instructions were executed; this took our ideal machine only 1,976 "clocks"—where every processor can complete an instruction every clock cycle. We term the number of steps required to complete the computation the *critical path*: there exists a sequence of 1,976 operations such that operation k requires the result of operation $k - 1$ for all k. That is, there is at least one inherently sequential thread in the computation comprising the critical path number of instructions.

---

[3] See [15] and [16] for a detailed discussion.

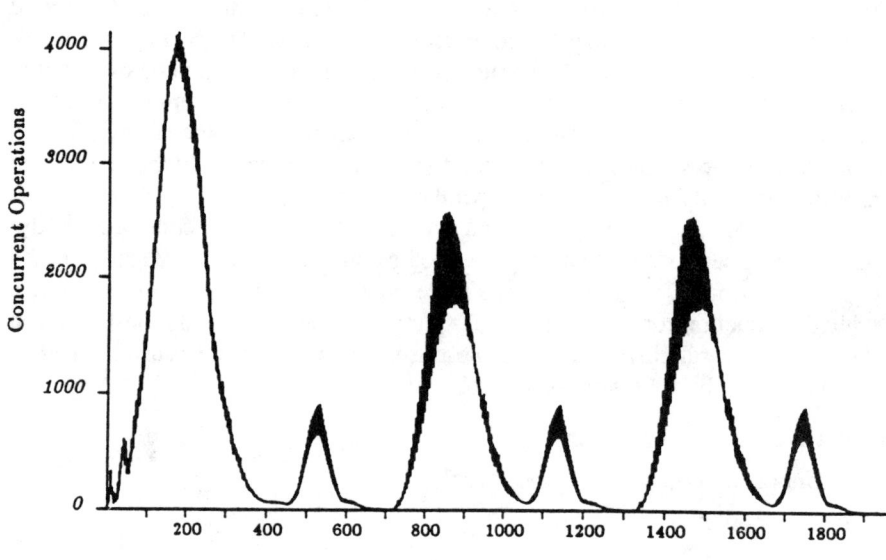

FIGURE 5.2
Parallelism profile for SIMPLE (3 iterations, 20×20).

We can also identify some important structural aspects of the parallelism. For example, as can be seen from iterations 2 and 3, there is no significant parallelism *between* the outer loop iterations of SIMPLE. The tremendous variability of the potential parallelism is also noteworthy, and typical of our experience with even the most highly parallel programs. This strongly suggests that reducing the profile to a single "average parallelism" number (analogous to the percentage vectorization) is apt to mask important dynamics, like the sections of inherently low parallelism. Yet even this highly idealized execution provides a hard upper bound:

No machine can complete the computation faster than the critical path number of instruction times.

Every instruction on the critical path depends directly on the result of its predecessor, thus these instructions *cannot* be rearranged to run in parallel nor can they be pipelined (pipelining requires independence of adjacent instructions). We can also conclude that a processor with an instruction pipeline depth of d cannot execute the program in fewer instruction times than the product of the critical path length and d.

5.3.2 Bounded Processor Profiles

Another clear consequence of the ideal parallelism profile is that a *single* processor machine will take at least as many instruction times to execute the program as the area under the curve—the total number of instructions executed. So now we know two extrema: the best time on an infinite collection of processors and the best time on a single processor. What about the space in between? Deriving the best performance achievable on n processors would establish an upper bound for evaluating real-time measurements. A "linear" speedup curve is often cited as the metric for performance comparisons for multiprocessors, but this is as naive as assuming that a linear improvement in the performance of a vector unit will cause a linear improvement in the execution of any application!

The intermediate points along the speedup curve have a fairly unremarkable relationship to the parallelism profile. Figure 5.3, shows the parallelism profile of the SIMPLE example where the number of processors has been limited to 1000, slightly greater than the average parallelism. As expected, the peaks of the profile have been truncated to 1000 parallel activities. The area under the curve is the same (the same number of instructions are executed in both cases) and the length of the critical path has increased from 1,976 to 2,763.

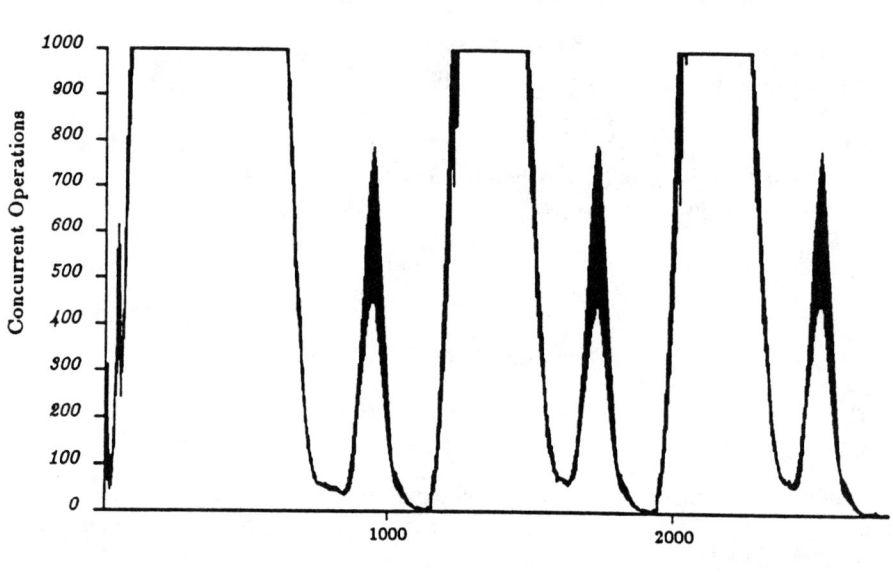

FIGURE 5.3
Parallelism profile for SIMPLE bounded to 1000 processors.

5.3.3 Accounting for Latency

The "processors" assumed in the bounded simulations really represent concurrent computations. For example, a pipelined processor of depth d would account for d "processors", as the pipeline computes d instructions in parallel. An alternative view is that the pipelined processor indeed represents a single "processor" but it introduces a *latency* between dependent computations equal to d time units. A model that incorporates latency could also account for the processor-memory and interprocessor communication times. Figure 5.4 shows the parallelism profile for the SIMPLE example where the number of processors has been limited to 100. The top profile has latency of zero while the bottom has latency of 10—it takes 10 time steps for the result produced by an instruction to be distributed to any dependent instructions.

Surprisingly, the critical path is increased by a factor of two, not a factor of 10. This suggests that excess parallelism can be invested in tolerating latency, and that the program has enough parallelism to perform well on a realistic machine comprising 100 processors.

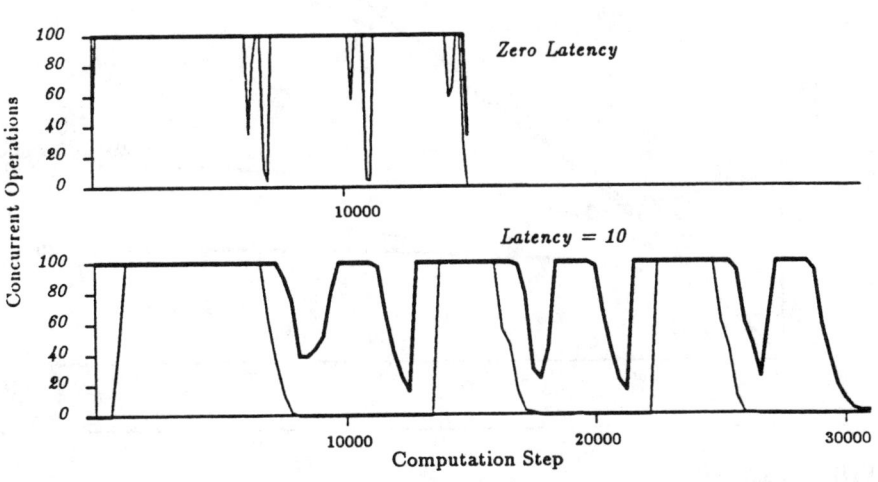

FIGURE 5.4
Parallelism profile for SIMPLE bounded to 100 processors.

5.3.4 Estimating Speedup from Ideal Profiles

Arvind, Culler and Maa [17] have shown that good estimates of the speedup expected on a finite number of processors with a given latency can be obtained from simple analysis of the *ideal parallelism profile*! Thus, we can avoid the costly computation of numerous scenarios of bounded processors and fixed latency. The derivation of the estimates is beyond the scope of this discussion, but we have shown the results on the SIMPLE example (this time, one iteration on a 32 × 32 mesh) in Figure 5.5. The curves (parameterized by latency) show the estimated performance derived from analysis of the ideal execution profile. The discrete points are the results of actually simulating the machine configuration on our graph interpreter.

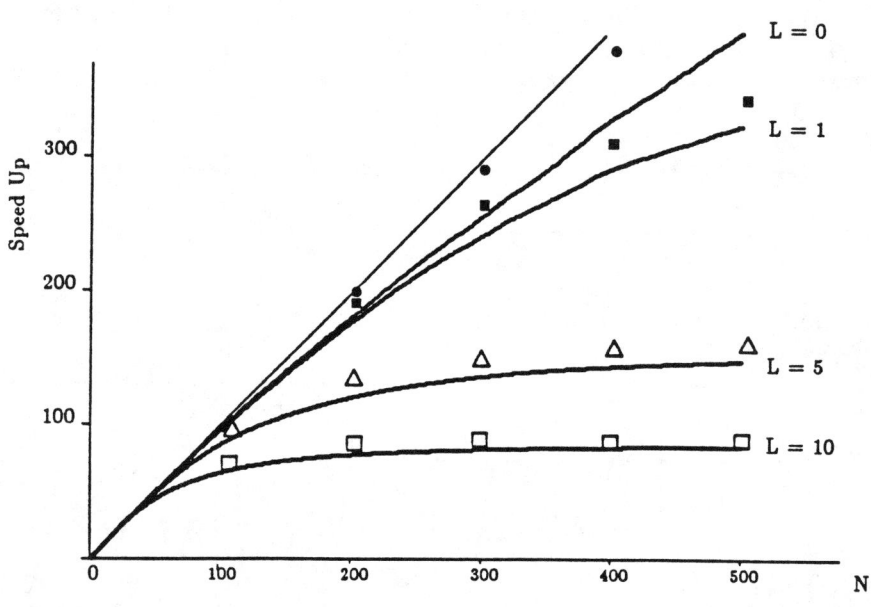

FIGURE 5.5
Speedup estimates for SIMPLE (1 iteration, 32 × 32) from the ideal parallelism profile.

5.4 Hardware Support for Idealized Execution

The ideal parallelism profile provides a solid foundation for predicting the performance of an application on a given multiprocessor configuration. However, even computing a single profile can be very expensive as it is a true simulation of the problem on given set of input data. Indeed, the idealized simulation produces the same numeric result as any real-time execution (Church-Rosser, again). This can be interpreted as a flaw—if the parallelism profile is highly dependent on the input data (it certainly is a function of problem size) then many ideal simulation runs would be required to characterize the program.

We believe that the parallel computation step abstraction can play such an important role in application development that hardware support for idealized execution should be developed. We have arrived at a simple hardware extension for the Monsoon dataflow that efficiently implements a parallel computation step, and appears to have general applicability among various dataflow architectures.

Monsoon, like most dataflow machines, is a collection of pipelined processing elements. The processing element pipeline independently transforms computation state descriptors called *tokens*. Tokens are the means by which data are communicated from instruction to instruction. A Monsoon processing element can consume a token and produce zero, one or two result tokens. Thus, a large buffer or *token queue* is required to store the transient of excess tokens that are generated during periods of high parallelism. Please refer to Figure 5.6. The token queue is analogous to a work queue. A processing element keeps consuming tokens from the queue and adding new ones. The only time it idles is when the queue is empty.

Our hardware trick is simple. Rather than have a single token queue we equip each processor with *two* queues. A parallel computation step works as follows (see Figure 5.7):

1. Let Q_0 contain the tokens that were produced by computation step j.

2. All processing elements consume the tokens from Q_0 but insert any result tokens into Q_1. This continues until all processors have emptied their respective Q_0 and all idle. Each processor counts the number of instructions executed.

3. The roles of Q_0 and Q_1 are reversed, and the next computation step is performed: dequeuing from Q_1 and enqueuing into Q_0.

Interprocessor communication is also accounted for: a token, which is produced by a processor and destined for another processing element, is automatically (by the normal hardware rules) transmitted over the network to the

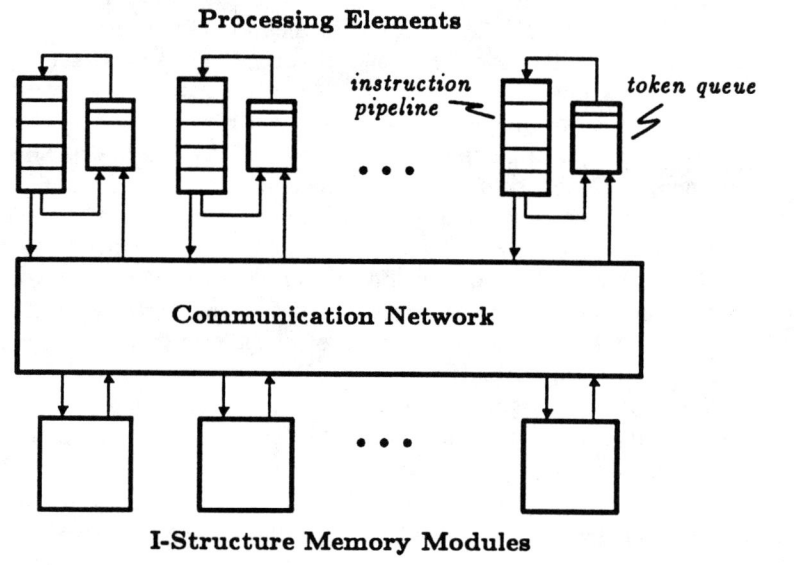

FIGURE 5.6
A collection of pipelined monsoon processing elements.

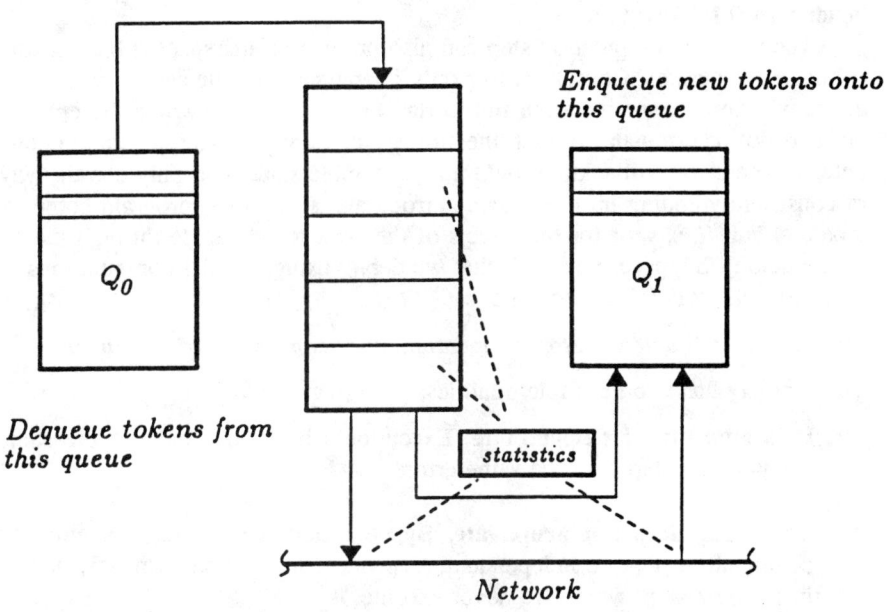

FIGURE 5.7
A modified monsoon processor for performing parallel computation steps.

destination processing element, that simply enqueues the token until the next computation step.

Notice that the actual processing of instructions is performed at full speed by each processor. The overhead from this technique arises from the implied barrier synchronization—no processor can flip its queues until all other processors have come to an idle. This overhead is incurred only as many times as there are steps on the critical path, so programs that exhibit even modest amounts of parallelism ought to run fairly well. We would view executing within an order of magnitude of real-time acceptable, and expect a typical degradation of about a factor of three. In contrast, even our fastest graph interpreters execute in no better than 0.1% real-time.

The parallel computation step can also provide an unexpected benefit for debugging programs. Church-Rosser only guarantees that the same *set* of errors will be encountered from run to run, but the *order* in which the errors occur is not determinate. In fact, the strategy of "stopping" the machine upon detecting an error will seldom yield a reproducible state. The only certain way of consistently ending up in the same error state is to let the program come to a natural halt (*i.e.*, wait for the effects of the error to propagate through the computation). Suppose, however, that we debug using parallel computational steps with the following error rule:

When an error is detected stop computation after completion of the current step.

This strategy has two desirable qualities:

1. **It is guaranteed determinate.** Execution will always halt on the same computation step with the same errors.

2. **The error does not propagate.** By definition, all instructions within a computation step are independent. Dependent instructions can only appear in the *next* step, which we never execute.

The technique applies equally well to programmer-inserted breakpoints and traces. In many ways, the parallel computation step is analogous to a *single-step* on sequential uniprocessors.

We think there are analogs of parallel computation step for course-grain models as well. In these settings, all tasks in the active task queue would execute until some blocking event, and then enqueue into the task queue for the next step. Statistics and error information could be gathered at the end of each step and *task parallelism profiles* could be generated.

5.5 Instruction Coloring

Between each computation step various processor and network statistics can be gathered from each processor for later analysis and display. They include:

- instruction mixes, *e.g.*, fixed and floating point operations, fetch, store,

- processor performance, *e.g.*, idle cycles, cache misses, pipeline bubbles, and

- network performance, *e.g.*, message counts, blocking statistics.

This same set of event counters can be sampled periodically during real-time operation to provide a trace of runtime performance data—with the usual concern over sufficient sample frequency. However, the sampling *between* computation steps during idealized execution is sufficiently frequent as the instructions processed during a step are, by construction, completely independent. So nothing "interesting" would be revealed by sampling the statistics counters in the middle of a parallel computation step.

We note that a programmer might also be interested in displaying statistics other than total instructions executed in the style of parallelism profiles. For example, the user might want to display only the floating-point operations per step, or the aggregate network traffic to identify potential network hotspots that might be exposed during real-time execution.

One often desires to filter the data to display the contribution of a *subset* of procedures (maybe just a single function) to the overall execution trace. This is accomplished on Monsoon by replicating the instruction mix counters in each processing element and then adding a field to every instruction (its *color*) that specifies which set of counters should be updated. All instructions belonging to the subset of procedures to be monitored would be assigned the same color.

For an experimental processor like Monsoon, the added hardware of this approach is tolerable. Replication of the statistics counters is relatively inexpensive. Because all instruction mix counters are mutually exclusive (only one counter from one color set will updated during a given cycle), we can store the current counts in a high speed memory and have only a single incrementer. Adding more colors only involves increasing the size of the memory. A more practical limit on the number of colors is dictated by the amount of time required to read all of the sets of counters during each sample period. Of course, we must also pay for a few extra bits on *every* instruction memory location. We have found four bits (sixteen colors) to be a reasonable compromise.

5.6 Performance Monitoring

At the other end of the development cycle is the performance tuning of a working program. In the purest of worlds, the ideal execution profiles would accurately predict the real-time performance of the application. At least, the ideal execution profiles provide reasonably tight bounds on the *best* we can hope to do on a given machine configuration. So when we observe performance that is poor, but matches prediction, we know not to indict the machine. If this performance is inadequate then the only choice is to adjust the application—for example by reformulating the problem with algorithms that exhibit greater parallelism.

What happens when the real-time performance is significantly *worse* than predicted? The first step is to try to relate the real-time statistics back to the predicted execution profiles. Instruction coloring can help identify a computation phase by indicating when certain procedures are active. Attention can then be focused on those phases where the measurements and predictions diverge—the places where aggregate machine utilization is significantly lower than projections. There is apt to be a small number of explanations for the divergence, as we have already factored out the inherent limitations of computation:

- **Poor workload distribution.** Some processors have a disproportionate share of procedure activations, inducing other processors to idle.

- **Excessive network contention.** The network traffic is imbalanced leading to restrictions in bandwidth or inordinate increases in latency.

- **Memory contention.** Memory requests are unevenly distributed causing certain modules to become bottlenecks.

We believe that of the divergence better analysis of the ideal execution statistics can also help reveal the cause of the divergence. After each computation step we can query the memory modules and discover any excessive loading. Similarly, the network elements can be examined to determine relative traffic and contention. It should then be possible to determine at each step the rate limiting term: be it the processors, network or memory.

All of this may be interesting to the programmer but not very helpful unless there is some way to *fix* the problem. Unfortunately, we will have to wait until we have gained more experience with large configurations before we know what mixture of programmer control directives are truly useful.

5.7 Conclusion

If we are to leave the reader with one thought, it is that it is possible to *systematically* develop a reliable, well-performing application for a parallel processor.

But this nice world of determinate debugging, theoretical performance prediction and relaxed execution instrumentation is only realizable if we make significant changes to our programming languages and constituent processor architectures. Declarative languages provide a natural basis for a robust parallel programming environment. Dataflow machines like Monsoon that provide especially efficient interprocessor synchronization and context switching can insulate the programmer from the vagaries of the underlying implementation.

References

1. Arvind and D. E. Culler, Dataflow Architectures, in *Annual Reviews in Computer Science*, Annual Reviews Inc., Palo Alto, CA, Vol. 1, pp. 225–253, 1986.
2. J. Backus, Can Programming be Liberated from the von Neumann Style?, *Communications of the ACM*, 21(8), August 1978.
3. J. R. McGraw, SISAL: Streams and Iteration in a Single Assignment Language, Language Reference Manual, Version 1.2, Technical Report M–146, Lawrence Livermore National Laboratory, March 1985.
4. R. S. Nikhil, Id Nouveau Reference Manual, Part I: Syntax, Technical Report, Computation Structures Group, MIT Laboratory for Computer Science, 545 Technology Square, Cambridge, MA 02139, April 1987.
5. G. M. Papadopoulos, Implementation of a General Purpose Dataflow Multiprocessor, Technical Report, Computation Structures Group, MIT Laboratory for Computer Science, 545 Technology Square, Cambridge, MA 02139, August 1988.
6. A. H. Karp, Programming for Parallelism, *Computer*, 20(5), May 1987.
7. J. R. McGraw and T. S. Axelrod, Exploiting Multiprocessors: Issues and Options, in *Programming Parallel Processors*, Addison-Wesley, Reading MA, 1988.
8. D. A. Mandell and H. E. Trease, Parallel Processing a Real Code — A Case History, Technical Report LA-UR 88-1836, Los Alamos National Laboratory, May 1988.
9. L. A. Henderson, R. E. Hiromoto, O. M. Lubeck and M. L. Simmons, On the Use of Diagnostic Dependency-Analysis Tools in Parallel Programming: Experience Using Ptool, Technical Report LA-UR 88-1968, Los Alamos National Laboratory, Los Alamos, NM 87545, June 1988.
10. G. Huet, Confluent Reductions: Abstract Properties and Applications to Term Rewriting Systems, *Journal of the Association for Computing Machinery*, 27(4):797–821, October 1980.

11. Arvind, R. S. Nikhil and K. K. Pingali, Id Nouveau Reference Manual, Part II: Semantics, Technical Report, Computation Structures Group, MIT Laboratory for Computer Science, 545 Technology Square, Cambridge, MA 02139, April 1987.

12. Arvind, K. Ekanadham and D. E. Culler, The Price of Asynchronous Parallelism: An Analysis of Dataflow Architectures, in *CONPAR 88, Manchester, England*, 1988.

13. K. Ekanadham, Arvind and D. E. Culler, The Price of Parallelism, in *Fifteenth Annual International Symposium on Computer Architecture, Honolulu, Hawaii*, May 30–June 2 1988.

14. K. R. Traub, A Compiler for the MIT Tagged-Token Dataflow Architecture, Technical Report LCS TR-370, MIT Laboratory for Computer Science, 545 Technology Square, Cambridge, MA 02139, August 1986.

15. Arvind and K. Ekanadham, Future Scientific Programming on Parallel Machines, in *Proceedings of the International Conference on Supercomputing, Athens, Greece*, June 1987.

16. W. P. Crowley, C. P. Hendrickson and T. E. Rudy, The SIMPLE Code, Technical Report UCID 17715, Lawrence Livermore Laboratory, February 1978.

17. Arvind, D. E. Culler and G. K. Maa, Programming for Parallelism, in *Computer*, 20(5), May 1987.

6
Instrumentation for Future Parallel Systems

Blaine Gaither

6.1 Introduction

The instrumentation of parallel systems has recently become a topic of interest because of the increasing number of researchers attempting to solve real problems with parallel systems. The crisis in parallel system instrumentation is analogous to the status of Single Instruction Stream-Single Data Stream systems (SISD) instrumentation in the early 70s. In the early 70s there were only a few experimental interactive debuggers, work on program profiling was done principally via hardware monitors, and system-level performance measurement was done with hardware monitors. Software monitors were in their infancy. Most importantly, there was no unifying model for system-level performance [1–9].

With the advent of operational analysis modeling techniques, the required instrumentation for prediction of system-level performance was identified and many modern commercial operating systems have been instrumented. Users of these systems have countless stories of success in predicting both the performance of systems and individual applications [10,11].

6.2 Parallel Processing Instrumentation

To date there has been no modeling breakthrough for parallel systems that is equivalent to operational analysis. Several modeling techniques with much promise are based petri nets [12]. If petri nets are the proper path to a breakthrough in modeling parallel systems, then the area of petri net languages may lead to insights useful for instrumenting parallel systems. Some of these areas are reviewed in [13]. According to this work, the most important instrumentation capability would be that of tracing events.

Since there is no generally accepted parallel modeling theory at this time, it is useful to step back and look at the general state of instrumentation for systems with less complexity than parallel systems. Refer to Table 6.1.

TABLE 6.1
Architecture versus Instrumentation Status

Architecture	Degree of Insight
SISD[a] Uniprocessor/Multiprocessor	High
	UNIX[b] world lags
	Poor timer resolution
SIMD[c] Vector and Array	Low
	Lack SIMD-specific instrumentation
	Chains
	Chimes
	Flop counters
MIMD[d]	Hardly any

[a] Single Instruction Stream/Single Data Stream
[b] Unix is a registered trademark of AT&T.
[c] Single Instruction Stream/Multiple Data Stream
[d] Multiple Instruction Stream/Multiple Data Stream

To date, UNIX based systems do not have the same level of performance visibility as commercial computers. Most have inadequate timer resolution to allow fast events to be easily measured. Finally, they often have instrumentation errors. An example is the violation of Bucher's timer rule [14]. Bucher's timer rule concerns the need to be able to de-pipeline timer requests in order to assure that the code being timed is completed before the time is read.

The state of the art of SIMD instrumentation is even more dismal. Some machines have floating-point operation (FLOP) and instruction counters, but the utilization of the internal "parallel" resources must usually be inferred.

Thus, the state of the art for instrumentation for parallel systems is being built on an inadequate foundation. The first step in building parallel instrumentation facilities must be to assure that the machine instrumentation is completely adequate for sequential problems.

6.3 Requirements for Instrumentation

An essential consideration in determining instrumentation requirements is the characteristics of the users of the instrumentation. The taxonomy in Table 6.2 categorizes the users of instrumentation.

Of the above types of users, the dusty deck customers pose a unique challenge. Dusty deck users don't really want to be aware of parallel processing while they are using it, and they are more comfortable using tools analogous to SISD tools for profiling and debugging.

The following section describes the instrumentation utilities built into the Gould NP1, as representative of the current state of mini-supercomputer instrumentation.

6.4 Gould NP1 Instrumentation

The Gould NP1 is a vector mini-supercomputer based on the vector register approach [15,16]. It consists of one to eight processors, and has a 308 Mbyte/s bus. I/O devices supported on this bus include a 7100 Mbyte/s supercomputer channel.

The NP1 processor is implemented with ECL MCA 1 gate arrays, occupying seven circuit boards including an optional floating-point accelerator board pair. Each CPU has its own instruction and data cache. A maximally configured system can have 2 Gbytes of shared memory.

TABLE 6.2
Characteristics of the Users of Computer Instrumentation

The System Designer	Needs very good visibility for debugging and some parallel application development; is very well informed about the internal architecture and timing of the systems; and has lots of resources to spend in tuning the systems, including custom hardware monitors.
The Dusty Deck User	Does not want to be required to have a detailed knowledge of the internal operations of the system; wants simple tools that stick as closely as possible to the sequential programming paradigm; will pay 5% of system cost for improved visibility; emphasizes debugging rather than tuning activities; and will accept a 5% measurement artifact.
High Performance User	Is very well informed on system architecture; wants total visibility; emphasizes performance tuning; is very sensitive to artifact; and will use a range of tools including trace-driven models, event traces, and hardware monitors.

The instrumentation built into the CPU includes the components shown in Table 6.3.

The operating system is based on BSD/UNIX with System V extensions. The operating system runs all processors tightly coupled and allows user tasks to share memory. A full 32-bit virtual address space is supported.

Operating system extensions that will assist measurement efforts include (1) process page nailing, and (2) uninterruptable user process execution. Other tools that have been developed for internal use include an instruction set interpreter and trace-driven multiprocessor models.

A supercomputer channel augments the NP1's interconnection capabilities. This full duplex channel obeys the Cray HSX protocol, and operates at up to 100 Mbyte/s. Several of these channels may be installed in a system.

The principal communication channels between systems are always an important point of interest. The supercomputer channel is provided with probe points (available on a special connector), that allow the following information to be determined:

□ bytes transferred, and received,

□ time and count of transmitter inhibits,

□ time and count of receiver inhibits,

□ time and count of receiver inhibits that caused No Transmit,

TABLE 6.3
NPI Instrumentation

Component	Description
System Timer	50- or 100-HZ resolution used as the default process time and elapsed-time clock.
Interval Timer	52-NS clock with a 223-second epoch. This is available for the user through timer calls.
TB Reference Count	Counts number of virtual address translations.
TB Hit Count	Counts number of address translation buffer hits.
Instruction Cache Fetches	Counts number of instruction fetches.
Instruction Cache Hit Count	Counts number of instruction cache hits.
Operand Memory References	Counts number of operand cache references.
Operand Cache Hits	Counts number of operand cache.

- time and count of firmware or memory conflict that caused No Transmit,
- time and count of software caused No Transmit, and
- buffer fill and empty statistics.

Figure 6.1 corresponds to a system built with the instrumentation listed above. The system being measured was a single processor NP1 with eight-way interleaving of 128- bit words. A maximum of 64-way interleaving is available on the NP1. The system was running a diagnostic that did not attempt to overlap processing with supercomputer channel I/O.

6.5 Parallel System Instrumentation

In order to speculate on useful instrumentation for future parallel systems, one should first specify a hypothetical parallel architecture for which the instrumentation is relative. In this light let us imagine the following architecture:

- shared memory,
- shared synchronization registers with a reasonable set of operations, and
- efficient fine-grain parallelism.

The system just described is capable of efficient fine- and coarse-grain parallelism. In many respects, fine-grain parallelism invites the most interesting instrumentation and debugging cases. For such a system, there are several forms of instrumentation that seem reasonable:

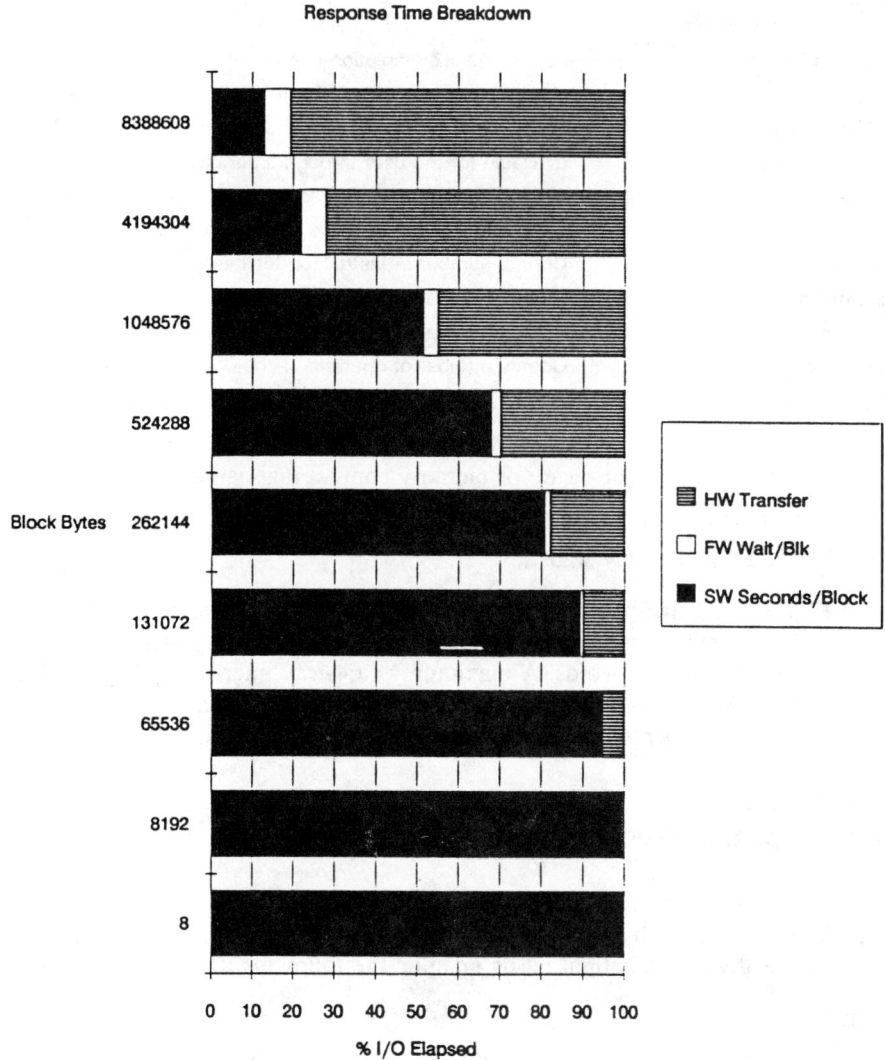

FIGURE 6.1
Response time breakdown.

6.5. Parallel System Instrumentation

- parallel trap,
- shared high-resolution real-time clock,
- hybrid instrumentation through shared registers; the values stored into one or more shared registers are made available to an external monitor, and
- built-in circular monitor buffer.

The parallel trap stops all or a subset of processors as quickly as possible. Upon receiving a parallel trap, each processor should be vectored into a local trap handler.

A parallel trap is useful in debugging because it can freeze a system state for subsequent analysis in performance evaluation because it allows the undertaking of useful parallel profiling.

Just how fast does a parallel trap need to be? For performance evaluation purposes, it is probably acceptable if not all systems stop simultaneously. The trap signal must propagate between the processors more quickly than any other form of communication. Communication here refers not only to intentional message passing, or values stored in shared resources, but also to the artifact of execution such as contention for shared resources. That is, the effect of a trap on one CPU must never be felt by another CPU before the trap itself has arrived.

The usefulness of the parallel trap is enhanced if all other system instrumentation is frozen when the trap is received. If a system has a few bits of state for each internal resource such as functional units and memory banks that indicate whether the resource is in use or whether it is blocked while awaiting some other resource such as a memory, the parallel trap can then be used by sampling routines, allowing very useful profiles of resource contention and utilization.

It is useful to discuss why parallel trap sampling is better than sampling performed independently and asynchronously by executives on each of the processors:

1. All artifacts occur after the trap is taken. With asynchronous schemes, the artifact of sampling on one processor may affect what is observed by sampling on another.
2. Events involving multiple asynchronous CPUs and memories may be sampled easily. With asynchronous sampling, this is not possible.

As mentioned earlier, the parallel trap would be quite useful for debugging. Do debugging requirements demand that parallel trap propagation occur faster than is required for performance instrumentation? Many codes still have branches that occur as frequently as once in four instructions. Trap propagation times of much over eight instructions would probably greatly increase debugging efforts.

A shared real-time clock is essential for determining the sequence of parallel events without incurring a substantial synchronization overhead. Clearly, the resolution of the shared real-time clock should be smaller than the execution time of the synchronization code it replaces. In general it is best if the shared real-time clock's resolution is smaller than the fastest interprocessor communication path. Of course, the ideal is for the shared real-time clock to have sufficient resolution in order to time the execution of a single instruction.

In general, high-resolution clocks and low trap propagation time, exceeding the minimums stated above, will make measurement experiments easier to carry out. They will also greatly enhance debugging efforts.

Hybrid instrumentation via a shared register should provide a fast mechanism for ordering events and allow them to be recorded externally from the system under test [17,18]. This could be combined with a circular monitor buffer that contains the last n timestamped values of the register. Other issues that must be considered, include (1) what other system state should be recorded along with a hybrid event, (2) how many entries (n) are required in the buffer, and (3) what ranges of behavior should be allowed in response to a full buffer event (parallel trap on full, set flag, and wrap around)?

The power of a parallel trap and a shared real-time clock may make hybrid instrumentation and hardware event buffers unnecessary. It is too early to be certain of this point.

6.6 Implementation

Both parallel trap and shared real-time clock utilities can be implemented by a single shared line that runs to each CPU. The shared real-time clock can be implemented by replicating clock logic on each CPU using a common frequency source for synchronization, or by placing it in shared registers.

Many systems have circular monitor buffers built-in for certain maintenance functions. These buffers are similar in function to special purpose logic analyzers. It is important to consider the difference in requirements between performance evaluation and hardware diagnosis. This is particularly true of buffer management and triggering policies.

None of the previously mentioned mechanisms are easy to retrofit onto arbitrary existing hardware designs. The parallel trap and the shared real-time clock are relatively easy to add to new implementations. Indeed, they would seem to be easy to implement even on distributed memory systems.

The implementation of the circular monitor buffer and the hybrid instrumentation facilities are certainly within the current state-of-the-art.

6.7 Conclusion

This paper has reviewed the current state of instrumentation, noting the lack of standard models, and hence the lack of standard metrics. A minimum set of instrumentation has been proposed for shared memory parallel systems, and its applicability to performance evaluation problems has been discussed.

These instrumentation mechanisms are generally useful for distributed memory parallel systems as well. The combination of the proposed facilities would allow the same degree of visibility into parallel events that is present today in sequential performance monitoring and debugging environments.

The area of instrumentation requirements still needs further study. Namely, what are the acceptable ranges of artifact and cost for each end-user type, what is the required resolution of counters and clocks, and how long an observation period is required?

References

1. T. Beretvas, System Independent Tracing for Prediction of System Performance, *Symposium on the Simulation of Computer Systems*, 1973, pp. 209–213.
2. A. Bonner, Using System Monitor Output to Improve Performance, *IBM Systems Journal*, No. 4, 1969, pp. 290–297.
3. P. Cheng, Trace-Driven System Modeling, *IBM Systems Journal*, No. 4, 1969, pp. 280–289.
4. D. Ferrari and M. Liu, A General Purpose Software Measurement Tool, *Software-Practice and Experience*, Vol. 5, 1975, pp. 181–192.
5. J. Hughes and D. Chronshaw, On Using a Hardware Monitor as an Intelligent Peripheral, *ACM Performance Evaluation Review*, December 1973, pp. 3–19.
6. K. Kolence, The Software Empiricist, *Performance Evaluation Review*, Vol. 2, No. 2, June 1973, pp. 31–36.
7. T. Peterson, A Comparison of Software and Hardware Monitors, *Performance Evaluation Review*, Vol. 3, No. 2, June 1974, pp. 2–5.
8. A. J. Smith, Two Methods for Efficient Analysis of Memory Address Data, *IEEE Transactions on Software Engineering*, Vol. SE-3, No. 1, January 1977, pp. 97–101.

9. S. K. Tripathi, S. Kaisler, S. Chandran, and A. K. Agrawala, Report on the Workshop on Design & Performance Issues on Parallel Architectures, *Performance Evaluation Review, ACM Sigmetrics*, Vol. 14, No. 3 and 4, January 1987, pp. 1631.
10. J. P. Buzen, Fundamental Operational Laws of Computer System Performance, *Acta Informatica*, Vol. 7, No. 2, 1976.
11. J. P. Buzen, On the Essential Properties of Operational Analysis, *10th IMACS World Congress on System Simulation and Scientific Computation*, Vol. 4, 1982, pp. 242–244.
12. M. K. Holliday and M. K. Vernon, A Generalized Timed Petri Net Model for Performance Analysis, *Proceedings of the International Workshop on Timed Petri Nets*, Torino, Italy, July 1985.
13. B. D. Gaither, Application of Petri Nets to the Documentation of System Instrumentation, *CMG Transactions* No. 48, June 1985, pp. 12–16.
14. I. Y. Bucher, Private Conversation.
15. D. Vianney and S. Heffner, An Overview of the Gould NP1 Parallel Multicomputer System, *Proceedings of the Second International Conference on Supercomputing*, Vol. 1, 1987, pp. 29–34.
16. D. Vianney, The Gould NP1 System Architecture, *Proceedings of the Second International Conference on Supercomputing*, Vol. 1, 1987, pp. 35–43.
17. L. Svobodova, Measuring Computer System Utilization with a Hardware and a Hybrid Monitor, *Performance Evaluation Review*, Vol. 2, No. 4, December 1973, pp. 20–33.
18. B. D. Gaither and E. D. Patrick, Hybrid Instrumentation on the NCR Criterion, *Proceedings of CMG X*, 1979.

7

Monitoring Experimental Parallel Machines

A.P.W. Bohm
J.R. Gurd
M.C. Kallstrom

7.1 Introduction

7.1.1 The Need For Monitoring

A key problem that is inhibiting the effective use of parallel computer systems is the absence of tools to support the process of effectively mapping an application problem onto the parallel resources of a machine. The processes of debugging the parallel code and tuning the performance of the debugged code, whether hand-crafted or automatically generated, require data about run-time events. Hence, an important group of tools are those that allow the users of various parallel systems to observe the run-time behaviour of their programs.

7.1.2 Levels Of Abstraction

In an attempt to master the complexity of the situation, it is commonly recognised that there are several important levels of abstraction at which computing systems can be described. The exact choice of levels is arbitrary, but the following are representative and can be readily identified in most computing systems:

1. the application level,
2. the programming language level,
3. the abstract machine level,
4. the computational model level, and
5. the realisation level of the hardware implementation.

The abstract machine usually operates at a level closely related to the programming language level. The first three levels are the province of the application programmer, whereas the last three concern the system architects (i.e. compiler writers, operating system and hardware designers). At present, it is only at the lower levels that there is some feeling for the way in which data should be assembled and presented. Most current practice is clearly derived from experience with conventional, sequential computer systems.

Monitoring at the abstract machine level can help an application programmer to debug a program and gain insight into its dynamic behaviour. Ideally, such monitoring would be completely machine independent. For example, the applicative programming language, SISAL, is implemented on several different parallel machines, such as a vector processor, a shared memory multiprocessor, and a dataflow machine, and the programmer does not want to be forced into thinking in terms of one particular implementation (e.g., dataflow) when trying to debug a program.

Monitoring at the computational model level reveals idealised machine level information, such as the maximum available parallelism and the maximum possible speedup based on ideal assumptions. Note that, for different computational models, the characteristics of a program measured at this level (e.g., its parallelism) may vary widely [1]. Information gathered at this level provides a target for performance to be achieved at the realisation level.

Monitoring at the realisation level is used by the computer architect to study real machine-level characteristics, such as precise elapsed time, data traffic, resource contention, and the utilisation of hardware modules.

7.1.3 Monitoring Methods

At each level, there is a choice to be made regarding the nature of monitoring information. At one extreme is the idealised concept of full tracing, in which the time and place of every event is recorded. This is useful for studying the relative timing of events and forming a complete picture of runtime behaviour. When simulating a parallel machine and running modest-sized experiments, full tracing can provide useful insight into program or machine behaviour. However, this method is infeasible in a real machine, due to the sheer amount of data that would have to be saved, and due to the drastic change in behaviour of a machine when monitoring itself with high frequency. In sampling, the required amount of storage is reduced by saving only a selected part of the full trace.

At the other extreme, information is condensed at the point at which it is collected, usually by counting the total number of selected types of event, or by summing, averaging, or taking maximum or minimum values. Recorded events cannot be distinguished by time, and so certain queries about them cannot be answered. However, such monitoring may be made feasible in a real machine by intelligent selection of the monitoring points and applying statistical interpolation techniques [2]. It is also possible to mix sampling and condensing modes, creating partially traced, condensed records of execution.

7.1.4 Summary Of Paper

The remainder of this paper investigates the application of program animation, and tracing and condensing monitoring tools in the implementation of simulators for a multiring dataflow machine on the T-Rack. In this case, the realisation level of the dataflow machine, i.e., the dataflow simulator, coincides with the application level on the T-Rack. Table 7.1 shows the levels of abstraction in this double hierarchy. The subsequent sections discuss these levels and the monitoring tool for each when appropriate.

7.2 The Manchester Dataflow System

7.2.1 Application Level

The dataflow computing system at the University of Manchester is an example of fine-grain message-passing parallelism [3]. It is assumed that the applications that are of interest can be expressed in the single assignment language, SISAL [4]. This language choice restricts attention to predominantly numerical and combinatorial computations operating on array-structured data. The choice of algorithms to take maximum advantage of any available hardware parallelism is an open issue that is not investigated further in this paper.

7.2.2 Language Level: SISAL

SISAL [4] is a general-purpose single-assignment language designed for efficient execution on a variety of parallel computers. Because of its single-assignment property, the language naturally lends itself to parallel execution; sequencing will only occur where it is enforced by data dependencies. Apart from the usual scalar types, the data structures of SISAL include arrays, streams, and records.

TABLE 7.1
Levels of abstraction in a parallel machine simulator

Level	Feature Dataflow Simulator	T-Rack	Tool
application	SISAL application		
programming language	SISAL		
abstract machine	IF1		TREE
computational model	dataflow graphs		
realisation = application	simulator	occam application	MatMet
programming language		occam	
abstract machine		processes, channels	GRAIL
computational model		transputers, links	
realisation		T-Rack	

Data objects of any type can be regarded as mathematical values. A SISAL program consists of a set of side effect free functions. The function called "main" communicates with the outside world; its parameters are the input and output of the program. SISAL has conditional expressions and two forms of the FOR construct: one forming an iterative loop, the other a parallel FORALL expression. As an example, "Binint," a binary integration program in SISAL is shown in Figure 7.1.

The single assignment and functional properties of SISAL make it particularly suited to translation into data-dependence graph format. In essence, this translation is what is achieved in the front end of the SISAL compiler. A machine-independent data-dependence graph form known as IF1 (Intermediate Format – version 1) has been defined specifically for translation purposes [5]. IF1 constitutes the abstract machine implementation for SISAL.

7.2.3 Abstract Machine Level: IF1

An IF1 program is a set of graphs, one for each SISAL function. Edges represent values travelling from node to node and are typed. Nodes represent operations and are of three main types, the most important of which are the compound nodes that recursively contain subgraphs and implement conditionals and loops [6].

```
export Main

function F(X: real    returns real)
    3.0*X*X*X + 2.0*X*X + 5.0
end function

function Trap(L, R : real   returns real)
    (R-L) * (F(L) + F(R))/2.0
end function

function Area(L,R,Est,Tol: real returns real)
let Mid     := (L + R)/2.0;
    A1      := Trap(L, Mid); A2 := Trap(Mid, R);
    Newest  := A1 + A2
 in if abs(Est - Newest) < Tol
    then newest
    else Area(L, Mid, A1, Tol/2.0) + Area(Mid, R, A2, Tol/2.0)
    end if
end let
end function

function Main(A,B,InitTol: real returns real)
Area(A,B,Trap(A,B),InitTol)
end function
```

FIGURE 7.1
Binint, a binary integration program in SISAL.

An important structure at this abstract machine level is the static call graph, which is a skeletal version of the IF1 representation in which nodes represent function and loop bodies and there is an edge between node A and node B if A activates B. During IF1 to dataflow compilation, the programmer may interact with the compiler using the static call graph to provide helpful information. For example, the programmer may wish to control the size of processes by inlining certain function calls (i.e., replacing them by their function bodies). It is possible to specify the maximum size of a function that is to be inlined and the extent to which recursive functions are to be inlined [7]. Figure 7.2 shows the call graph of the example SISAL program in various stages of inlining.

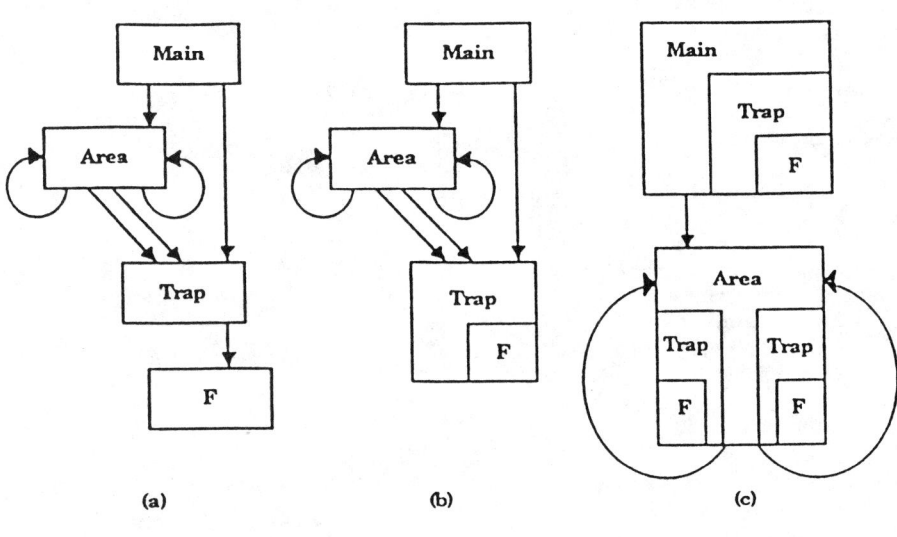

FIGURE 7.2
Call graph of example SISAL program.

A program monitoring tool used at this level animates the call graph by means of a dynamic process tree [6]. Process animation illustrates the runtime behaviour of the IF1 processes. Nodes denote activated function or loop bodies, and edges represent actual function calls or loop activations. When a function or loop body terminates, the node representing it, and the edge representing its activation, disappear. Figure 7.3 shows the dynamic process tree of the example SISAL program drawn by a graphics package TREE [8], running on a Sun[1] workstation. TREE takes its input from a monitor file created by the dataflow simulator. Currently the only events recorded in this file are the creation and termination time of processes and the process names. This is clearly inadequate. More information should be made available, such as the values of function parameters and other SISAL data objects local to the activation, and the access pattern to data structures.

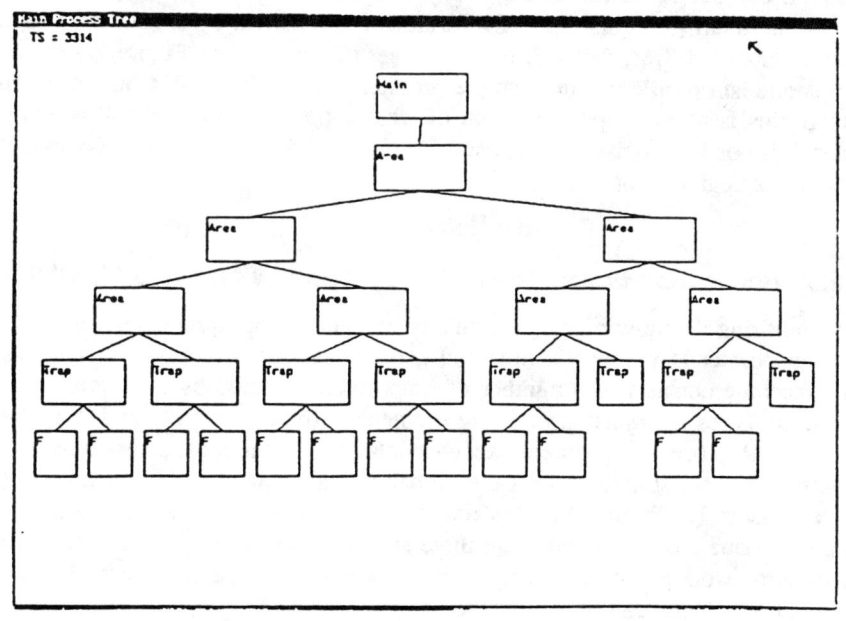

FIGURE 7.3
A snapshot of the process tree of Binint.

---

[1] Sun is a registered trademark of Sun Microsystems, Inc.

7.2.4 Model of Computation Level: Dataflow Graphs

The IF1 static call graph structure is converted into machine code by a machine-specific code generator. In the case of the Manchester Dataflow Computer, the machine-level instruction set has been developed in close conjunction with the code generator [7]. The resulting code is often drawn in graphical form; the code drawing can also be animated to illustrate instruction-level execution [3].

At the machine level, it is common to approximate machine behaviour by assuming, for example, that all instructions take the same time to execute, or that all instructions eligible to execute at any time are executed together. This approximation leads to an idealised machine in which maximally parallel execution proceeds along a critical path via a sequence of indivisible time steps, called Sinf, when an infinite number of processors are available, in lock step fashion. The average parallelism of the program can be assessed by dividing the total number of instructions executed by the number of Sinf steps required to execute them [3]. This kind of information is recorded by a dataflow graph interpreter called SIM, that will not be further discussed here. Figure 7.4 shows the parallelism profile of our example program derived from SIM output. Even though this is a crude approximation of what happens in a real dataflow computer, it is possible to use the idealised figures to predict real machine behaviour with a fair degree of accuracy.

7.2.5 Realisation Level: The Multiring Dataflow Machine Simulator

The multiring dataflow machine simulator emulates a multiprocessor version of the Manchester Dataflow Machine and gathers machine and program statistics. The machine consists of a number of rings interconnected by a switch. There are three types of rings: processing elements, structure stores, and a global allocator. A processing element executes dataflow instructions, a structure store manipulates data structures, and the global allocator manages global resources such as large (interleaved) arrays and processes. In principle, there could be more than one global allocator, but there are unsolved problems associated with distributing work among multiple allocators, and more research is needed before a complete scheme can be simulated.

For each type of ring, there are a number of characteristics to monitor. For the processing elements these include token queue length, matching store occupancy, and functional unit utilisation; for the structure stores, token queue length, the number of store accesses, the number of allocations, and the store occupancy; and for the global allocator, the number of active and suspended processes.

Information for each type of ring can be displayed conveniently as a matrix of meters. Every row of the matrix represents one ring and every column represents a characteristic. The authors are using a graphics package, MatMet [8],

7.2. The Manchester Dataflow System   129

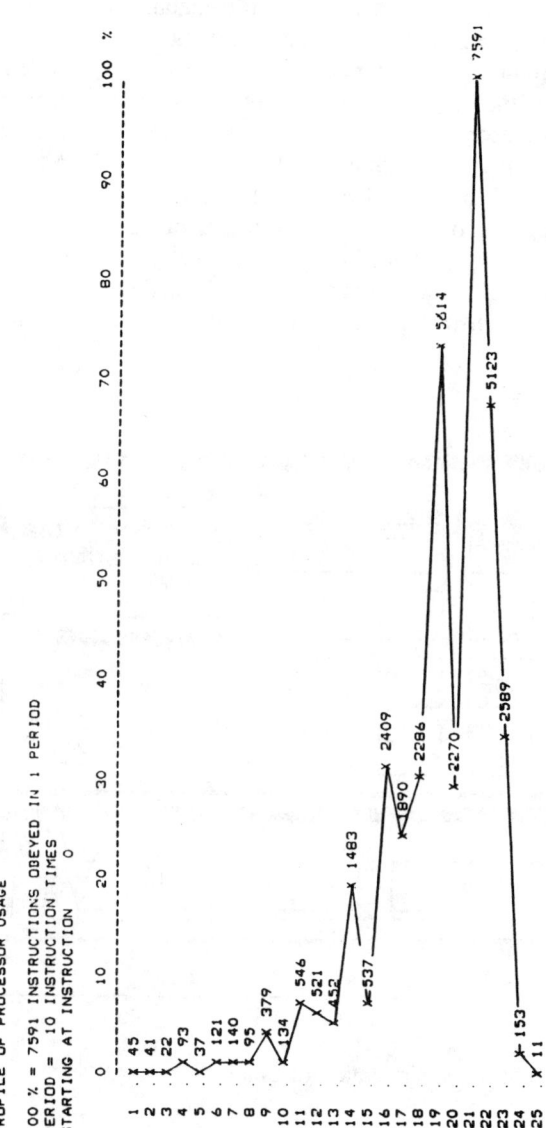

FIGURE 7.4
Parallelism profile for example program.

running on a Sun workstation, to observe the behaviour of dataflow machine simulations. The simulator produces a monitor file containing a description of the machine followed by measurements of the phenomena to be monitored. MatMet transforms this information into matrices of graphs and/or values, continuously displaying the state of the machine. The display can be played forward, stopped, and played back. The user can specify which phenomena are to be dumped in so-called history files. Figure 7.5 shows matrices of meters for a four-processor dataflow machine run of Binint, and Figure 7.6 shows the histories of the token queue and matching store occupancies, and processor utilisation. Even though the program is excessively parallel most of the time (see Figure 7.4), the machine controls the parallelism well, which can be concluded from the low storage occupancies [9]. Notice also that the work is equally distributed over the four rings.

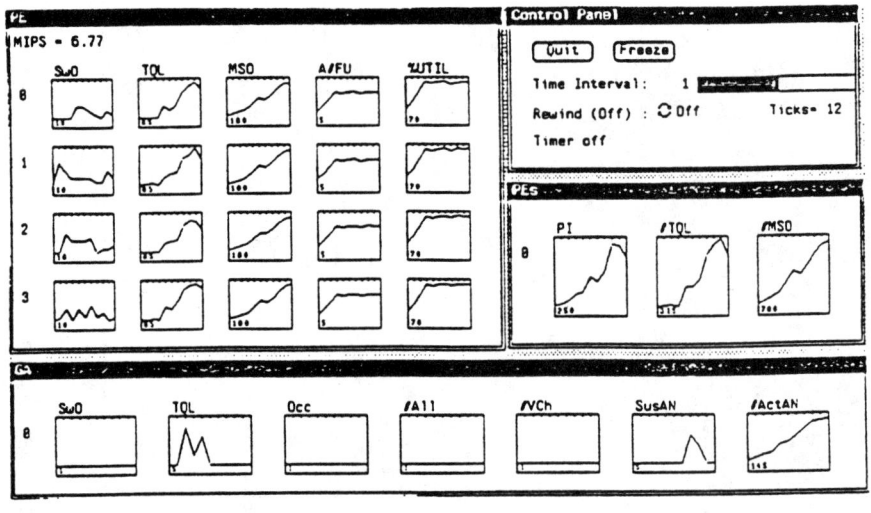

FIGURE 7.5
Matrix of meters of a four PE simulation of Binint.

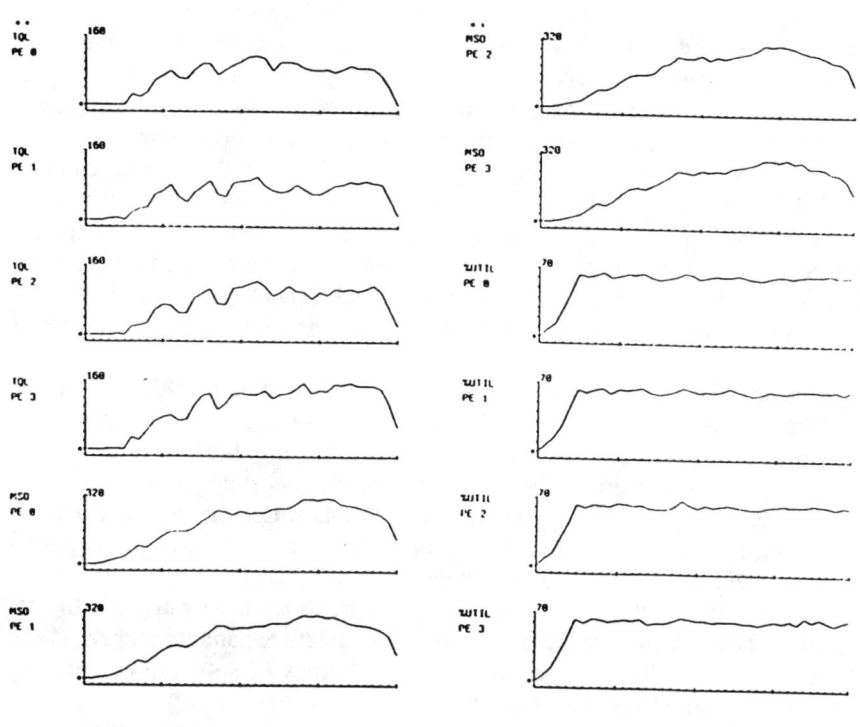

FIGURE 7.6
Histories of store occupancies and processor utilisation.

7.3 ParSiFal

7.3.1 Application Level

The ParSiFal project is developing a coarse-grain message-passing parallel computing system based on Inmos transputers [10]. This system focuses on applications that can be expressed in the static communicating process language, **occam**. An interesting application using this type of language is distributed simulation of parallel computer architectures. An experiment is in progress in which the multiring simulator for the Manchester Dataflow Computer is being implemented in **occam** and executed on the ParSiFal T-Rack.

Simulators of parallel computer systems are characterised by their level of abstraction (e.g., block, register transfer, or gate level) and by the way they model time. In time-driven simulators, time forms an increasing arithmetic sequence, whereas in event-driven simulators, time grows monotonically but not arithmetically. A simulator is tight if simulation time is equal in all components of the system at a certain moment in the simulation, and loose otherwise.

Currently, we are using a tight, time-driven block-level simulator running on VAXs[2] and Sun workstations [9] as a basis for experimentation with novel dataflow architectures. The advantages of this simulator are that it is simple, it models time straightforwardly, it has no problems with distributed clocks [11], and it is possible to trace and relate events at clockbeat rate (or at any other sampling rate). Its disadvantages are that it is slow and it uses large amounts of memory.

A distributed, loose, event-driven version of the simulator that will run on the T-Rack is being implemented. The parallel nature of this simulator introduces new design issues, such as the method of modelling time, and the method of mapping the **occam** processes that form the simulator onto the T-Rack transputers. In this paper we will concentrate on the latter. Our strategy has been to start with a simulator for a multiprocessor dataflow machine with a simplified computational model, known as one input dataflow (1DF).

Unlike real dataflow instructions, 1DF instructions have only one logical input. 1DF has sufficient expressive power to simulate expanding and shrinking parallelism, and it allows us to concentrate on issues of software engineering related to distributed event-driven simulation.

The basic **occam** process structure for a three-processing element (PE) 1DF simulator is shown in Figure 7.7. Circles and crosses (the switches) are **occam** processes; rectangles are arrays used in the processes attached to them.

7.3.2 Language Level: occam

The language, **occam** [12], is an explicitly parallel language based on the concept of communicating sequential processes [13]. A process is similar to a procedure written in any familiar, sequential programming language. There are variables, which can be assigned values by assignment statements, and there are various control constructs that allow conditional (ALT) and iterative (WHILE) execution (recursion is not permitted by current implementations). There are also constructs that allow explicit sequential (SEQ) and parallel (PAR) execution of statements. The main additional feature of the language is that processes are allowed to communicate with one another through channels, by using send-message (written !) and receive-message (written ?) operations. Figure 7.8 shows the **occam** code

---

[2] VAX is a registered trademark of Digital Equipment Corporation.

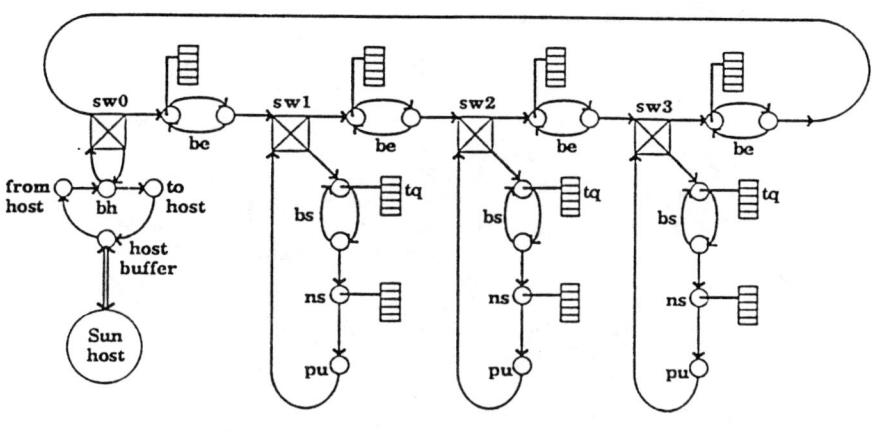

FIGURE 7.7
Process structure of the 1DF simulator.

for the switch processes from Figure 7.7. Sections of code are hidden in "folds" indicated by ...; comments are delimited by –.

7.3.3 Abstract Machine Level: Communicating Sequential Processors

In the abstract machine for **occam**, each process resides on a processor and each channel is represented by a physical link between the processors corresponding to the processes that send and receive messages across the channel. Only two processors can be connected together by one link. Each processor effectively interprets the **occam** statements within the corresponding process, and so monitoring is in terms of the **occam** statements executed and the messages transmitted and received by each processor.

A commonly used scheme for illustrating the intended process(or) behaviour is to draw a schematic diagram of the process structure of a program, just as in Figure 7.7.

A graphical monitoring tool, known as GRAIL (Graphical Representation of Activity, Interconnection, and Loading) has been implemented for the ParSiFal project [14]. GRAIL either simply counts the total number of statement

```
PROC switch(CHAN n, s, e, w, VAL INT id)
  ... declarations
  SEQ
    state := Alive
    WHILE (state <> Dead)
      SEQ
        ALT
          w ? data
            SKIP
          n ? data
            SKIP
        IF
          data[Ix.Type] = Type.Stop
            ... adjust current state (Alive, Coma, Dead)
          TRUE
            IF
              data[Ix.Ring] = id      ?-- for my ring
                s ! data
              TRUE                    ?-- for another ring
                e ! data
```

FIGURE 7.8
occam code for a 2*2 switch.

executions during a complete program run or counts "weighted" versions of them (weighted, for example, according to the expected number of execution cycles associated with each one). The weights can be changed by the user. As occam is a static language, these loads can be meaningfully incorporated in a structured block diagram of the program. There are no topic utilities as yet for monitoring the corresponding interprocess message traffic. GRAIL is clearly a condensing tool (see Section 7.1.3).

7.3.4 Model of Computation Level

The underlying model of computation is a slightly modified form of the traditional von Neumann (state-based) model. Conventional sequential processors with integral memory are used to implement each process(or), using traditional compilation techniques. These processors need not necessarily be transputers, although these devices are commonly cited as an ideal implementation vehicle. Point-to-point links are used to implement the channels.

At the computational model level, the costs of memory accesses and communications can be assessed more accurately than at the level of the abstract machine, since realistic machine code is being studied. However, simplifications are still present in the model because it is assumed that there are no limits on the number of processors and links or on the number of links per processor.

At present, there are no tools for monitoring at the computational model level. An accurately timed simulator for a distributed multiprocessor with unconstrained interconnection is required as a basis for such a tool. There are no plans within the ParSiFal project to produce such a simulator for transputer-based systems.

7.3.5 Realization Level: The T-Rack

The ParSiFal T-Rack comprises an extensible, reconfigurable array of 64 transputers (plus up to 2 Mbytes of memory each) with certain of their communication links interconnected via a pair of crossbar switches, as shown in Figure 7.9. A transputer consists of a processor, a local memory, four links, and a bus interface, all on one chip. The instruction set supports context switching, so multiple processes can run on one transputer efficiently.

The fixed horizontal path connecting all the transputers together is known as the necklace, and forms, in graph theoretic terms, a Hamiltonian path between the computational nodes. The two crossbar switches provide high connectivity beyond that afforded by the Hamiltonian path. A host transputer system is provided to set the crossbar switches and to load and run the multiprocessor code. The host system can also be used to compile **occam** programs. The complete T-Rack resides in a triple height Eurocard module and interfaces through the host (across a VME bus) to a Sun workstation.

Expanded versions of the T-Rack system can be constructed by replicating and interconnecting the "64-transputer plus 2-crossbar switch plus host system" configuration an appropriate number of times.

Low-level monitoring tools have been implemented on the T-Rack [15]. These involve transputer code that interacts with the host system via a special backplane bus, rather than through the normal T-Rack links. In principle, it would be possible to provide the same kind of monitoring utilities tools as the MatMet tool provides for the Dataflow system (see Section 7.2.5). However, a fully timed T-Rack simulator would be required before this could be implemented.

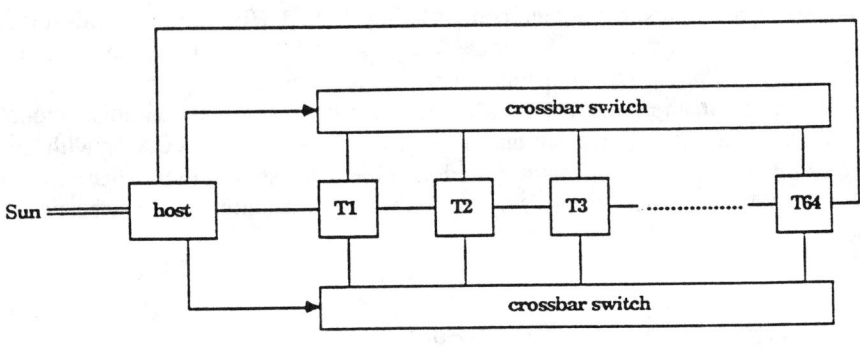

FIGURE 7.9
The ParSiFal T-Rack hardware configuration.

7.3.6 A Preliminary Experiment in Partitioning And Mapping

The process of "fitting" an **occam** program onto a particular configuration of transputers and links involves two major phases: partitioning and mapping. In the partitioning phase, the processes constituting the **occam** program are divided into groups that will be executed on the same transputer. In other words, partitioning is the process of identifying connected components in the process graph such that the components are linked to each other by not more than four channels. There is no such restriction for processes inside a component.

Mapping is the process of assigning the partitions of the program graph to transputers such that channels coincide with T-Rack links. Not every graph with nodes of degree less than or equal to four can be mapped on the T-Rack. For example, graphs where all nodes have degree four and the number of nodes is less than sixty-four, cannot be mapped because of the static configuration of the necklace.

As the dataflow machine consists of boxes connected to each other by not more than four links, and the simulator is written with this in mind, a number of partitions and mappings are feasible. Each process could be mapped on a separate transputer. On the other hand, all processes could be run on one transputer. The ideal fit depends on the run-time behaviour of the processes and the tradeoff between computation and communication on the T-Rack. A first approximation is to measure, either by using the GRAIL tool or by analysing the program, the complexity of the various processes (in terms of the number of occam instructions they execute), and then to partition the process structure into components with equal complexity. Notice that this approach is rather naive, as the time interdependence and communication complexity of the processes is not taken into account.

Naturally, the deciding factor that determines whether a certain fitting onto the T-Rack is a good one, is run time. However, timing and termination detection in a distributed environment present the problem that the distributed processes cannot detect when they have finished processing. A first solution is to let the program generate a statically known number of "termination signals" and to let the Buffer.to.Host process (BH in Figure 7.7) collect these. The Buffer.to.Host process receives a trigger token and registers the time on the transputer's clock. When all termination signals have been collected, it stops its clock and resets the machine.

GRAIL helps to explain timing results by showing the comparative workloads of the various occam processes. Alternately, GRAIL can be used to suggest new configurations by pointing out hot and cold spots. Figure 7.10 shows two possible configurations of the 1DF simulator on the T-Rack. With configuration I of the 1DF simulator, a simulation runs in 3.2 seconds. This same simulation takes 80 seconds with the time-driven version of the simulator running on a VAX 780. When examining the first configuration using GRAIL (see Figure 7.11), it becomes clear that the "hottest" components are switch elements and buffers on transputers 3, 8, and 9. The workload distribution displayed indicates that the output buffers, **bs** and **be**, work harder than the switch (sw). It is therefore worthwhile to allocate either **bs** or **be** to a private transputer. The "coolest" processes in configuration I are the node stores, transputers 4, 7, and 10, and processing units, transputers 5, 6, and 11. We can therefore further modify the configuration by mapping these two processes onto one transputer. The result of both of these modifications appears as configuration II in Figure 7.10, which takes 2.4 seconds to run the above mentioned simulation, reducing the run time by 25%.

7.4 Conclusions

Two kinds of parallel-message passing computers have been introduced, and tools for monitoring their behaviour at different levels of abstraction have been presented. Examples of the ways in which these tools can be used to aid the design of such machines and the implementation of application software on them have been given.

A multilevel experiment, in which a distributed simulator for one parallel machine architecture is implemented on another parallel computer, has been sketched. A preliminary attempt at fitting a parallel program on a course-grain message-passing multiprocessor using monitoring tools has been described.

138　Chapter 7. Monitoring Experimental Parallel Machines

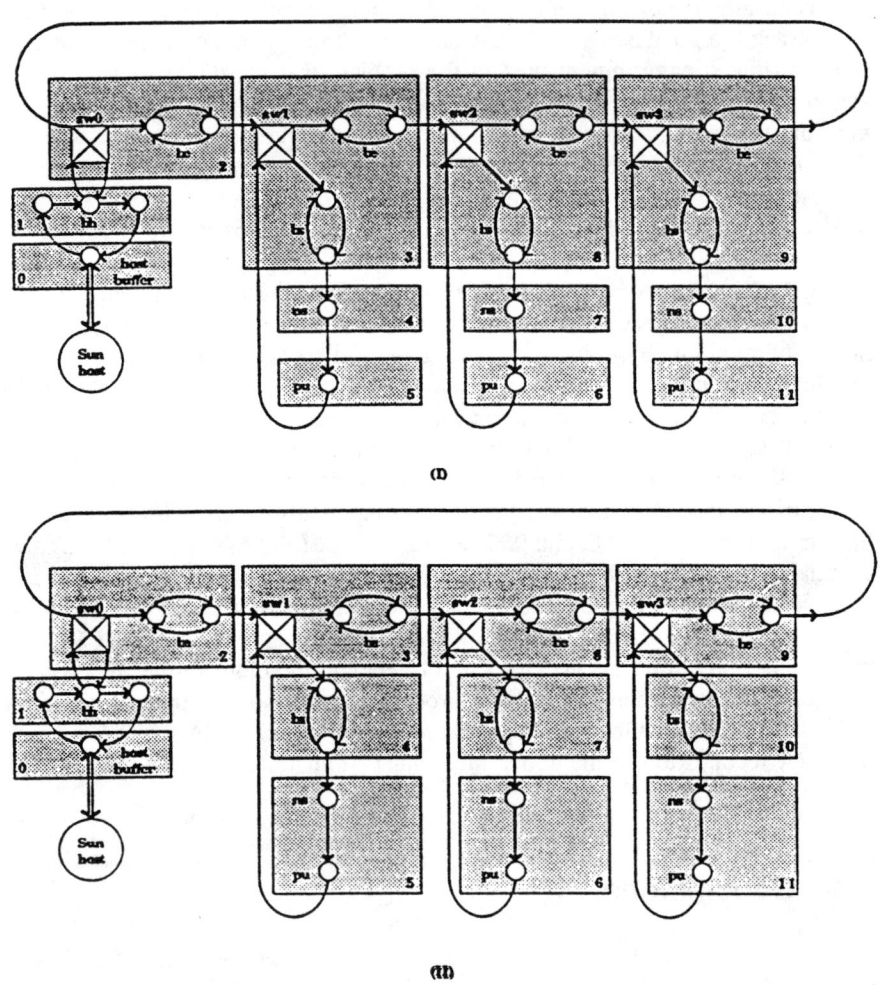

FIGURE 7.10
Two possible configurations of the 1DF simulator on the T-Rack.

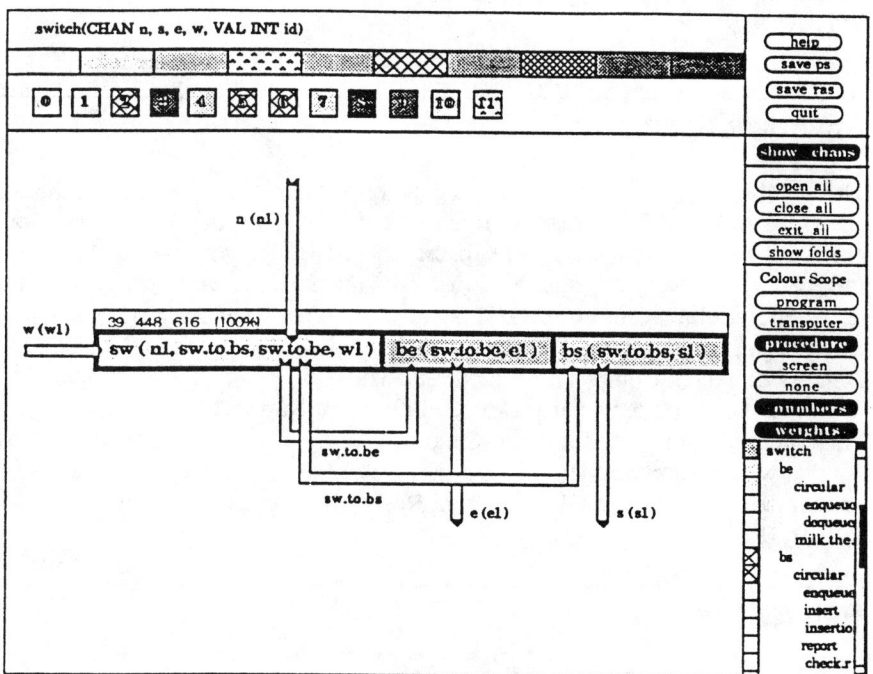

FIGURE 7.11
GRAIL snapshot of 1DF simulator on T-Rack in configuration I.

It is too early to comment on the relative merits of the various tools. Clearly, tracing gives more detailed information than condensing, but at the expense of requiring more accurately timed simulation and large amounts of storage. However, it is not at all clear how much more valuable tracing detail is in terms of the end objective of the monitoring. A considerable amount of experimentation with the tools is needed before any objective judgement can be made. The "levels of abstraction" view of parallel computer systems helps to organise and structure our understanding of these systems and to categorise the debugging and monitoring tools needed to visualise program and machine behaviour.

Acknowledgements

The authors wish to acknowledge the help of their many colleagues in the Dataflow and ParSiFal research groups at the University of Manchester. Both projects have received support from the UK Alvey Programme in Advanced Information Technology, and have involved interactions with partners in industry, polytechnics, and other UK universities. The Dataflow project has also received support from the UK Science and Engineering Research Council and Digital Equipment Company, Limited. The SISAL/IF1 system was implemented in conjunction with teams at Lawrence Livermore National Laboratory, Digital Equipment Corporation, Colorado State University, and the University of East Anglia, which also designed the languages. The GRAIL software was designed and written by a team at GEC-Marconi Research Laboratories.

References

1. Arvind, D. E. Culler, and G. K. Maa, Assessing the Benefits of Fine-grained Parallelism in Dataflow Programs, CSG Memo 279, Laboratory for Computer Science, MIT, March 1988.
2. M. M. Gorlick and C. F. Kesselman, Timing Prolog without Clocks, *Proceedings Symposium on Logic Programming*, San Francisco, IEEE Computer Society Press, August 1987.
3. J. R. Gurd, C. C. Kirkham, and A. P. W. Bohm, The Manchester Dataflow Computing System, in Dongarra J.J. (ed.), *Experimental Parallel Computing Architectures*, North Holland, 1987, pp. 177–219.
4. J. R. McGraw et al., SISAL — Streams and Iteration in a *Single-Assignment Language*, Language Reference Manual, Lawrence Livermore National Laboratory, 1983.

5. S. Skedzielewski and J. R. W. Glauert, IF1 — An Intermediate Form for Applicative Languages, Reference Manual M–170, Lawrence Livermore National Laboratory, 1985.
6. A. P. W. Bohm and J. R. Gurd, Tools for Performance Evaluation of Parallel Machines, in Polychronopoulos C. (ed.), *Proceedings International Conference on Supercomputing*, Springer-Verlag, 1987.
7. A. P. W. Bohm and J. Sargeant, Efficient Dataflow Code Generation for SISAL, Technical Report UM–CS–85–10–2, Department of Computer Science, University of Manchester, 1985.
8. H. W. H. Tang, Monitoring Tools for Parallel Systems, M.Sc. Thesis UM–CS–87–12–3 Department of Computer Science, University of Manchester, December 1987.
9. Y. M. Teo, Performance Evaluation of a Heterogeneous Multi-ring Dataflow Machine, M.Sc. Thesis UM–CS–87–12–2 Department of Computer Science, University of Manchester, December 1987.
10. A. E. Knowles, ParSiFal — A Parallel Simulation Facility Based on the Transputer, Internal Report, Department of Computer Science, University of Manchester, 1987.
11. L. Lamport, Time, Clocks and the Ordering of Events in a Distributed System, *CACM*, Vol.21 No. 7, 1987, pp. 558–565.
12. D. May, R. Shepherd and C. Keane, Communicating Process Architecture: Transputers and occam, *Lecture Notes in Computer Science*, Vol. 272, 1987, pp. 35–81.
13. C. A. R. Hoare, Communicating Sequential Processes, *CACM*, 21, 8 (1978), pp. 666–677.
14. S. Stepney, *GRAIL — Graphical Representation of Activity, Interconnection and Loading*, Report PSF/GEC/WP3/88/3, GEC-Marconi Research Laboratory, Great Baddow, Essex, January 1988.
15. A. E. Knowles and M. S. Illiev, Monitoring Facilities on the ParSiFal T-Rack, *Proceedings CONPAR88*, Manchester, September 1988.

8

Instrumentation for Application Performance Tuning: The M31 System

Matthew Reilly

8.1 A Statement of the Problems

It would be futile (as has been demonstrated fairly often) to embark on building a tool of any sort without first stating the problems that the tool is meant to address. The task discussed here is that of extracting information from a running parallel processor to answer questions that fall into one of the following three categories:

- Hardware and architectural questions
- Software performance enhancement
- Software functional debug

Typically, engineers interested in building parallel processors are interested in the stresses placed on a system by an application. Software engineers may be interested in optimizing the management of resources by the application and operating system and in ensuring that the application performs correctly.

8.1.1 Hardware and Architectural Measurement

The design of a measurement tool to address hardware and architectural research is strongly dependent on the architecture to be measured. It is not likely that much can be said about this task that would not be either obvious or irrelevant to the designer of the target machine.

That said in general, the hardware measurement task is aimed at identifying hardware bottlenecks and evaluating resource allocation and communication strategies. To do this well, the designer must provide measurement "hooks" at the access points to each major junction and resource. For a shared memory multiprocessor, hooks will likely be included at each processor-cache, cache-bus, and bus-memory connection. The events that occur at these points are very short-lived and most often are characterized by short interarrival times. Sampling behavior at the measurement points is often sufficient to answer the questions of interest.

8.1.2 Software Performance Enhancement

The task of designing measurement support for performance enhancement is the most interesting of the three introduced previously. Implementation must be inexpensive and easy to use to make it accessible to users. On the other hand, neither users nor computer manufacturers are willing to include hardware support for software performance enhancement if the performance of the hardware will be adversely affected. It is the tradeoff between maximal utility and minimal cost that makes the task of designing measurement support challenging.

Typically, an application developer approaching the task of "tuning" a particular implementation asks questions like the following:

- What portion of the code accounts for the most run time?
- What resources cause interprocess contention?
- What part of the code is running during the "serial" phase of a computation?

Instrumenting a parallel processing system poses some interesting problems for the designer. It is not yet clear whether traditional (uniprocessor-oriented) software measurement techniques (*e.g.*, program-counter sampling) can work in a general parallel environment. Further, any technique must account for the effect that the measurement activity itself has on the behavior of the system being measured. Finally, the user's demands on the measurement system are likely to be strongly affected by the user's model of computation. This is very clear in comparing users of loosely-coupled systems with users of closely-coupled systems. Similar arguments can be made for the different models implemented on shared memory architectures. [1]

---

[1] Note that some Cray X-MP users have found that program counter (PC) sampling has been quite satisfactory even with large sampling intervals. This indicates that it is possible (in the case of at least one model of computation) to use a very invasive monitoring strategy in a parallel processing environment.

8.1.3 Software Debugging

The use of hardware support for debugging multiprocessor applications looks promising but is not well understood. It is likely that much of the information gathered from a performance enhancement tool might be helpful in answering questions such as "what part of the code was running when event X occurred?" and "which process last modified location A before event Y occurred?" The difficulty arises in attempting to allow the developer access to the program state at the time an event occurs. The standard uniprocessor approach is to halt process execution when an event of interest occurs and pass control to some tool (a debugger) that allows the developer to examine program state. Implementing such a function for even a closely-coupled multiprocessor is extremely difficult (How are events detected in real time? What if an event of interest is composed of two or more "primitive" events occurring at different physical locations? How are such compound events detected? How is the order to "halt" propagated to the several processors?).

It seems clear that any effective software debugging tool requires some kind of event detection facility. The design of such a tool could aid the research directed at understanding the problem of designing a performance measurement facility.

8.2 Useful Features for a Measurement System

This section will concentrate on enumerating the useful and necessary features to provide a facility for software performance enhancement. The following sections will describe the implementation of a facility that provides these functions and describe the experience gained with such a tool.

8.2.1 The Measurement Model

The features described here are those that are necessary for an event trace facility. Such a facility would provide a developer with a time-correlated log of system activity for each active process. The log is a series of events, recorded in order of occurrence, with each event represented in triplets: event-type, event-data, and time-of-occurrence. From such a log, a developer may gather significant information about application *vs* system interactions, flow of control within the application, and even the flow of data among the cooperating processes.

8.2.2 A Brief Word About Time

Any hardware assistance for performance evaluation must provide a basic facility for measuring time. Ideally this facility is in the form of a register accessible to the monitor hardware at a constant cost in time. The resolution of the timer must be such that it can determine which of two memory transactions occurs first. Typically, such a timer is incremented at a rate similar to the memory access time or the instruction execution time.

Further, the timer should be large enough so that it does not overflow in the course of a normal experiment. If this is not practical (for instance, if such a width is incompatible with the natural data path width for the monitor hardware), then some "anti-aliasing" technique must be provided.

Finally, if there is more than one such timer register in the system, there must be a mechanism for ensuring that all of the timers are synchronized with each other.

8.2.3 Detecting and Collecting Events

The monitor hardware should be capable of recognizing event signals. Events are signaled by explicit action on the part of the software being monitored.

The simplest signaling mechanism is a write to a particular physical address. Each type of event in the active process would be assigned a distinct physical address. The measurement hardware would be designed to recognize the occurrence of a write to this address and capture the data being written as the event-data component of the event triplet.

Once the event triplets have been formed by the event-detection hardware, they must be deposited in the event log. Instrumentation hardware must provide a mechanism for intermediate storage of this data, as well as a communication path to some mass storage device for later analysis.

If the sensor stores the event log in a random access memory (RAM) (as opposed to a first in, first out (FIFO) queue) then it may be possible for the RAM to serve a more general purpose. The hardware can use such a feature to build histograms and accumulate performance measures rather than record events in some time sequence. This feature can be quite useful in collecting statistics on system behavior (*e.g.*, cache hit ratio, memory access time histograms, and cache state profiles).

8.3 An Experimental Implementation

An instrumentation system with the features described in Section 8.2 has been built as a part of Digital Equipment Corporation's M31 VAX[2] multiprocessor The following sections will describe the M31 system and its measurement support.

[2] VAX is a registered trademark of Digital Equipment Corporation.

8.3.1 The M31 VAX Multiprocessor

The M31 system is a thirty-two-processor shared memory VAX system. Each processor-cache module (PC) contains four MicroVAX[3] processors and a single shared cache. Automatic cache coherence is maintained using a modified version of the snoopy cache scheme presented in [1]. The software environment is Version 4.4 of the VAX/VMS asymmetric operating system. For a more detailed description of the M31 project, see [2].

8.3.2 The Instrumentation System

Each processor-cache module in the M31 system is connected to a companion processor-monitor module (PM). The PM is capable of monitoring signals from three of the four MicroVAX processors on the attached PC. The PM is composed of three microprogrammable *sensors* and one programmable *preprocessor*.

Each sensor is capable of "watching" the signals from a single MicroVAX processor and the connection between the processor and the shared cache. The preprocessor is connected to the three sensors and controls them. The fourth, unmonitored processor, can be disabled for the duration of an experiment. (See Figure 8.1.)

The Sensor. The sensor is a microprogrammable device that supports a rich variety of branching operations that are dependent on the result of a pattern-matching operation. (See Figure 8.2.) The sensor microprogram controls a data path that contains:

- two sixteen-bit counters,
- one thirty-two-bit counter,
- two registers containing the last accessed physical address and data,
- a thirty-two-bit by 8192 entry trace memory,
- a twelve-bit pointer to an entry in the trace memory,
- a thirty-two-bit register used to communicate with the preprocessor, and
- a thirty-two-bit timer that may be synchronized to all other timers in the instrumentation system via microprogram control.

The trace memory is partitioned into two halves of 4096 entries each. While one half is accessible to the sensor, the other half is accessible to the preprocessor. This arrangement allows the sensor to continue collecting data while the preprocessor is transmitting data to the instrumentation host.

Each microinstruction is composed of four fields:

---

[3] MicroVAX is a registered trademark of Digital Equipment Corporation

148   Chapter 8. Instrumentation for Application Performance Tuning: The M31 System

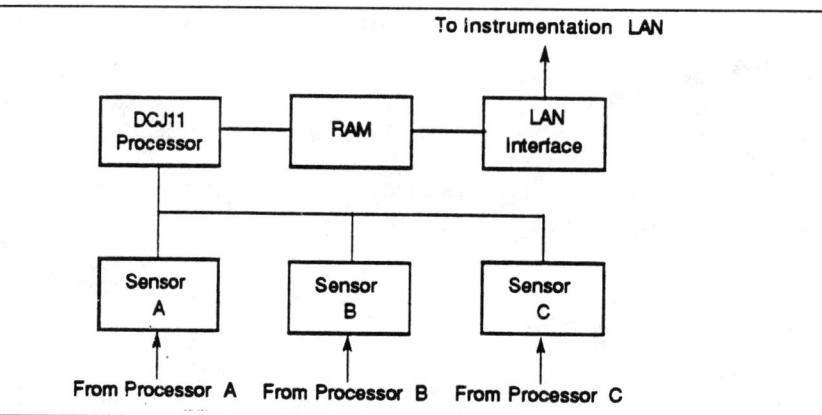

FIGURE 8.1
The processor-monitor and processor-cache components.

1. **Branch Control.** This field selects the contents of the next microprogram PC depending on the results of the current pattern matcher operation. Branch operations are provided that allow "looping" on the current instruction until or unless the pattern is matched (DO UNTIL or DO WHILE), and jump on condition. (Additionally, there is a facility that allows vectored microinterrupts in response to MicroVAX accesses to "magic" locations.)

2. **Match Pattern.** The pattern field allows each microinstruction to check the state of the attached MicroVAX and its cache interface, as well as to test the state that is internal to the sensor. The pattern is comprised of a logical *AND* of five subfields. If a subfield is unspecified in an instruction, then the subfield evaluates to *TRUE*. The fields allow the microinstruction to test for

    ▫ memory access type (*i.e.* data-read, instruction-read, write, read-lock, write-unlock, interrupt-vector-fetch),

    ▫ cache response (cache-hit, cache-miss) and the cache cell state (single, multiple, dirty, or invalid),

    ▫ pending interrupt request to the MicroVAX,

    ▫ results from the address/data lookup table, and

    ▫ data path status.

3. **Data Path Assignment.** Data may be copied from any of the readable registers to any of the writable registers in the sensor by a microinstruction.

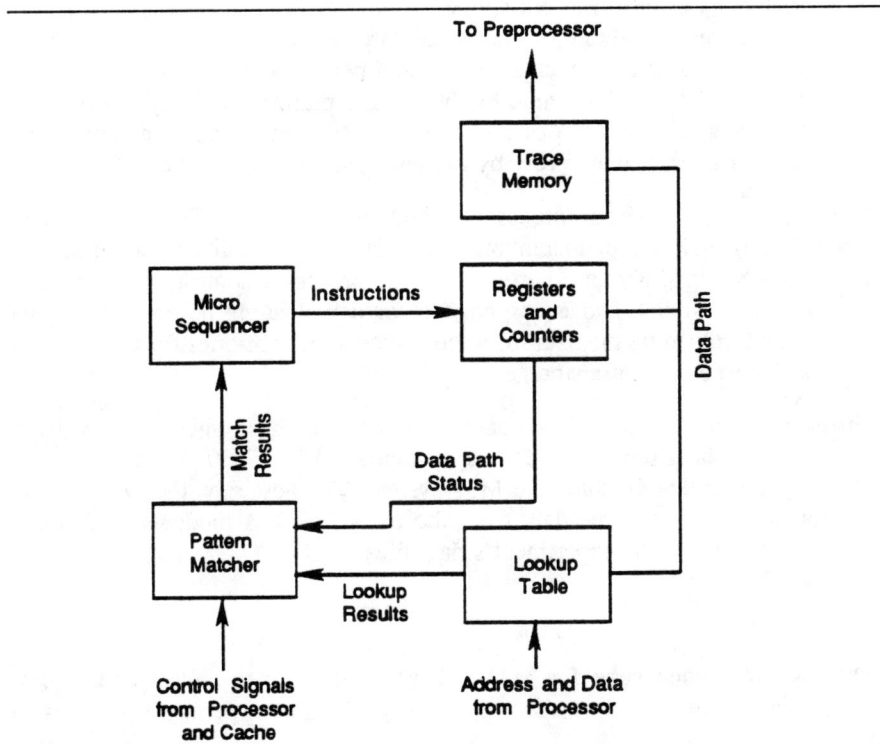

FIGURE 8.2
The processor-monitor sensor.

4. **Register Control.** Certain of the registers may be incremented, decremented, and/or complemented by a microinstruction. Additionally, the register control field is used to control part of the interface between the sensor and the preprocessor.

The rich variety of microprogrammed features allows the sensor to filter out irrelevant events and, in some experiments, accumulate statistics in histogram form. This allows the PM hardware to be used for architectural research as well as for collecting event traces for application tuning.

The most useful feature of the sensor hardware is a 512-entry lookup table that raises a signal if the attached MicroVAX performs an access to an address contained in the table. The same hardware also performs a comparison of the current address with a range of addresses set aside in physical memory. This later function is used extensively by the program event-trace microcode.

The Preprocessor. The preprocessor is built around a single DCJ-11 microprocessor (a single-chip implementation of the PDP-11 instruction-set architecture), and a single-chip Ethernet controller. The preprocessor controls the three sensors on a PM module and is responsible for downloading microcode into the sensors, and uploading the data from the sensor trace memories for transmission (via the Ethernet) to mass storage.

The Instrumentation Host. The final component in the instrumentation hardware support is the host processor. This is a standard VAX 8650 running as a part of same cluster that contains the M31 system. The host runs the experiment's control programs, receives data from the individual PM modules, and finally stores these data in the experiment's data files.

8.3.3 A Typical Experiment

The instrumentation suite for M31 is used most often to collect and analyze event traces from a multiprocessor application. Such an experiment involves six steps:

1. Insert event probes into the program to be monitored.
2. Load and start the instrumentation hardware.
3. Run the program to be monitored.
4. Shut down the instrumentation hardware when the program has run to completion.
5. Postprocess the collected dataset to provide the per-process event trace, the per-process activity graph, and the per-process call trees.
6. Use the graphical tools to examine the activity graphs and call trees.

    Of these steps, the first and last are most interesting.

8.3. An Experimental Implementation

Inserting Event Probes. As mentioned previously, an "event" is marked by a write to a "magic" physical address. Every event type is associated with its own address. Table 8.1 describes the event types used in a typical experiment.

Components of the operating system have been modified to signal events associated with their execution. Each time a process is switched onto (or off of) a processor, a process-activation (process-deactivation) event is recorded. Similarly, the system records instances of some page-fault occurrences.[4] Work is in progress to signal entry and return from system service code as well.

TABLE 8.1
Event-Types and Their Physical Addresses

Event	Event Name	Event Data
Primary Activate	NA	Process Number
Primary Deactivate	NA	Process Number
Secondary Activate	NA	Process Number
Secondary Deactivate	NA	Process Number
Subroutine Entry	entry_signal	Subroutine Number
Subroutine Return	return_signal	Subroutine Number
Alternate Entry	aux_entry_signal	Subroutine Number
Loop Entry	loop_entry_signal	Loop Number
Loop Exit	loop_exit_signal	Loop Number
Loop Iteration	loop_iteration_signal	User Defined

---

[4] At this writing, only page faults that occur on the "slave" processors are recorded.

The application program is instrumented by the user. Two alternatives exist: (1) for an application written in MODULA-II, a switch to a specially modified MODULA-II compiler will cause probes to be inserted automatically at each subroutine entry and return as well as at loop entry and exit and (2) if the application is written in Fortran, the experimenter may pass the sources through a preprocessor (called FORTPROBE) that automatically inserts probes at each subroutine entry and return.

The probes are simple in nature. For reasonable compilers, a probe will compile to a simple VAX MOVL instruction. At the source level for Fortran, the probe consists of an assignment to a variable held in a common block. This common block is mapped to the "magic" address region in physical memory by initialization code that is invoked by the operating system before the program is started.

Each Fortran subroutine entry is marked with an assignment similar to the following.

```
entry_signal = 1001
```

The number on the right-hand side of the assignment corresponds to the subroutine identifier. Each subroutine in the application is assigned a unique identifier. In Figure 8.3, subroutine XXOR is assigned the identifier 18501. Both `entry_signal` and `return_signal` are declared in the include file.

Per-Process Displays. Once the trace data have been captured by the instrumentation system, the traces must be converted into usable information. This is the task that is the most difficult and is likely to be most dependent on the user's model of computation.

For the M31 project, the dominant model of computation assumes a pool of processes communicating via shared memory. All the processes execute identical copies of the same program image. In some cases there is a master-slave relationship between the processes, but this is not mandatory. For the test case, CAYENNE [3], described here, there is a single parent process and five child processes. CAYENNE is a multiprocessor version of the SPICE circuit simulator.

It is unrealistic to expect an experimenter to wade through the reams of paper that it would take to print an event trace for each of the cooperating processes. Instead, the M31 project has begun to develop a set of tools that allow a programmer to explore the important characteristics of a program's behavior. So far, the aspects that the tools present are an execution profile (Figure 8.4) and a call graph (Figure 8.5).

The execution profile displays a graph of process activity for the entire run. The horizontal axis corresponds to "wall clock" time and the vertical axis corresponds to the portion of time the process spent running. Where two curves are visible, the lower curve shows the portion of time that the process spent

```
            INTEGER FUNCTION XXOR(A,B)
            IMPLICIT DOUBLE PRECISION (A-H,O-Z)
            INCLUDE 'INST$LIBRARY:INST_SIGS.CMN'
            entry_signal = 18501
            XXOR=1
            IF(A.EQ.B) XXOR=0
            return_signal = 18501
            RETURN
            END
```

FIGURE 8.3
Subroutine XXOR with Probes.

running on the primary or "master" processor. With this graph, the user may determine, among other things, whether the primary processor is acting as a bottleneck. Corrective action for such a condition may be to reduce the incidence of system service calls by the child processes.[5] Such a graph can also provide immediate insight into any actual serial bottlenecks inherent in the algorithm.

In addition to the execution-time profile program, the instrumentation support includes a program that allows a user to examine the call graphs for each of the processes in an application. The program displays the call graph on a VAX workstation screen and allows the user to browse through the tree. The user may select a node (routine) for more detailed examination and cause the call-graph viewer to display detailed statistics for each routine. The statistics include:

- the amount of time the process spent executing code in this routine,

- the number of times the routine was called,

- the amount of time the process spent *not* running (*i.e.*, stalled) while executing code in this routine,

- the number of times the process was "swapped off" a processor while executing code in this routine,

- the amount of time the process was running alone on the multiprocessor while executing code in this routine (A large amount of time here indicates that this code is a serial bottleneck.),

- the number of times the process became the sole active process while executing code in this routine,

---

[5] Calls to certain VAX/VMS system services require the calling process to be scheduled on the primary processor. In many instances this may result in inordinate amounts of lost time while waiting for the primary processor to become available.

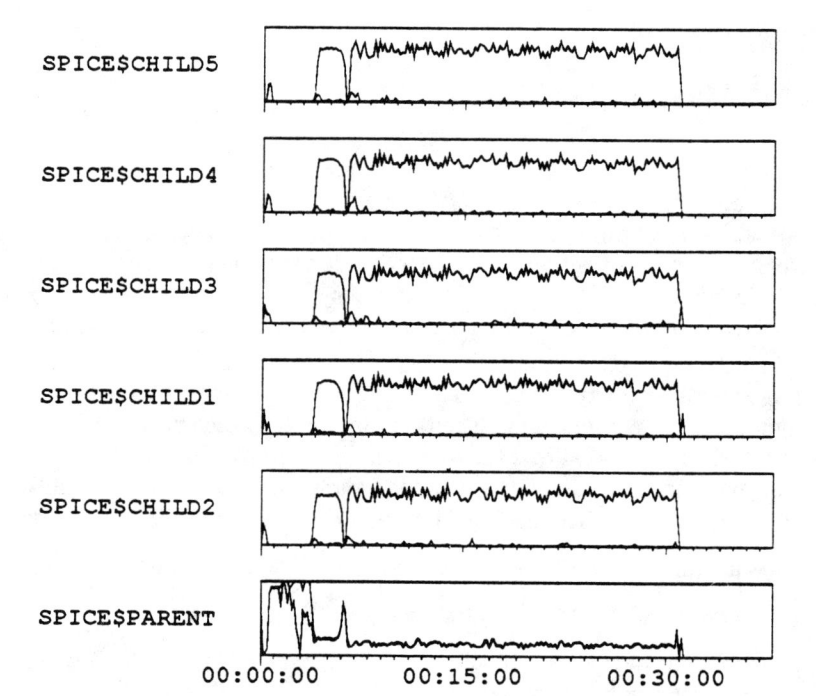

FIGURE 8.4
Execution Time Profile for CAYENNE.

8.3. An Experimental Implementation   155

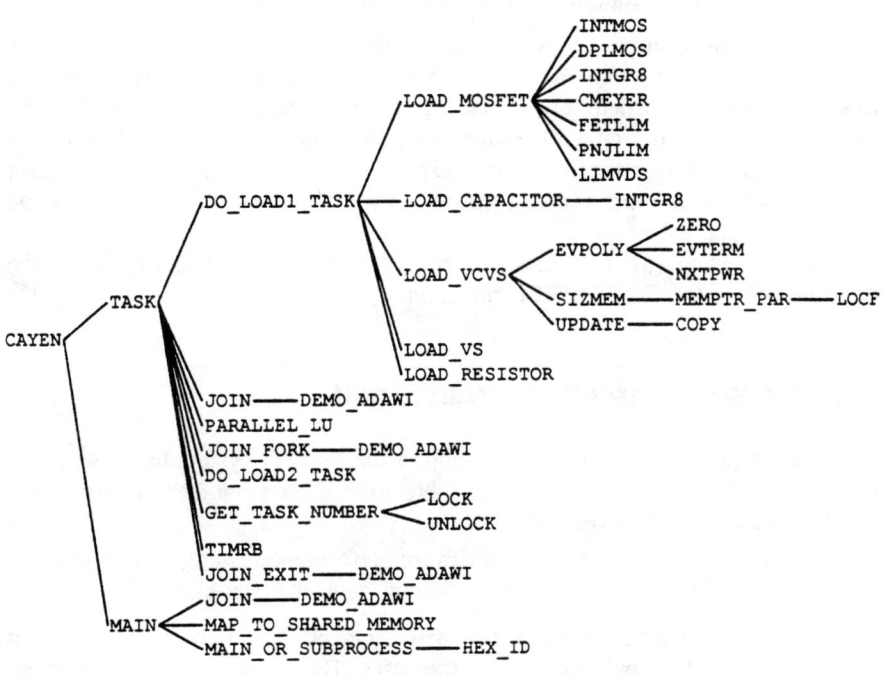

FIGURE 8.5
CAYENNE Child Process Call Graph.

- the amount of time the process spent executing code in routines called by this routine,
- the amount of time the process spent *not* running while executing code in routines called by this routine, and
- the amount of time the process was running alone on the multiprocessor while executing code in routines called by this routine.

Figure 8.6 is an example of the statistics display.

By browsing through the call graphs for the parent and child processes in CAYENNE, it was determined that the parent process spent most of its time (almost 20 minutes during a 30 minute run) in a routine called FORK. For almost all of this time the parent process was suspended, waiting for the child processes to finish their work. Further investigation showed that the bulk of the work done by the child processes was in the LOAD_MOSFET routine.

Work is in progress to make use of this information while improving the performance of the CAYENNE application.

8.4 Some of the Lessons Learned

The work of providing measurement support for the M31 system has been going on for almost five years. In this time there have been a number of false starts and unfortunately late revelations.

Noninvasive measurement for software performance tuning is not practical. Several facts of life conspire to make this problem inescapable:

- Hardware to support measurement activity takes space in the system cabinet and power that could be put to other uses. The existence of measurement hardware will affect the performance or cost of the system. Noninvasive software measurement seems to require large amounts of hardware support.
- Unless the virtual address stream from the processor is visible, the monitor system must acquire and maintain knowledge about the mapping of addresses from the virtual space to the physical space. The trend in microprocessors is to make the virtual addresses unavailable outside the processor chip.
- Non-invasive tracing of subroutine call and return usually requires keeping track of the process call stack (at least in the case of the VAX architecture). Passing this state around as part of the process state (when the process moves from one processor to another) is a complex operation that requires some assistance from the operating system.

The latter problems can be mitigated somewhat, but at the cost of imposing some restrictions on the system (adding hooks to the memory management code,

```
LOAD_MOSFET
     Local Call Time/Count:
          6:57.503997 / 8082
     Local Off Time/Count:
          0:02.733650 / 1686
     Local Serial Time/Count:
          0:00.600283 / 261
     Agregate Call Time:
          14:22.302429
     Agregate Off Time:
          0:03.098733
     Agregate Serial Time:
          0:02.347606
```

FIGURE 8.6
Statistics for CAYENNE child process subroutine LOAD_MOSFET.

for instance). It remains to be seen whether this kind of invasiveness is more or less intrusive than inserting probes into the application.

Processor monitors themselves are expensive, both in component cost and in their effect on system size. Such monitors are indispensable for certain hardware-related measurements, but it seems clear that, for shared-bus multiprocessors, a single central monitor should be quite sufficient for software performance measurement. The publication [4] describes TRAM, a centralized monitor designed to collect event traces for a shared-bus multiprocessor.

Research on the M31 system is beginning to demonstrate the effectiveness of several measurement techniques. Future research will allow comparisons among the techniques to ascertain which are appropriate tools to realize the end goal of providing a toolset for developing more efficient applications.

References

1. J. R. Goodman, Using Cache Memory to Reduce Processor-Memory Traffic, Technical report, University of Wisconsin, Department of Computer Science, 1983.
2. M. H. Reilly and J. R. Sopka, M31: A Large-Scale Multiprocessor VAX for Parallel Processing Research, in *Thirty-Third IEEE Computer Society International Conference (COMPCON '88)*, 1988.

3. G. Bischoff and S. Greenberg, CAYENNE: A Parallel Implementation of the Circuit Simulator SPICE, in *Proceedings of the International Conference on Computer Aided Design*, 1986.

4. G. Nacht and A. Mink, Recommended Instrumentation Approaches for a Shared-Memory Multiprocessor, Technical Report NBSIR 87-3663, National Bureau of Standards Institute for Computer Sciences and Technology, 1987.

9

Performance Measurement Instrumentation at NBS

Robert J. Carpenter[1]

9.1 Introduction

A wide range of multiprocessor computer architectures exist, and there are a number of implementations of them. Our interest is the use of multiple processors to get a single job done faster. To succeed, there must be a reasonable match between the algorithms, the data set, and both the architecture and its implementation. The quality of this match is hard to determine *a priori*, even for specific instances of hardware and software. Even where only one machine is available, various algorithms and programming paradigms may be used. Thus the user needs to be able to measure the response of the computer to various paradigms, test programs, and the algorithmic solution that is eventually chosen. The comprehensive measurement of complex machines is extremely difficult. Little effort has been made in today's machines to facilitate accurate measurement of the internal operations that are critical to performance. There is a trade-off between

---

[1] Work reported here was partially supported by the Defense Advanced Research Projects Agency. This work was performed at the National Bureau of Standards (NBS), an agency of the U.S. Government and is not subject to U.S. copyright. The identification of commercial products in this paper is for clarification of specific concepts. In no case does such identification imply recommendation or endorsement by NBS, nor does it imply that the product is necessarily the best suited for the purpose.

cost and accuracy of measurement. The cost can be monetary, physical size, or reduced performance caused by the mere presence of the measurement system. Attempts to measure multiprocessor parallel computers can create so much perturbation to normal operation as to render the results useless, and the (perturbed) operation must be correctly quantified.

A range of approaches to performance measurement, without incurring excessive perturbation, are presented here. Other approaches are possible, for example the SySM system from Harris for the Concert multiprocessor [1,2]. Data, once obtained, must be analyzed and presented to the user. Though important, this is not discussed here, nor is testing for fault-tolerance and maintenance purposes.

9.2 What to measure?

"How long did it take?" is the most obvious question asked about the performance of a computer system doing a specific task. But once that question can be answered without inducing significant experimental perturbations, there remains the question of "what caused this limited performance?" The characterization of a computer system involves:

- measurement of the time required to execute the test software, and

- measuring the utilization of the system's computing resources to discover bottlenecks that may be corrected by hardware redesign, system reconfiguration, system expansion, use of another algorithm or a different programming paradigm, etc.

These measurements are most useful if they can resolve performance to chosen segments of the test software. Gross overall execution measurements give little insight on the best corrective action to take.

9.3 Cost Considerations in Measurement

A number of measurement approaches are actively being pursued at the National Bureau of Standards. Our goal is techniques that would allow manufacturers to offer the measurement hardware as an option, with essentially no incremental hardware cost to purchasers who did not want the measurement option.

9.4 Measuring Execution Duration

There are two critical *events* in the measurement of execution duration: starting time and ending time. If the execution duration is long enough, the user may be able to use the timing service provided by the operating system without significantly perturbing the results. Unfortunately the requirement for long execution duration usually means that either the test software is very large and hard to characterize, or that a very unrealistic synthetic test routine has been created. One needs to be able to insert time-measurement *events* freely, and without significant perturbation to the system under test. It is important to provide the user with a means to start and stop data taking to avoid filling data storage while the desired starting state is being created. Various measurement approaches are summarized in Table 9.1, and will be discussed below.

Each time one resorts to the timing service of an operating system, perhaps 500 extra instructions are executed. The tolerance of computations to time-gathering perturbations of this sort can be divided into two classes: computations with one instruction stream, and those with multiple (simultaneously executing) instruction streams or with time-critical external relationships.

Systems with a Single Instruction Stream. If there is but one instruction stream and no machine state to upset (no pipelining, no fetch-ahead, no cache), and no external time-critical interactions, execution can be suspended at any time by an operating system call without great perturbation of execution characteristics. This implies no time-critical user or mass-storage I/O. With these limitations, measurement can be accomplished by recourse to operating system services, and little hardware measurement support is required. This observation applies to both single- and multiple-data-stream processors with a *single instruction stream* (SISD as well as SIMD).

Systems with Multiple Instruction Streams. All other computer systems, including "single-instruction-stream" machines with real-time I/O or separate I/O processors, are effectively multiple-instruction-stream machines (MIMD), wherein the time relationships between the various instruction paths contributing to the solution of a single problem must be maintained. Calls to an operating system for measurement services would delay one processor while allowing the others to proceed—seriously perturbing execution. The amount of perturbation that can be tolerated is related to the program *granule* size: how much computation is done between times that processes must interact and measurements must be taken. In general, the longer this time, the more time perturbation that can be tolerated.

TABLE 9.1
Performance Measurement Approaches

Event Trigger	Hardware Enhancement	Comment	Resource Utilization Preprocessing
	No measurement hardware	Only appropriate for SISD and SIMD non-real-time systems	Can be used; started, stopped, and read by operating system routine
	Central time counter register	Requires globally-accessible memory or input-output; much less perturbation than above	Can be used, but causes more perturbation since counters must be read
	Synchronized local time counters	Suitable for both loosely- and tightly-coupled systems; less perturbation	Can be used; increased perturbation; should be local to each processor
	Time counter and global "report" interrupt served by microcode	Reduces amount of local measurement memory needed; not for real-time systems	Same as above
Inserted code	As above with global "capture" interrupt served by microcode	Allows correlation of activity of all processors; even more perturbation	Same as above
	Single central off-machine event data collection system including clock	Reduced perturbation since clock tags data automatically; not for loosely-coupled systems	Automatic collection of resource utilization data with no *extra* perturbation
	As above with global "capture" interrupt served by microcode	Much perturbation because the captured state must be written to central hardware	Same as above
	Off-machine event data collection with "head end" for each processor	Useful on both loosely- and tightly-coupled systems; doesn't use shared data paths so less perturbation	Automatic collection of resource utilization data with no *extra* perturbation
	As above with global "capture" interrupt served by microcode	Less added perturbation because of distributed data collection	Same as above

9.4. Measuring Execution Duration

TABLE 9.1 (continued)

Event Trigger	Hardware Enhancement	Comment	Resource Utilization Preprocessing
Pattern monitor	Pattern-matching unit for each processor	*No* perturbation to execution; hard to set up; requires many internal connections; activity of all processors known at each trigger; triggering on virtual address often prevents process identification	Cause *no* perturbation
	Same, except that a sequence of patterns required for trigger	Same, except less ambiguous triggering; even harder to set up	Same as above
Hybrid trigger	Trigger from both inserted-code and patterns	Inserted-code trigger allows process-address correlation; pattern trigger causes no perturbation	Same as above

These MIMD and real-time systems require at least some hardware support to obtain reliable measurement [3]. One approach could be to assign measurement as the sole task of one of the processors, surely a major distortion of system resources. Hardware for the support of measurement without significant perturbation will be discussed below.

9.4.1 Identifying Time Events in Test Program Execution

Events in the execution of a program can be identified in two ways: by inserting extra instructions in the software to explicitly trigger data capture, or by recognizing use of a specific instruction or data (address or value) by passive monitoring and pattern matching. The recognition of a user-specified event during test program execution generates a *trigger* to cause capture of the current time and other measurement data.

Inserted-Code Triggering. In some situations, the perturbation from extra measurement instructions may be tolerable [3]. On the other hand, the perturbation may be insidious. Instruction fetch-ahead queues will be affected, caches will be perturbed, and memory management translation look-aside buffer entries may be affected. Inserted-code event triggering should only be considered for measurement events separated by at least dozens of instructions in the same instruction path.

The advantages of inserted-code triggering are substantial. Child processes can easily identify themselves, as can processes sharing code. There is never false triggering as might occur in an address-monitor trigger when instructions or data are fetched but never used. It is relatively easy to identify processor-process association. In tightly-coupled systems, hardware measurement support can be accomplished centrally at relatively low cost.

Pattern-Matching Triggering. Time-measurement events can be recognized without any program perturbation by use of a pattern-sensitive monitoring system. This relatively-complex trigger hardware is designed to recognize certain instruction or data addresses or values and *must usually be replicated for each processor in the system*. While pattern-matching has the great advantage of being non-perturbing, it suffers practical operational problems in addition to high cost. The first problem is that the desired signals may not be easy to reach; they may be buried inside a VLSI chip. One usually needs access to the logical address, but often only the physical address is available outside the chip. Many processors prefetch instructions or data, but may not in fact use all of the prefetched information. This can cause extraneous triggers. Additionally, the addresses (of the type that *can* be accessed) of the instructions or data that are to cause the triggers must be known. The association between virtual and physical addresses may change during execution. The same virtual or physical address used by multiple processes will cause indistinguishable triggers. Moreover, one cannot distinguish between different entities that are sharing code. Of course processes can be "locked" in place in memory during execution, but this is often a gross distortion of normal operation [4].

To make pattern-matching triggering practical, details of determining patterns to match must be done *for* the user. The user should be allowed to insert measurement pseudo-instructions in the source code, with the system software such as compilers, linkers, and loaders creating the corresponding trigger patterns. These patterns would then be down-loaded to the measurement hardware.

Triggering on a Sequence of Patterns. False triggers caused by use of the same virtual addresses in multiple tasks can sometimes be reduced if triggering is based on a required *sequence* of patterns. Some kinds of events can only be identified by a sequence of patterns. Sequences will require a substantial increase in the size of the pattern storage memory and its control hardware.

9.4.2 Timed Trace Support Hardware

There exists a progression of time measurement hardware support techniques in which additional difficulty or cost is rewarded by more accurate or more detailed information.

Central Time Counter Register. Measurement of MIMD machines requires that at least the same notion of time be readable with very low delay and overhead by each processor. In a shared-memory architecture, this could be a globally-accessible register as illustrated in Figure 9.1.

Each processor could refer to the time register by a simple read instruction, greatly decreasing the perturbation as compared to an operating system call. Once data are obtained by a processor, they must be stored either in local or central memory. The obtaining of time data and storing them demand processor cycles on the single processor where the time trigger occurred. This

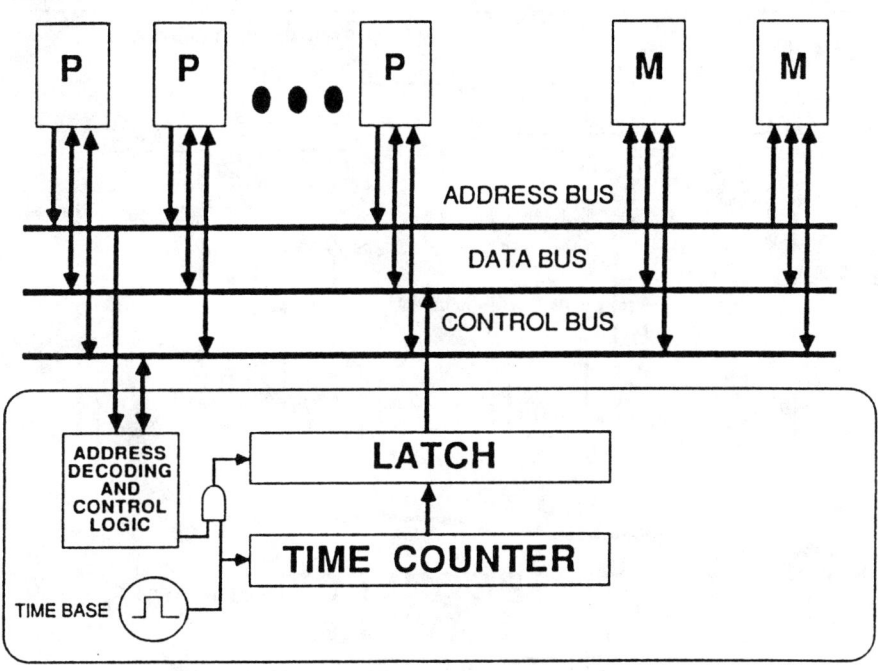

FIGURE 9.1
Central readable time counter.

may tie up the memory path for all processors and may perturb register, cache and memory management state. This technique only allows elapsed-time and process-processor association measurements; data about utilization of resources such as caches, buses, etc., require the addition of some resource measurement hardware to be discussed later.

Distributed Time Counters. Anything less than very tight coupling discourages use of a single central time counter. The extra communication delay to read a central register in machines, such as the Butterfly and RP3, may be excessive. Loosely-coupled systems certainly require a time counter local to each processor due to the long communication delays. All such counters in a system have to be synchronized. The counters could be internal to a VLSI microprocessor and would require only a time-base and a synchronizing or reset signal from the outside, as illustrated in Figure 9.2. No additional pins would be needed should there be additional processors on each chip.

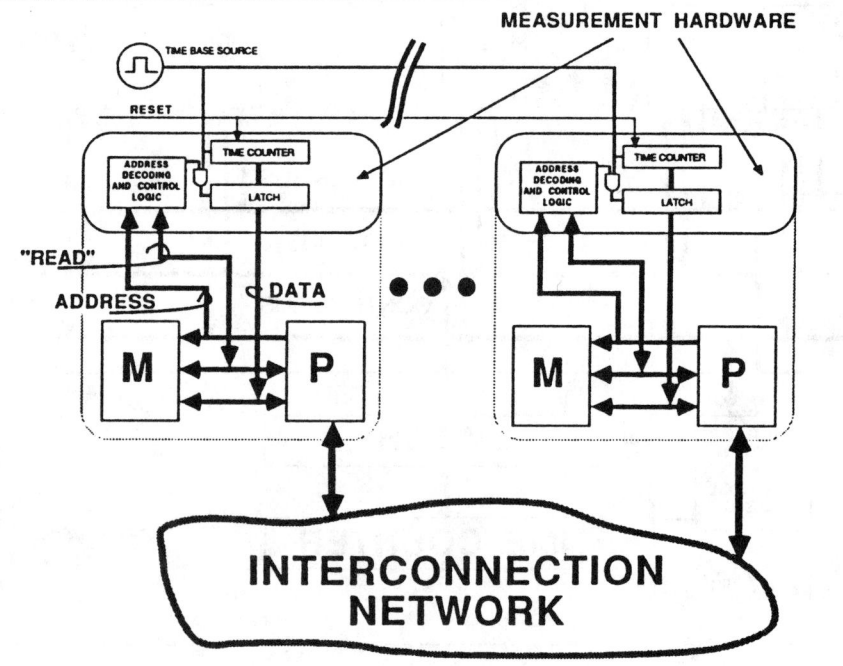

FIGURE 9.2
Distributed time counters.

In a loosely-coupled system, all measurement data would have to be collected locally at each node and reported after the experiment. This has the benefit of no extra load on the interconnection network to perturb the experiment. In a tightly-coupled system, distributed time counters would reduce perturbation since reading of the time register would not use the normally-shared memory data path. Local storage of the measurement data would further reduce perturbation that would otherwise be caused by writing of the event data to central memory during the experiment.

This is a relatively low-cost addition, requiring only a time-counter register. It *should* be connected by a path that avoids disturbing the cache and memory management system.

Global Measurement Interrupt. Inserted-code event triggering has the deficiency that only the state of the processor executing the *event* is captured. The situation at other processors must be inferred from their surrounding events. A global measurement interrupt can overcome this deficiency. By this means any processor serving an inserted-code measurement *event* can command all other processors to cease normal activity and save information about their current activity, such as process and time information. Since all processors in the system stop executing the application program, time relationships are not perturbed. Perturbation will result if the instructions and data of the interrupt handling process perturb machine state such as cache and memory management systems; local program and data storage, as illustrated in Figure 9.3, will greatly reduce this perturbation.

The global interrupt circuit should be driven by "open collector" devices. Once asserted by any processor, all processors should hold the signal in the asserted state until finished with their measurement interrupt service routine. They should not resume normal processing until all processors have released the global interrupt circuit. Because the processor is not executing user code when servicing the measurement interrupt, the time counters must pause the entire time the interrupt line is asserted. For the same reason, the measurement interrupt may be inappropriate in some real-time systems. The global interrupt signal would add one more pin to a VLSI processor package, independent of the number of processors in the package.

The previously mentioned timed trace systems suffer from either the perturbation of accessing a *central* measurement data memory area, or the cost of providing substantial measurement data storage memory locally at each processor. Much smaller local measurement data memory could be used (in some cases) if the global measurement interrupt were used to cause all processors to simultaneously abandon their normal tasks and dump their local measurement data memory to a central memory area. Execution would continue, without distortion to inter-processor timing, after all interrupt processing was completed.

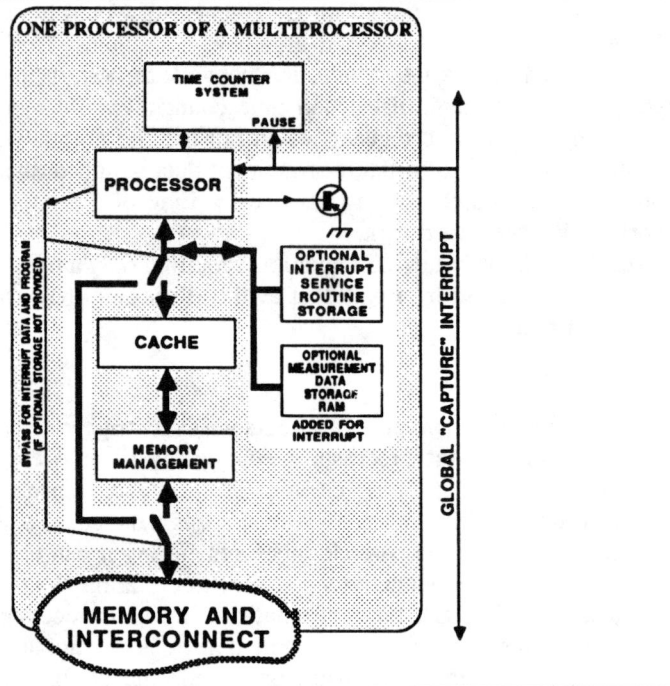

FIGURE 9.3
Adding a global "capture" interrupt.

Off-Machine Timing Event Data Collection. The code that must be executed for a time measurement event may be further reduced if each timing measurement *event* consists solely of writing a single value to special data collection hardware addressed as a memory or I/O location. This external hardware contains the time counter; the mere act of writing data to the collection hardware causes the current time to be captured in off-machine memory, along with the written data and other information such as the identification of the writing processor. It is important that the identification of the writing processor be made available to the collection hardware. It must be possible to start and stop data collection and the time counter (to ignore execution of non-user software). Either additional addresses or certain data bits may be used for these functions.

Central Off-Machine Timing Event Data Collection. In a shared-memory architecture, a single central location can be the target of all of the system's event data writes. This approach is only suitable for machines with an easily-accessible global memory or I/O area. The factor-of-three-or-more time penalty to reach a global location in switch machines (Butterfly, Ultra, RP3, etc.) would make this central-collection approach fairly perturbing. Placing the data collection address in memory space (instead of I/O) usually results in less system perturbation because of more efficient transfer protocols. Each process should identify itself in the data it writes. There should be hardware identification of the processor at each event data write. In a bus-oriented machine, the writing processor should be identified on the machine's bus so that the experimenter will not have to make special internal connections to the machine. User design of processor identification circuitry is usually impractical, given the proprietary nature of the details of present-day computer hardware. The NBS Trace Measurement System (TRAMS) [5,6] is an example of off-machine timing event data collection applied to a commercial multiprocessor, as illustrated in Figure 9.4. We required very detailed proprietary hardware information about the multiprocessor computer in order to design the processor identification hardware because that information was not present on the bus. In TRAMS a single added board serves an entire tightly-coupled shared-memory system.

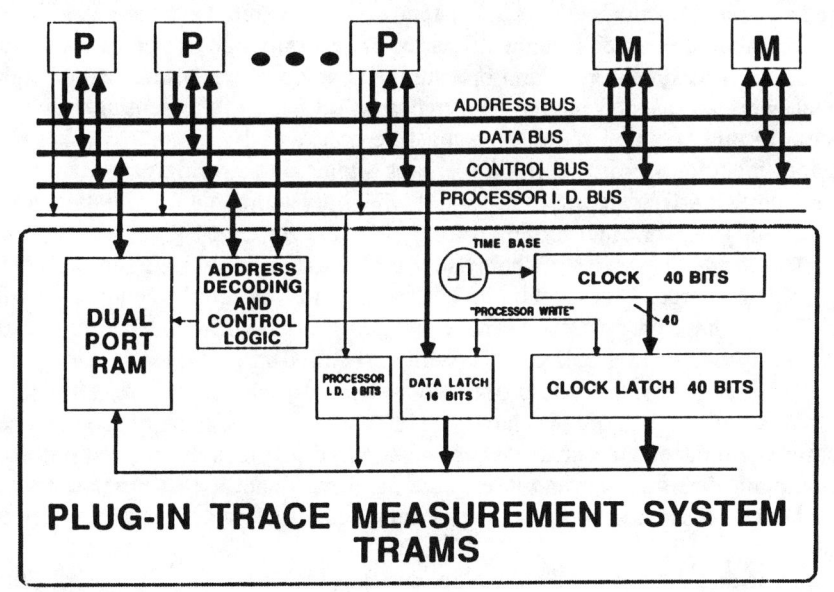

FIGURE 9.4
Plug-in trace measurement system TRAMS.

Note that a global measurement interrupt can be useful in this type of system.

Distributed Off-Machine Timing Event Data Collection. The advantages of off-machine data collection can also be applied to loosely-coupled systems (and in switch-connected "tightly"-coupled systems), where the collection of timing event data must be distributed throughout the system being measured to avoid serious perturbation. Here the communication speed and bandwidth available over the normal loosely-coupled interconnection network to a central point is too low to permit its use for real-time time distribution and performance data collection.

An attractive solution involves replication of at least some of the data capture hardware (including a synchronized time counter) at each processor. Each such measurement "head end" should include a FIFO buffer to smooth out the peak rate of the collected measurement data and allow serial (or byte-parallel) transmission of the captured data back to a central collector by means of a special time and data collection network. This approach is illustrated in Figure 9.5. As in other distributed-counter systems discussed above, only one or two global wires are sufficient to synchronize and operate the time counters. Either one or eight global wires are needed for the data transmission back to the central collector. Access to this common return path must be arbitrated by a suitable local area network medium access algorithm (perhaps a logical token ring network, or the simple collision-free algorithm used in the Digital Equipment Corporation VAX Cluster(TM) network and proposed for ANSI X3T9.5 LDDI [7]).

The headend portion of the system that must be replicated for each processor is not large. It could be either an application specific integrated circuit (ASIC)—perhaps gate array—or might be incorporated within a VLSI processor itself. Only one central collection system is required in each system.

There is substantial traffic over the network on which data are returned to the central collector. Examples are given in Table 9.2. For example, at 64 bits per measurement event and one event per one hundred instructions at each processor (each taking one microsecond to execute), and with data for 32 processors collected over the same network, a total of ten megabits of data must be transferred each second.

Some additional central collection hardware would thus have to be provided for each 10 to 50 processors in the system, depending on processor execution rate, and the size of program "granules" being time traced.

Distributed off-machine data collection can also reduce measurement perturbation in tightly coupled machines, since it avoids use of the computer's shared data path for collection of measurement data. The headend should be a special integrated circuit.

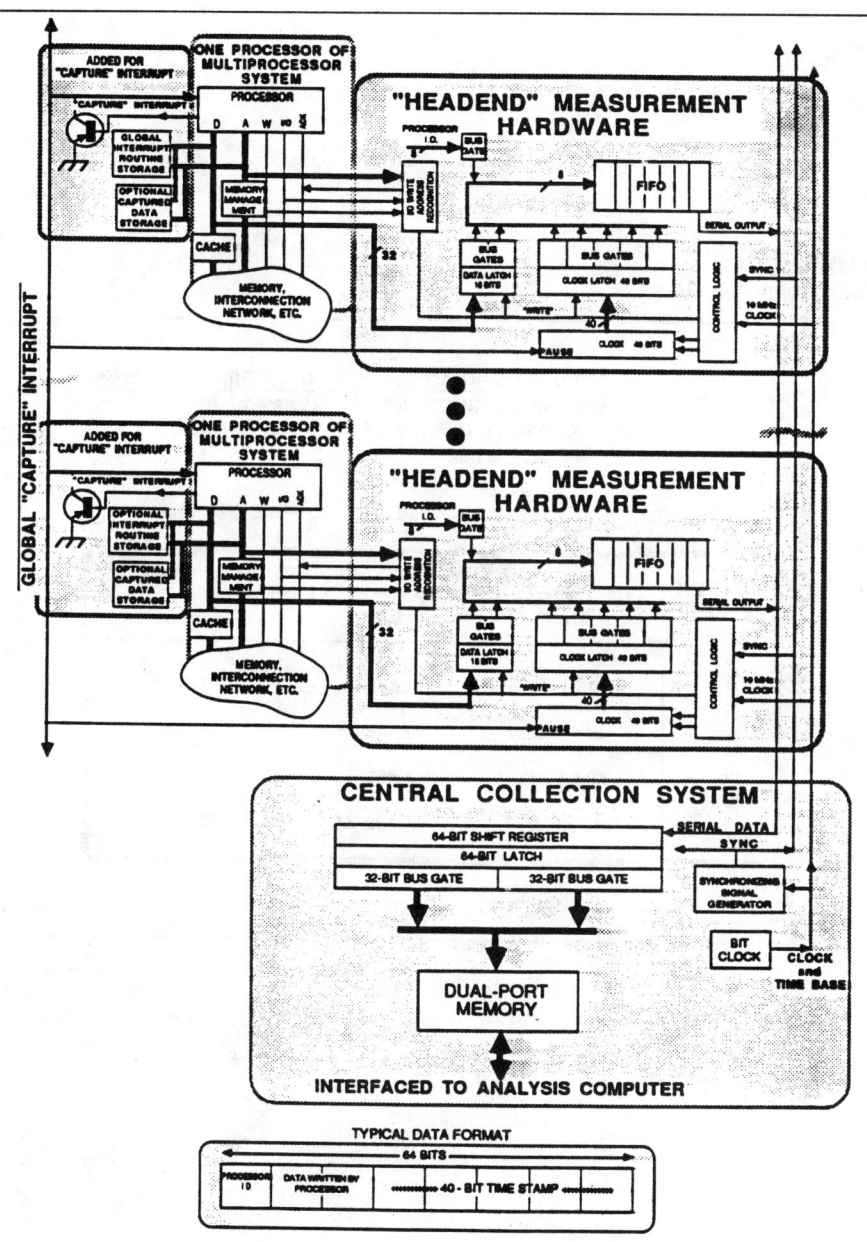

FIGURE 9.5
Distributed off-machine data collection with "capture" command.

TABLE 9.2
Data Collection Rate

$$\text{TRAFFIC} = \frac{\text{NUMBER OF NODES}}{\substack{\text{NUMBER OF INSTRUCTIONS}\\ \text{BETWEEN DATA EVENTS}\\ \text{AT EACH NODE}}} \times \frac{\text{DATA PER DATA EVENT}}{\text{AVERAGE INSTRUCTION DURATION}}$$

$$= \frac{32}{100} \times \frac{64 \text{ BITS}}{1 \text{ }\mu s} = 20\ 480\ 000 \text{ bits per second}$$

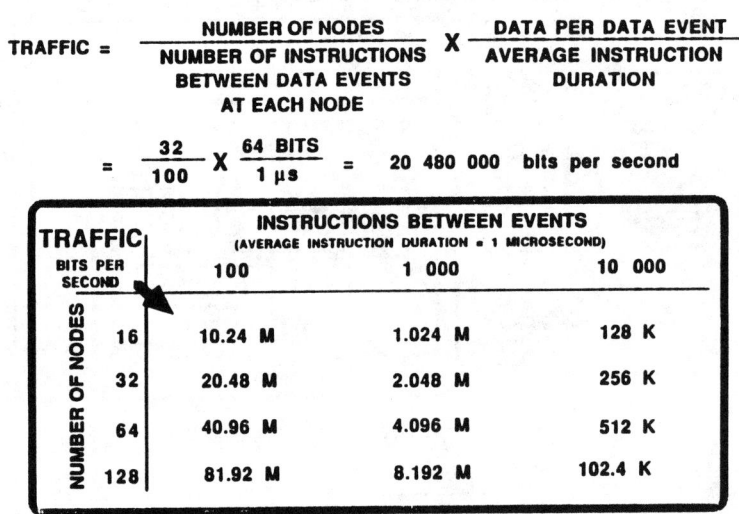

TRAFFIC BITS PER SECOND	INSTRUCTIONS BETWEEN EVENTS (AVERAGE INSTRUCTION DURATION = 1 MICROSECOND)		
NUMBER OF NODES	100	1 000	10 000
16	10.24 M	1.024 M	128 K
32	20.48 M	2.048 M	256 K
64	40.96 M	4.096 M	512 K
128	81.92 M	8.192 M	102.4 K

9.4. Measuring Execution Duration

Distributed Off-Machine Data Collection with CAPTURE Command. The perturbation caused by a CAPTURE command would be reduced by distributed event data collection (as compared with central data collection) since the FIFOs in the return paths would allow the processors to write their state data without having to wait for the shared data path. The upper left hand corner of Figure 9.5 illustrates the additions needed to add the CAPTURE command to a distributed off-machine collection system. Of course, the time-stamp counters must be *stopped* during the the time the CAPTURE signal is active. Again, the CAPTURE command might cause too much perturbation to be used in systems with external timing constraints.

- Built-in Hardware - The addition of a CAPTURE command always involves major modification of the data paths in or near the the processor itself, as illustrated at the upper left in Figure 9.5. A special interrupt must be added, and it is desirable to be able to bypass the normal instruction and data paths. There would be much less impact on the design of the central off-machine collection hardware, except that much more data would be collected. This substantially-increased traffic over the serial data link to the central collector reduces the number of processors that could be served by each central front-end shift register and dual-port memory.

- Optional Hardware - The CAPTURE command has little effect on the add-on distributed measurement hardware, except that the timing clock must be stopped during CAPTURE interrupt service. Since it has such a major impact on the processor itself or the close-by data paths, it would either have to be included in all processors, or as a special processor version.

Non-Perturbing Triggering. All of the above time-event triggering systems require execution of "measurement code" that perturbs the operation of the system being measured. On the other hand, recognition of time trigger *events* can be based on passive monitoring of the addresses or values of instructions and data, along with the state of the processors.

Non-Perturbing Pattern-Matching Timing Event Triggering. The trigger addresses or values can be detected by matching the information on the address or data lines with stored patterns. Because of at-processor caching, or lack of a single central monitoring point, this trigger hardware must usually be replicated for **each** processor in the system. A number of different patterns, one for each event, must be matched. In a system with 32-bit matching, one cannot afford to be able to match *all* possible combinations (some four billion), nor would one need to. Breaking the 32 bits into groups the size of the address space of high speed static random access memories (RAM) allows a fully-programmable matcher to match any desired subset containing many combinations; more can be matched if there are a number of common subterms. This results in combinations recoding a sparsely populated state space into a small, manageable state space.

The general outline of a pattern-matching event-trigger detection system is illustrated in Figure 9.6. Instead of basing the match on a single logical product of all 32 inputs, a multistage approach with simpler products to generate intermediate terms is sufficiently flexible and more economical. The 32 input signals (where the input patterns appear) are first separated into groups of 10, 11, and 11 bits. These groups of bits are used to address RAMs. The contents of locations corresponding to trigger events contain unique 7- or 8-bit codes (a minimum of 127 unique event codes). These codes are further combined to address the second rank of RAMs. The uniquely encoded locations in this second rank produce two 8-bit event codes. The sixteen bits from the second rank of RAMs address the last rank. There is one RAM in the last rank for each *type* of trigger (global trigger, selective trigger 1, selective trigger 2, etc.). Ones are loaded in the last rank of RAMs at addresses corresponding to trigger events. The accumulated RAM access delay may become excessive at some point in the above process. One must then insert a pipelining register at this point—for example between the second and last ranks of RAMs in Figure 9.6.

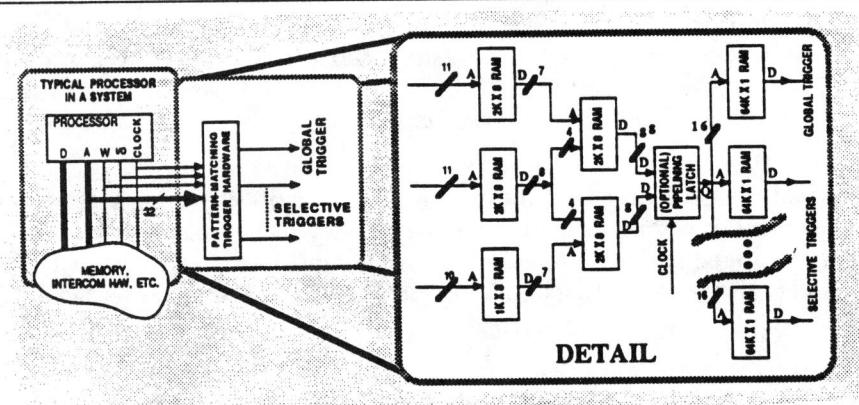

FIGURE 9.6
Pattern-matching triggering.

9.4. Measuring Execution Duration

System software must be provided to allow the experimenter to define trigger points as pseudo-instructions; these would eventually generate the patterns to be down-loaded to the matching RAMs. This measurement setup software must select non-colliding intermediate terms for the matching process. More details can be obtained from the report on the NBS REMS system by Nacht [8].

Once the timing-event trigger has been created, both the trigger pattern (or the encoded event identification) and a time-counter value must be captured. This trigger can be used with on- and off-machine data collection in most of the same ways as inserted-code triggers. The REMS system captures data in a distributed, off-machine manner. The *global* trigger from any pattern matcher causes data to be captured at all processors. Actual "trigger" patterns are captured, rather than encoded events, because the full patterns present the easiest way of determining the execution progress at the processors that did not cause the trigger event. Only a single time-stamp is needed in the REMS systems because data from all processors are captured at the same time. Use of the "selective" triggers will be covered in the discussion of resource utilization measurement using preprocessors.

Because of the cost and the difficulty in obtaining unambiguous event identification, pattern-matching triggering will probably never be attractive alone.

- Built-in Hardware - While a pattern-matching trigger mechanism could be incorporated with each processor, this may require *more* external connections than would an off-board implementation. Not only would all of the resulting trigger signals need to lead out, but the pattern itself would have to be available for capture in order to identify the trigger cause. In addition some means would have to be provided to load the matcher RAMs. This system is quite complex and would occupy a lot of real estate.

- Optional Hardware - All of the address (or other) lines of interest, along with timing signals, have to be made available to add-on hardware. This requires a substantial interconnect path. Some way must be provided to load the patterns into match storage RAMs from the measurement control computer. Logical addresses are often not visible from outside VLSI processors. One possible answer to the problem of inaccessible signals in VLSI circuits is to provide an additional connector on the **top** of the IC package, and to bring out the extra measurement signals to it. This is a variant of an idea used by Zilog. They provided a version of their Z8 single-chip microprocessor with a top socket for an industry-standard EPROM. The EPROM took the place of the normal internal mask-programmed ROM during the software development process and the processor would still mount in the normal Z8 socket.

Triggering on a Sequence of Patterns. Some additional selectivity in triggering can be obtained by requiring a specific sequence of patterns. The general case of recognizing a sequence of patterns is very expensive to implement. Any "first" match would be followed by a tree of state machines of arbitrary branching width at each layer. A great simplification results if the branch width is limited to **one**; no branching is allowed beyond the first match, as illustrated in Figure 9.7. In this case, each "first" match may only lead to a single correct sequence of patterns. The resulting loss in flexibility may be acceptable.

If **M** different sequences of length **N** (or less) were allowed, then an added sequence matching memory of **M*(N-1)** locations would be required. Each location in sequence RAM would need a word-width equal to the matching word length - say 32 bits. A pattern-matching system similar to that in Figure 9.7 is used to detect the first trigger. Its output is a pointer to the remaining sequence that must be followed exactly in order to recognize any event. Each of the following steps in the sequence merely requires comparison of the incoming pattern with a single correct pattern from the "sequence" RAM. This is a state machine that must be traversed in the proper order to create a trigger.

- Built-in Hardware - As in the case of matching simple patterns, incorporating the matching system on the processor board may actually *increase* the number of external connections required by the measurement system. This system would occupy even more real estate than the simple pattern matching system, but might be well worth it.

- Optional Hardware - All of the address (or other) lines of interest, along with timing signals, have to be made available to add-on hardware. This requires a substantial interconnect path, but no more than the simple matcher.

Both Event and Pattern Triggering. A hybrid system with triggering from both inserted *event* code and passive pattern-matching hardware has many of the advantages of both systems: the easy correlation of data with program execution, association of process and processor, etc. Since the execution address of all processors can be captured at each trigger in a passive monitoring system, the state of all processors at the time of each measurement trigger is captured, even when the triggers come from the inserted-code route.

9.5 Measuring Resource Utilization

As soon as the time required for execution of selected code segments is known, the reasons for that particular length of time are of interest. Bottlenecks can be identified by measurement of the utilization of the component resources of the computer system. Duty cycles must be measured, for example, the amount of time the processor-memory path is busy. Pulse widths must be measured, for example, the duration that processors wait for data or instruction fetches. What

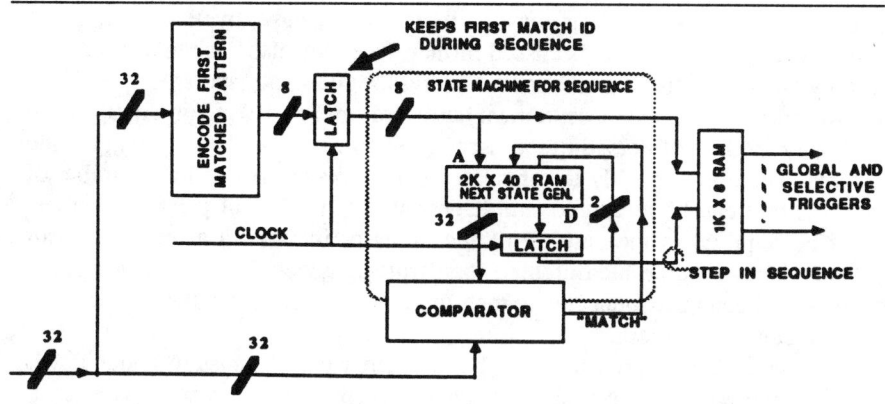

FIGURE 9.7
Sequence matching triggering systems (sequence length of 4, branching factor of 1).

fraction of the memory accesses are satisfied by the caching system? Since data must be captured for each system cycle, the addition of resource measurement "preprocessing" hardware is necessary. Roberts [9] has discussed a wide range of possible resource utilization measurements.

Often one is satisfied to learn average values taken over specified sections of the test program. Many parameters are actually the ratio of two counts. Real-time calculation of the ratio, on-the-fly, would seem to be too expensive. As a compromise, average values can be obtained by collecting both the numerator and denominator counts and later doing the division during the measurement data analysis processing.

To obtain average values, one counter (A) counts "all" of a class of events, while the other counter (B) counts a subset of the events. For example, the loading on a backplane is measured by counting all backplane time slots in counter A and just the occupied time slots in counter B. For another example, average backplane access delay (at a given processor) can be measured by counting all access attempts in counter B and summing in counter A the backplane time slots or processor cycles that occurred during all the waits for access. The ratio, A/B, is the average access delay. The values in counters A and B can be read as timing-event triggers. If the preprocessor ratio counters are reset after reading, the measurement of the resource can be resolved to different periods in the test routine execution without reduced precision. Certain measurement *events* should generate *selective triggers* that cause preprocessor counter resetting.

While accumulation of time-resolved *average* values of these parameters may be sufficient, capturing the distribution of the individual data items in "buckets" by ranges of values may be more useful, but is well known, much more costly, and will not be discussed further. One may also wish to characterize memory activity according to selected address regions (hot spots).

Resource utilization measurement hardware can be used in conjunction with nearly any method of detecting the user-specified events to be time-tagged and captured. There is a roughly linear relationship between cost and the number of resources that can be measured simultaneously. A number of pairs of counters would be required to measure all of the items of interest in a multiprocessor system. Since resource measurement hardware is generally non-perturbing, in many cases it can be reconnected to measure other resources and the test stimulus software can then be rerun.

It is vital that all preprocessors be disabled when the system under test is *not* executing test code. No data should be taken when the system is executing the overhead of "measurement" calls to the operating system, etc. Special measurement events can be used to start and stop the data accumulation.

- Resource Monitoring with Inserted-Code Triggering - The means of generating data collection triggers is not closely related to collection of resource utilization data. Even operating-system measurement calls can be used. The operating system would then manage the preprocessor counters—albeit with considerable extraneous effect on their values due to the operating system's own code. Inserted-code event triggering, using off-machine data collection hardware, can use resource measurement preprocessing very effectively. Specific event codes, or bits, can be used to reset certain preprocessors, giving all the resource-measurement flexibility of the NBS REMS system previously mentioned.

- Resource Monitoring with Non-Perturbing Triggering - The **global** triggers from a a pattern-matching trigger system cause collection of the current state of all of the resource utilization counter data. In addition, any global trigger can be accompanied by one or more *selective triggers*, which reset certain preprocessor counter pairs after their data have been captured. The NBS Resource Monitoring System (REMS) [8] is an example of this class of system.

9.5.1 Resource Utilization Preprocessor Implementation

Present computer systems pay scant attention to providing access to the "test points" needed for resource utilization measurement. At NBS we have observed that the vital resource status signals are not explicitly and simultaneously present because the designer has chosen logical minimization or reduced pinouts to reduce costs. It then becomes necessary for the measurement hardware to perform combinational and sequential logical operations to derive the signal to be measured. The signals to be combined often occur at different times. This makes the measurement hardware very special-purpose, and requires a lot of costly study of usually-proprietary system details before the measurement apparatus can be modified and attached.

The computer designer should consider the types of signals that are likely to be of interest for resource measurement. Status signals are most useful if they are continually present and only unstable at specified times, or always present in a certain relation to the clock phase or system state. A daughter board could contain logic so that these signals are explicitly present. With these "standardized" resource measurement signals thus made available, the interface with the measurement equipment is extremely straightforward, and can be the same for many systems. This could allow performance measurement equipment to become a commodity product, usable by people with a wide range of technical skills.

Ratio Counter Preprocessors. The ratio counters are conceptionally numerator (A) and denominator (B) counters. As mentioned above, there are two obvious modes of use:

- Counter B counts all events and counter A counts a subset. This can be used for parameters such as cache hit ratio and bus occupancy.
- Counter A counts time ticks at all times some condition is TRUE and counter B counts the number of occasions that the condition changes from FALSE to TRUE. This can be used for parameters such as average pulse duration and bus access latency.

For some parameters such as duty cycles, there will be a count *every* bus cycle (once each 5–500 ns). In order to allow a reasonable interval before the counters overflow (between places where measurement data capture events *must* be inserted), a counter of perhaps 32 bits will be needed. Because the value of the ratio is never exactly known before an experiment, the two counters should be of the same size. Capturing both counters with 32-bit precision would require a great deal of measurement data memory, which is essentially wasted since experimental *accuracy* in the computer measurement field is rather poor due to the many unquantifiable perturbations. Why store 32-bit data with 14-bit accuracy?

One is certainly justified in compressing the ratio counter data using a reduced-precision floating point format, by employing a self-normalizing ratio counter technique as illustrated in Figure 9.8. If 14 bits of data are captured from each counter, adequate resolution should result if **both** counters are normalized by the factor appropriate to the one containing the greater value.

A counter - 14 bits — B counter - 14 MSB — Exponent - 4 bits

32-bit Ratio Counters Compressed into 32 bits

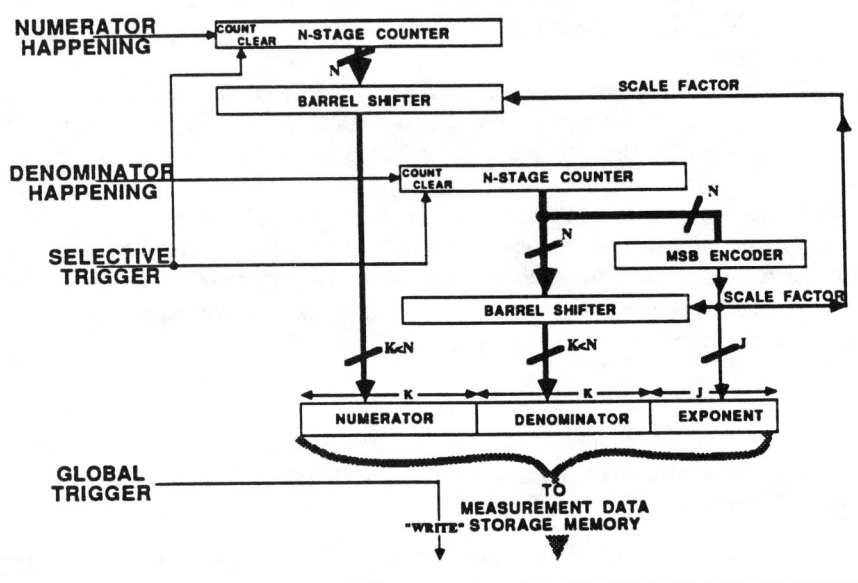

FIGURE 9.8
Ratio counter preprocessor.

Compressing into 32 bits allows a precision of about 0.01 percent of full scale.

- Built-in Hardware - The cost of providing ratio counters for a vast array of parameters would be great even if they were reduced to VLSI; the cost might be silicon or board area. A more likely approach would be to accept the incremental costs of combining and retiming the signals needed for resource measurement, and to provide logic in the computer under-test to route selected subsets of the resource signals to a small number of ratio counters. The user could then set up the desired measurements by programming the routing logic to select the subset of interest.

- Optional Hardware - One could just as well include, in all systems, the hardware to combine and retime the signals, and to provide logic to route selected subsets of the resource signals to "standardized" interface connectors. This would allow performance measurement equipment to become a commodity product, usable on a number of systems by *ordinary* people.

A number of possible preprocessors have been discussed; their applications are summarized in Table 9.3.

TABLE 9.3
Resource Utilization Preprocessor Uses

Parameter	Preprocessor Use	
	Counters to Obtain Averages	
	Numerator	Denominator
Event duration	Number of events	Total duration
Access latency	Number of accesses	Total duration of all waits
Memory access distribution	Not Used	Not Used
Event ratio	Special events	All events
Cache hit ratio	Cache hits	All accesses
Bus occupancy	Occupied time elements	All time elements
Percent time writing	Time spent in write instructions	Total elapsed time
Percent time writing data	Time spent in write data instructions	Total elapsed time
Processor idle	Clock cycles when processor idle	All clock cycles
Number of events	Not used	Count all events
Translation look-aside buffer misses	Not used	Count misses
Transactions		Count transactions

9.6 System Software Aspects

Measurement events must be placed at all entries and exits from the operating system so that user code and operating system characteristics may be separated (cf. [1]). The system software must assure that data collection addresses are always present in the page tables; the delay and perturbation of a page fault caused by measurement reading or writing is unacceptable. As stated above, in order to make pattern-matching triggering practical, the details of determining the patterns to match must be done *for* the user. In any case, the user should be allowed to insert measurement pseudo-instructions in the source code, and the system software such as compilers, linkers, and loaders should assemble the corresponding trigger patterns. The effect of optimizing compilers is an open question. These trigger patterns would then be written in a file for down-loading to the measurement hardware and for use in the data interpretation process. It will be impossible for most computer purchasers to make any required measurement changes to the operating system and other system software because of the highly proprietary nature of system software source code for parallel machines, and the level of understanding and skill required to make the changes. In any case it makes more economic sense for the measurement "hooks" to be inserted in the system software by its supplier.

9.7 Summary

The variations among computers has been greatly increased by the many architectures and implementations of multiprocessor machines. Some are particularly unsuited to certain algorithms and programming styles. This has greatly increased the difficulty of designing, choosing, and using computers. Performance measurement can help the designer and user obtain the best results. Performance may vary greatly depending on apparently minor changes in the program or data set, therefore measurement and tuning are pivotal. Performance measurement of multiprocessor computers can be accomplished over a wide range of cost, accuracy and completeness. Measurement accuracy can be drastically impaired by perturbations caused by the measurement process. Reduction in perturbation increases the cost and complexity of the measurement equipment and process. Some measurement techniques require hardware support to be built-in by the manufacturer, others can be offered as options with little cost to customers not requiring them, *if the hardware design provides access to the required signals.*

Measurement is accomplished in two parts: (1) the establishment, recognition, and timing of *events* in program execution, and (2) the collection of facts about the operation of the computer at and among events. As a practical matter, completely non-perturbing *event* detection is either ambiguous or very complex and costly; it appears that one must tolerate a minimal level of perturbation at each event to achieve an affordable system. This implies that there is a minimum practical granularity in measurement. In MIMD machines, accurate timing and resource utilization collection requires hardware support. There is a roughly linear relationship between cost and the number of resources that can be measured (in detail) simultaneously. In many cases the test stimulus software can be run while other resources are being measured because resource measurement hardware is, in general, non-perturbing.

Acknowledgments

This report could not have been written without the many suggestions of my colleagues in the NBS Parallel Processing Group. Particular thanks are due G. Lyon, A. Mink, G. Nacht, and J. Roberts. Dr. Mark Pullen of the Defense Advanced Research Projects Agency also contributed useful suggestions.

9.8 References

1. S. Mitchell, SySM Functional Requirements Description, Harris Government Information Systems Division, Melbourne, FL, 1986.
2. J. G. Whitman, Private communication, Harris Government Information Systems Division, Melbourne, FL, May 1986.
3. G. Schrott and T. Templemeier, Monitoring of Real Time Systems by a Separate Processor, in *Real Time Programming 1983*, Proceedings of the 12th IFAC/IFIP Workshop, Hatfield, UK, 29-31 Mar 1983. Pergamon Press, Oxford, UK.
4. M. Reilly, Telephone conversation regarding how to better accomplish process identification with pattern-matching triggering, Digital Equipment Corp. and Carnegie-Mellon U., 10 Mar 1987.
5. A. Mink, J. Roberts, J. Draper, and R. Carpenter, Simple Multi-Processor Performance Measurement Techniques and Examples of Their Use, NBSIR 86-3416, National Bureau of Standards, Gaithersburg, MD, July 1986.
6. A. Mink, J. Draper, J. Roberts, and R. Carpenter, Hardware Assisted Multiprocessor Performance Measurements, NBSIR 87-3585, National Bureau of Standards, Gaithersburg, MD, June 1987.
7. R. Carpenter, A Comparison of Two 'Guaranteed' Local Network Access Methods, *Data Communications*, Vol. 14 No. 2, February 1984, pp. 143-152.

8. G. Nacht and A. Mink, Recommended Instrumentation Approaches for a Shared-Memory Multiprocessor, NBSIR 87-3663, National Bureau of Standards, Gaithersburg, MD, October 1987.

9. J. Roberts, Performance Measurement Techniques for Multi-Processor Computers, NBSIR 85-3296, National Bureau of Standards, Gaithersburg, MD, February 1986.

10

Problems in Characterizing Barrier Performance

Harry F. Jordan

10.1 Introduction

The barrier is a synchronization among all executing processes, all of which encounter a barrier construct at some point in their execution. The synchronization requires that all processes execute the barrier construct before any process can proceed past it to the next executable statement. It was introduced in connection with hardware support for global synchronization in the Finite Element Machine [1] and has since been used in various parallel languages [2-4] and incorporated in parallel language standards proposals [5], [6].

The barrier is usually used to satisfy a number of data dependences simultaneously by imposing sequentiality on the production and use of data items. A common usage, as suggested in the definition of a barrier appearing in Figure 10.1, is to synchronize the production and use of many parts of a complex data structure simultaneously, without dealing with data items individually.

The barrier is one of a class of synchronizations that can be called "generic," to indicate that processes are not identified by name. The synchronization condition is specified by the quantifier "all". An example of a synchronization that is not generic is the rendezvous, in which two specifically named processes wait for each other.

Barrier Synchronization
All processes must enter a Barrier statement
before any process can complete it.

Process A	Process B	...	Process P
.	.		.
.	.		.
.	.		.
Compute part of Q	Compute part of Q	...	Compute part of Q
Barrier	Barrier	...	Barrier
Use Q	Use Q	...	Use Q
.	.		.
.	.		.
.	.		.

FIGURE 10.1
Use of the barrier synchronization.

There are several variations on the semantics of the barrier. Perhaps the most important is the way in which the set of processes quantified by "all" is defined. In some systems, implicit knowledge of a parallel execution environment defines the set; in other systems a simple count of the number of processes to arrive before the barrier is satisfied is used. In the Force language [2], the semantics is modified by including a section of code between the beginning and end of a barrier construct. This code is executed sequentially by one processor after all processors have arrived at the barrier and before any process leaves it.

10.2 Implementation of the Barrier

There are numerous ways of implementing barriers on existing multiprocessors, and the alternatives have performance implications for specific architectures. A discussion of the linear versus the logarithmic organization of barrier implementations was given by Axelrod [7]; a broader set of barrier implementations was studied and measured in [8]. A number of the choices made in implementing barriers are summarized in Figure 10.2. For simplicity, they are given as simple dichotomies that can be combined in various ways to yield a number of very

Shared memory	—	Message passing
Prescheduled	—	Self-scheduled
Master-slave	—	Symmetric
Test&set	—	Readwrite
Logarithmic structure	—	Linear structure
Distributed exit	—	Broadcast exit

FIGURE 10.2
Alternatives for barrier implementation.

different implementations with potentially different performance, depending on the underlying multiprocessor architecture.

This discussion will be focused primarily on shared-memory multiprocessors, since the performance measurements to be studied were selected from shared-memory machine examples. Most of the interprocess communication patterns for barriers can appear in either shared-memory or message-passing systems. The only exception is the self-scheduled updating of a shared-arrival count, which is difficult in message passing machines without prescheduling at least one process to maintain the count. In the prescheduled case, processes report arrival at the barrier in some predetermined order, while a self-scheduled barrier allows processes to execute their arrival-reporting code in any order. Because the barrier's purpose is to eliminate time-skew between arriving processes, the situation illustrated in Figure 10.3 is the normal case for a self-scheduled barrier using a critical section to update shared-arrival variables.

If the arrivals were prescheduled so that processes had to execute their critical sections in a fixed order, say from left to right in the figure, then the arrival section of the barrier would take longer for most arrival orders.

The master-slave barrier structure is often associated with prescheduling, but it is possible to have the first process arriving at the barrier become the master and execute code distinct from that executed by the slaves. The characteristic of a symmetric implementation is that all processes execute the same synchronization code, which differs only in that the indices of certain synchronization variables, or the destinations of some synchronization messages, may be computed from the fixed identity assigned to the process. The main advantage of the master-slave structure is that communications between the master and the slaves can be arranged so that any one synchronization variable is written by only one

188   Chapter 10. Problems in Characterizing Barrier Performance

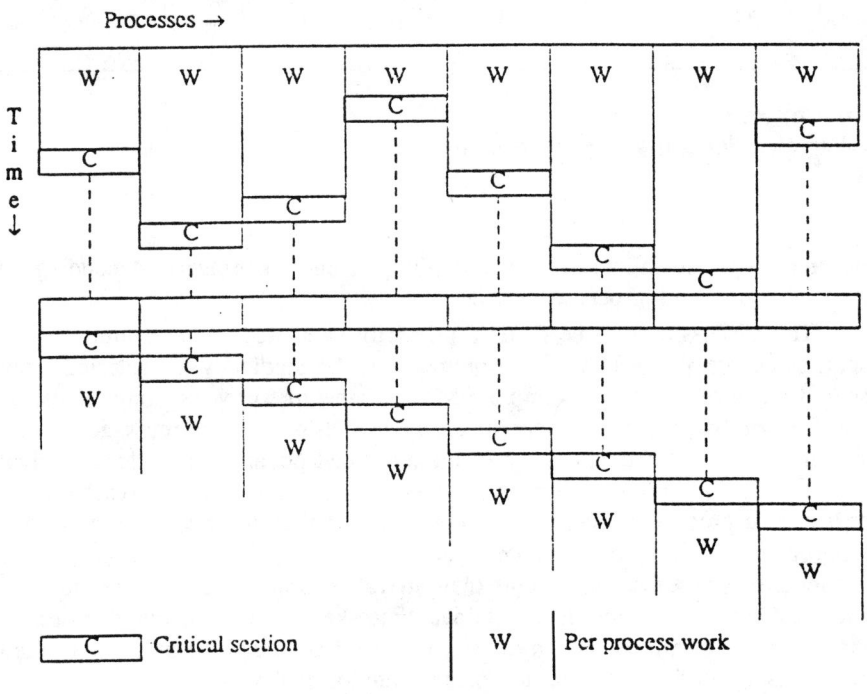

FIGURE 10.3
A self-scheduled barrier with skewed process arrival.

process. This allows the use of memory cells for which only read and write are indivisible. Symmetric implementations require something like **test&set** to indivisibly test and update a synchronization variable. For machines with hardware support for synchronization, the difference is small, but it can become large if all synchronizations are mediated by the operating system.

The most clear-cut choice in an implementation is whether to use a linear or logarithmic pattern of communication among the processes. For systems with many physical processors, the logarithmic organization makes far better use of the system parallelism. In systems with only a few physical processors, the slightly higher computational complexity of the logarithmic structure may mean that the linear barrier can be more efficient. Depending on the nature of a machine's synchronization support, 16 processors is usually enough to make the logarithmic barrier a better choice. Figure 10.4 shows two examples of logarithmic barriers. The first is the double tree barrier, which has distributed, master-slave arrival and exit phases. The second is the butterfly barrier, which is symmetric and self-scheduled, and whose arrival and exit phases are not distinct.

The choice of broadcast versus distributed exit is also dependent on the particular machine hardware. If the machine supports efficient broadcast from one source to multiple destinations, say by having one process write a variable that is read by many others, then the exit phase of a barrier may use this capability. If the barrier arrival code distinguishes a unique process, either the master or the last to arrive, this processor may broadcast a release to all other processes. For example, in the double tree barrier of Figure 10.4, the inverted exit tree may be replaced by a one level broadcast from the master. Of course, if some distributed mechanism is used by the system to support the broadcast, there may be no performance gain.

10.3 Accounting for Barrier Performance

There are several different influences on time accounting in measurements of barrier performance. The major ones are:

- delays in arrival of processes,
- the waiting mechanism,
- the code of the barrier implementation,
- synchronization delays, i.e. critical sections, and
- swapped processes, perhaps due to interrupts.

The purpose of the barrier is to synchronize processes arriving at different times, so the ideal performance is to wait for the last arriving process. In addition to the ideal behavior, a differential delay among the arriving processes can mask

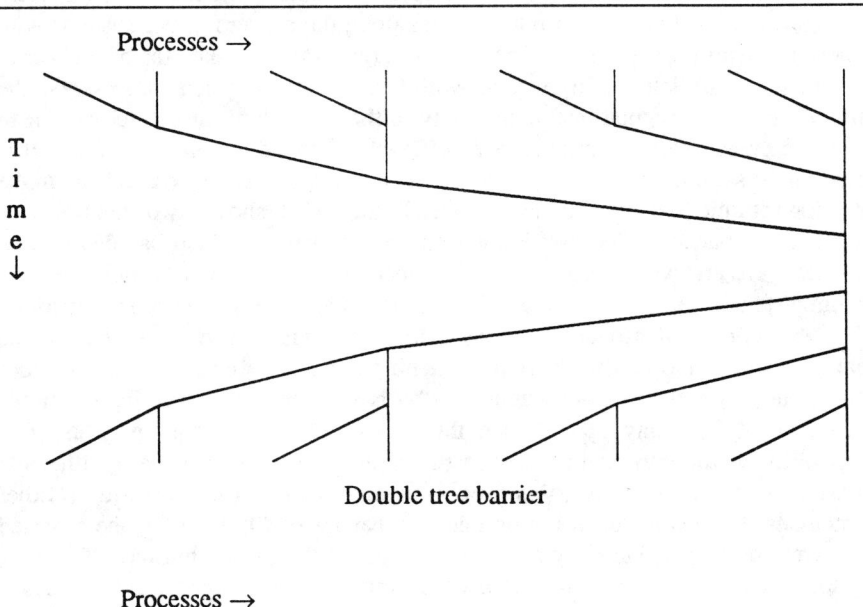
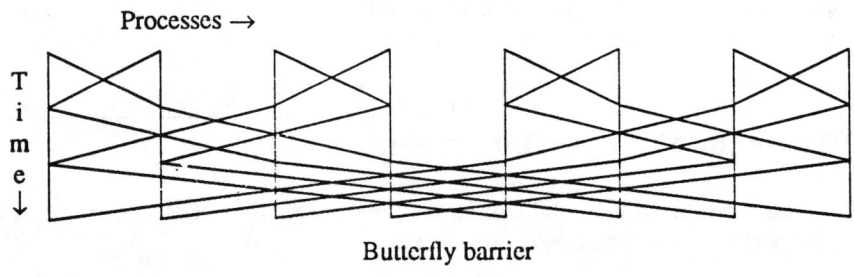

FIGURE 10.4
Two examples of logarithmic barriers.

some of the barrier code execution. This masking is most effective for a self-scheduled barrier that uses a critical section to update a shared count of arriving processes. If a prescheduled, master-slave barrier implementation is used, then the order of arrival of processes makes a large difference in the amount of barrier code that can be masked by the arrival-time differential. Thus, in measuring the performance of such barriers, either a fixed arrival order must be specified and guaranteed, or a sufficiently large sample of random arrival orders must be taken to obtain average performance. The arrival order for self-scheduled, symmetric barriers is irrelevant, and no measurement precautions need be taken with respect to arrival order.

Once processes start arriving at the barrier, the early arrivals must wait for the later ones. The waiting mechanism may be busy-waiting, virtualization of processes (swapping them out), or something intermediate between the two. Busy-waiting wastes processor cycles during long delays, while virtualization is associated with an irreducible minimum overhead that is often quite long. Intermediate positions are possible in systems that support a lightweight process model or by giving up the processor only after an initial busy-waiting period, the duration of which is determined by the swapping overhead of the particular system. Our interest has been primarily in tightly-coupled parallel scientific codes, so the use of process virtualization for waiting has been avoided wherever allowed by the underlying system.

The actual code executed by processes in a specific barrier implementation depends on the structure of the barrier implementation chosen, as well as on the system primitives used to implement it. The major implementation influence is the choice of linear or logarithmic barrier organization. The logarithmic organization requires somewhat more code. This can make it slightly slower than a linear barrier when used with only a few processes, but is more than compensated for by the increased parallelism possible in executing the code for even a modest number of processes. Much more important than the amount of code is the nature of the synchronization primitives on which the barrier is built. For tightly-coupled parallel processing, it is important to avoid operating system overhead wherever possible. Hardware locks used to support critical sections or to implement interprocess synchronization directly are one good choice. Another is to use a master-slave implementation based on shared variables capable of atomic read and write. The time processes spend waiting for synchronization messages from other processes or for a critical section to be released is a major factor in barrier time accounting.

10.4 Instrumentation for Barrier Measurement

The most important instrument for measuring performance in a parallel system is a low-overhead timer. Timers are also important in measuring sequential systems, of course, but their effect is much easier to subtract out of a strictly serial execution history. In considering the structure of timers, there are two main aspects to take into account: the timer update mechanism and the timer sampling mechanism. The time may be updated by a mechanism that is completely transparent to the processes involved in the parallel computation. This is usually done by hardware, but it is possible to allocate an independent process to do a transparent software update in some systems. The timer update can involve processor cycle stealing, in which case it is nearly, but not entirely, transparent. It can also be done by a periodic interrupt, which usually performs other periodic operating systems functions in addition to updating a timer. Timer sampling can either be done by simply reading a shared variable, or it may require the more substantial overhead of a call to the run-time or operating system.

Another important aspect of timers for multiprocessors is whether there is a single system clock, which is accessible to all processors, or whether each processor maintains a separate hardware or software timer. Having separate timers for each processor eliminates competition when many processors try to sample the time simultaneously, but a single timer gives a more coherent measure across the processors. If it is important to keep track of the distinction between system time and user time on a per-processor basis, then a timer for each processor may well be a natural choice. Systems range from having a single hardware timer that is readable by any processor as a shared memory location, as in the Encore Multimax, to having a software timer per processor that is updated by a periodic kernel interrupt, as in the Flexible Computer Systems Flex/32.

An important parameter for a software timer is the uncertainty introduced by the time spent in the timer interrupt handler. This uncertainty can be expressed as

$$\Delta H = \frac{\text{Timer interrupt service}}{\text{Interrupt interval}}.$$

Since the timer interrupt may support periodic operating system functions of different frequencies, ΔH may vary, so that it may be appropriate to use an average value.

There are several aspects of barrier performance that may be measured. Most obvious is the effect of an ideal barrier (one with no overhead), on the behavior of a section of a parallel program. In a simple case, the effect of delaying all processes until the last one arrives can be calculated analytically, but in more complex situations, especially data-dependent ones, it may be necessary to measure the effect. In addition to the ideal synchronization performed by the barrier, there are synchronization delays introduced by interprocessor synchronizing communications used to implement the barrier. Typical would be critical section delay protecting the update of a shared arrival mechanism. Finally, there are the processor cycles used to execute code associated with a particular barrier implementation. If it is assumed that barriers are the right synchronization to use for a particular parallel algorithm, then the important thing to measure is the difference between the ideal barrier behavior and the behavior that includes the synchronization and code of the real implementation.

Given a specific parallel applications program, some simple probes of barrier behavior are possible using only an elapsed time measurement. This assumes a system dedicated to the applications program so that no substantial time is used for systems functions or time-multiplexed users during the course of program execution. If the flow of program control is not altered by the violation of data dependences imposed by barriers (only the answers are wrong), then a program can be run and timed both with and without barriers to get a measure of their total effect. Another possibility is to change the barrier implementation in a known way, say by doubling the processor cycles used in the barrier code, and to measure the effect of this change on the overall execution time. These methods are primarily useful for measuring the influence of barrier synchronization on a specific parallel program to determine whether it is important to find a less costly synchronization method.

If measurements are made for the purpose of comparing different barrier implementations for the best performance, as was done in [8], then barriers should be measured independently of surrounding code. It is not possible to separate barriers completely from their execution environment as a result of the dependence of implementation overheads on skew and order of arrival times for different processes. A careful set of measurements on barriers with such a dependence will include different types of arrival loading. A common arrival pattern occurs when two successive barriers are separated by a fixed amount of computation that is the same for each process. The order of arrival at the second barrier is then determined by the order of their release from the first one. A configuration having two barriers, separated by random, and different, amounts of work for each process, represents another useful measurement. Enough samples must be taken to average both the latest arrival time and the effects of different arrival order, if any. Another form of arrival loading that occurs commonly corresponds to two barriers separated by a fixed amount of work that containing a critical section. The time-skew introduced by processes waiting to enter the critical section may influence barrier performance. For example, a self-scheduled, linear barrier does an excellent job of masking critical-section skew.

The nature of the timers used to measure barrier performance is important, and in at least one case, has a drastic effect on the reliability of the measurement. Since barriers synchronize all processes, a single clock per system is most natural to their measurement. This assumes, however, that the whole system is used for the measurement. In shared or time-multiplexed systems the situation is more complicated. A case presenting considerable difficulty is a dedicated system that has one software timer per processor. In addition, the timer interrupts in different processors are asynchronous. The effect of the measurement uncertainty

ΔH interacts with the synchronization function of the barrier in an unpleasant way. A worst-case situation can occur in which all processors are interrupted while executing a barrier in a sequential order that causes the other processors to wait on the return of each interrupted processor in order to complete the barrier. Thus with P processors, the uncertainty of the measurement of barrier completion is not just ΔH but can be as large as $P \times \Delta H$. An example of this situation will be reported in the next section.

10.5 Examples

Barrier performance is one aspect of measurements performed on the Denelcor HEP shared-memory multiprocessor system [9]. The system involved in the measurements consisted of four pipelined multiprocessor modules, called PEMs. Each PEM could obtain a speed of 10 MIPS (or MFLOPS) by executing 12–15 processes in parallel. The system could support up to 200 processes executing in parallel, but the pipelined structure implied that improved performance could not result, even theoretically, for more than about 64 processes. Each PEM was equipped with a hardware performance monitor known as the System Performance Indicator, or SPI. The SPI kept track of clock cycles of 10^{-7} seconds along with numbers of completed instructions in several categories. The instruction categories were: floating point instructions, other register to register instructions, memory reference instructions, and wave-offs (instructions that could not be issued because of synchronization).

The barrier measurements made on the HEP system were with respect to a parallel Gaussian elimination program that used barriers for its synchronization. The flow of control in Gaussian elimination is not influenced by the correctness of the floating point computations, which are the operations synchronized by the barriers. At most the time for pivoting could be influenced, but this was not the case in this program. Figure 10.5 shows the execution time versus number of parallel processes for the Gaussian elimination program with and without its synchronizing barriers. A summary of the results shows that the synchronized version obtained a maximum speed of 7.5 MFLOPS, corresponding to 32 MIPS, while the program with barriers removed ran at 9.5 MFLOPS, or 40 MIPS, which is the maximum speed for a four PEM HEP. The decrease in execution time as the number of processes increases beyond the point at which all pipelines are filled is a result of process contention for shared synchronization variables in the barriers, and of the increase in barrier complexity with number of processes.

Measurements were also done by making changes in the barrier implementation. The initial implementation counted processes entering the barrier and blocked them with a single shared-memory locking variable until the last process had arrived. The compiled code for this implementation amounted to about

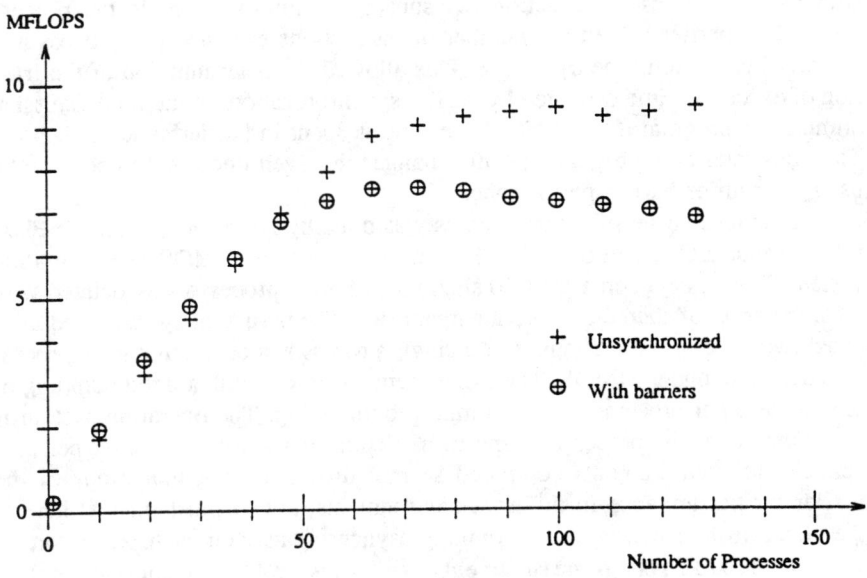

FIGURE 10.5
Barriers in Gaussian elimination on a 500 by 500 Matrix.

20 instructions per process. Since four PEMs could generate memory reference retrys at four times the rate that a single memory module could handle them, it was suspected that memory access congestion made this implementation inefficient on the four PEM system. An alternate implementation of the barrier, that suspended processes as they arrived and used the last one to restart them, executed about 100 instructions per process but reduced execution time by 20%, verifying the memory contention effect. It should be noted that process suspension in this machine did not involve the operating system, but was possible with four or five user instructions. A subsequent improvement in the process suspending barrier halved the number of instructions executed per process and improved execution time by 11.8%. This allowed the determination of the fraction of execution time occupied by barrier synchronization. In the final Gaussian elimination program about 14% of the time is spent in barrier synchronization. This illustrates how program-specific changes in a well understood code can be used to examine barrier performance.

An extensive set of measurements was done by Arenstorf [8] on the Flexible Computer Corporation's Flex/32 running under the MMOS [10] operating system. This system consists of 20 single board microprocessors associated with a combination of shared and private memories. The particular system used allocated two processors to running in a single processor mode, leaving 18 processors available under MMOS. The experiments were run with a fixed mapping of one process per processor with no multiprogramming. The operating system is distributed over the processors, and in particular, has a software timer per processor. The measurements compared several different implementations of the barrier for performance in different environments, but of most interest here is the effect of the software timers running asynchronously on each processor.

The Flex/32 system measurements exhibit the problem, mentioned earlier, of multiplying the measurement uncertainty ΔH due to the service time for timer interrupts by the number P of processes. The standard configuration of the MMOS operating system uses a 20 millisecond (ms) interrupt interval with a service time of 0.3 ms. The resulting $\Delta H = 1.5\%$ is acceptable for timing single stream phenomena, but using 18 processors synchronized by barriers presents a significant problem. In the worst case sequence of timer interrupts using all 18 processors, some processor is unavailable to satisfy the barrier synchronization 27% of the time. The resulting uncertainty in barrier measurements is not a result of inaccurately sampling the value of the time but of overheads involved in updating the time. The problem of obtaining accurate times was solved by increasing the timer interval to one second, thus reducing ΔH to 0.03% and the worst-case influence on barrier measurements to 0.54%. Of course, it was necessary to make very long timing runs to reduce the effect of the one second accuracy of the time to an acceptable percentage of the measurement.

A final measurement of barrier performance is of interest in demonstrating an extreme case of the effect of all processors not being available to execute the barrier simultaneously. In this case, it is not timer interrupts that occupy the processors but multiprogramming activity. The measurements were performed by Benten [11] on the Sequent Balance 8000, a bus-connected, shared-memory multiprocessor. This system had eight processors, organized as two per board sharing a cache memory. All memory is shared and is connected to the bus, so that it is uniformly accessible to all processors. The version of the system to which we had access ran a Unix[1]-style operating system that was highly multiprogrammed and treated processors as a schedulable resource. We had no way of locking processes to processors other than ensuring that there was no other load on the system, and no reason in our own program to time-multiplex processors.

A barrier synchronized Gaussian elimination program, similar to the one measured on the HEP, was run for varying numbers of processes. The character of the results is not surprising, but the magnitude is interesting. As shown in Figure 10.6, when the program was run on an unloaded system, normal speedup results were observed until multiprogramming was forced to occur by virtue of the number of processes exceeding the number of physical processors. With nine processes time-multiplexed on eight processors, the execution time is significantly longer than that for one process. This reflects the fact that all processes must be cosheduled for a barrier that is implemented independently of the operating system to perform reasonably. An alternative to the barrier must be used for synchronizing parallel programs unless the operating system's scheduler can cooperate with the barrier construct. Figure 10.7 shows that the presence of a multiprogramming load on the system merely causes the effect to be seen for fewer processes and to increase in magnitude.

10.6 Conclusions

The barrier is a convenient synchronization mechanism in multiprocessors, especially of the shared-memory type. Measuring the performance of barriers may be used to determine their effect on the performance of a parallel program, in order to optimize the program, and to choose the best method and arrangement of synchronization. Measurements can also help select between different types of barrier implementation to suit it to the machine environment. The measurement of barrier performance offers some unique difficulties that result from the global nature of the synchronization. All processes must be available for the barrier to complete, and any virtualization of processes will have a noticeable effect. Another problem is to separate overhead due to a specific barrier implementation from the waiting time imposed purposely on processes by the nature

---

[1] Unix is a registered trademark of AT&T.

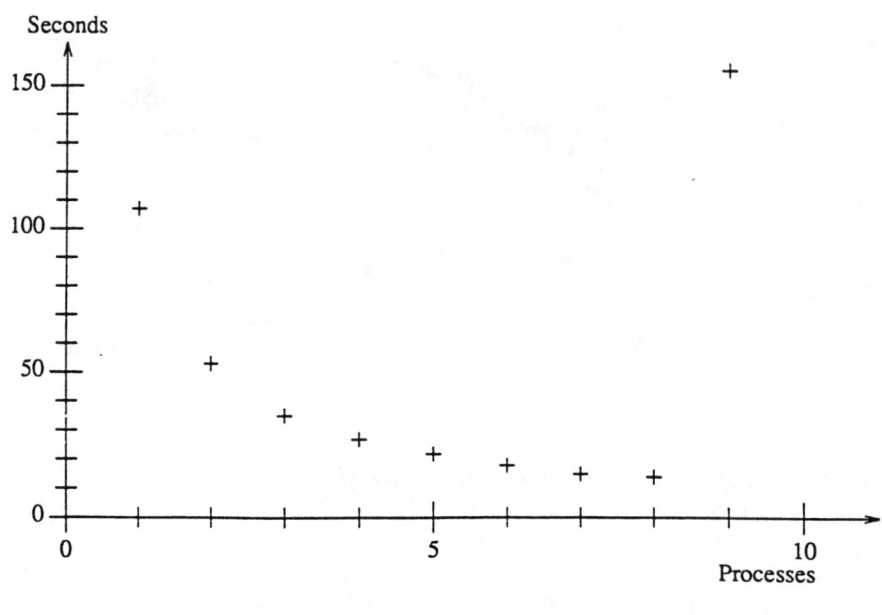

FIGURE 10.6
Effect of lack of coscheduling, single program.

of the synchronization. Hardware or software support for measuring the waiting time of processes directly would significantly aid barrier measurement. In the work done to date, waiting times must be inferred from several indirect time measurements.

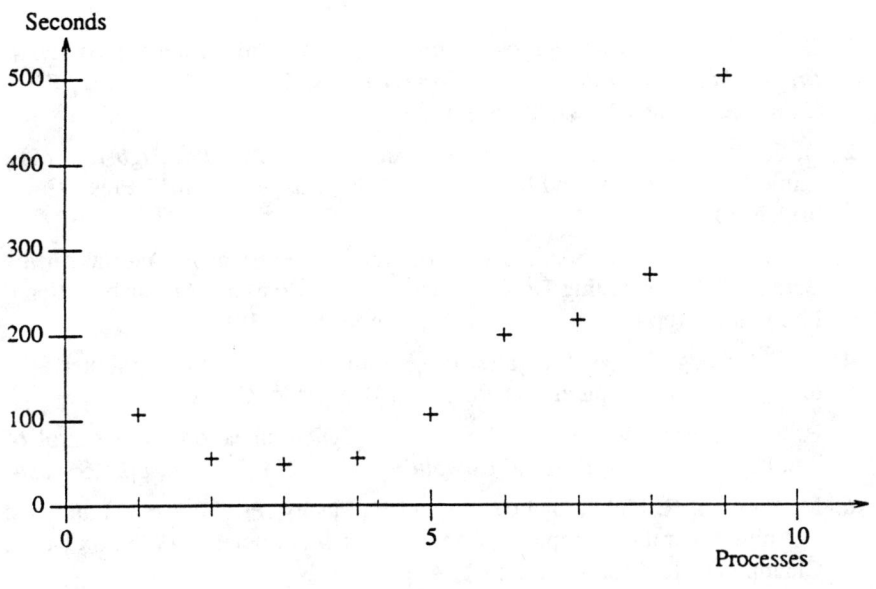

FIGURE 10.7
Effect of lack of coscheduling, with multiprogramming load.

References

1. H. Jordan, A Special Purpose Architecture for Finite Element Analysis, *Proceedings 1978 International Conference on Parallel Processing*, IEEE Computer Society Press, 1978, pp. 263–266.

2. H. Jordan, The Force, in *The Characteristics of Parallel Algorithms*, L. Jamieson, D. Gannon and R. Douglass, Eds., Chapter 16, MIT Press, Cambridge, MA, 1987.

3. E. Lusk and R. Overbeek, Use of Monitors in Fortran: A Tutorial on the Barrier, Self-scheduling Do Loop and Askfor Monitors, Argonne National Laboratory Report No. ANL-84-51, Argonne, IL, 1985.

4. A. Osterhaug, Guide to Parallel Programming on Sequent Computer Systems, Sequent Computer Systems, Inc., Beaverton, OR, 1985.

5. P. Frederickson, R. Jones and B. Smith, Synchronization and Control of Parallel Algorithms, *Parallel Computing*, V. 2, No. 3, 1986, pp. 265–254.

6. M. Furtney, R. Kuhn, B. Leasure and E. Plachy, PCF Fortran: Language Definition, Parallel Computing Forum, Kuck & Associates, 1906 Fox Drive, Champaign, IL 61820, Version 1, Aug. 1988.

7. T. Axelrod, Effects of Synchronization Barriers on Multiprocessor Performance, *Parallel Computing*, V. 3, No. 2, 1986, pp. 129–140.

8. N. S. Arenstorf and H. F. Jordan, Comparing Barrier Algorithms, ICASE Rept. No. 87-65, NASA Langley Res. Ctr., Hampton, VA, September 1987, to appear in *Parallel Computing*.

9. H. F. Jordan, Performance and Program Structure in a Large Shared Memory Multiprocessor, in *New Computing Environments: Parallel, Vector and Systolic*, A. Wouk, Ed., pp. 201–217, SIAM, Philadelphia, PA, 1986.

10. Multicomputing multitasking operating system (MMOS) reference manual, Flexible Computer Corporation, Dallas, TX, 1986.

11. M. S. Benten and H. F. Jordan, Multiprogramming and the Performance of Parallel Programs, *Proceedings 3rd SIAM Conference on Parallel Processing for Scientific Computing*, Los Angeles, CA (December 1987).

11

Experiences With Performance Monitors

Harry Nelson

11.1 Introduction

After asking vendors to supply us with built-in performance monitoring hardware for our large scale supercomputers for at least 20 years, we at Lawrence Livermore National Laboratory (LLNL) felt particularly fortunate to receive a machine, the CRAY X-MP/48, which has some designed-in monitoring features.

Specifically, each X-MP CPU contains eight counters that can be assigned via programming to accumulate the total number of particular events occurring in the hardware without affecting the performance of the programs being monitored. Though this counting facility is not nearly the ultimate that we would like to have, it is enough to provide accurate statistics for some performance measures which, in the past, we could only estimate.

11.2 What Can be Monitored?

Table 11.1 lists the 32 events that can be monitored. This table is slightly modified from Table C-1 of CRI's X-MP/48 hardware reference manual, and I have added the two right-hand columns [1]. For any given run, one of the four 8-event groups must be selected, but the particular group may be changed as

TABLE 11.1
Performance-monitor counter groups. Total number of clock periods monitored in example = 112891×10^8

Monitor Group	Performance Counter	Description	Increment per CP	Example (10^8 counts)	Ctgy
j=0		Number of:			
	0	Instructions issued	+1	30506	
	1	CPs holding issue	+1	64544	1
	2	Fetches of instruction buffer	+1	302	
	3	I/O references, port 3	+1	86	2
	4	CPU references, ports 0, 1, 2	+3 max	29929	
	5	Floating-point add operations	+1	11983	
	6	Floating-point multiply operations	+1	13462	3
	7	Floating-point reciprocal operations	+1	1351	
j=1		Hold issue conditions:			
	0	Semaphores	+1	214	
	1	Shared registers	+1	<1	
	2	A registers and functional units	+1	9831	
	3	S registers and functional units	+1	22087	4
	4	V registers	+1	12650	
	5	V functional units	+1	12116	
	6	Scalar memory	+1	1011	
	7	Block memory	+1	13178	
j=2		Number of:			
	0	Fetches of instruction buffer	+1	302	
	1	Scalar references	+1	6578	
	2	Scalar conflicts	+1	3009	
	3	I/O references	+1	59	5
	4	I/O conflicts	+1	26	
	5	Block references, B + T + V	+3 max	23285	
	6	Block conflicts, B + T + V	+3 max	4797	
	7	Vector memory references, V only	+3 max	22567	
j=3		Number of:			
	0	000-017 instructions	+1	2122	
	1	020-137 instructions	+1	26699	
	2	140-157, 175 instructions	+1	243	6
	3	160-174 instructions	+1	630	
	4	176, 177 instructions	+1	822	
	5	Vector integer operations	+3 max	9390	
	6	Vector floating-point operations	+3 max	23903	7
	7	Vector memory references	+3 max	22708	

desired by a system call. In addition to the values returned by the counters, an actual count of the (real-time) machine cycles for which monitoring was performed is also accumulated by the system, and is made available as a ninth event. A machine cycle (CP) is 9.5 nanoseconds.

11.3 Results of an Example Run

The column of Table 11.1 headed "Example" gives the values collected by the counters during a 30-hour weekend run covering all X-MP activity on July 13 and 14, 1985. These data were gathered by locking each of the four CPUs of the LLNL machine into monitoring a different one of the four groups by using the appropriate system call.

The operating system was the Livermore Time-Sharing Sytem (LTSS); extensive tests have shown that each of the four CPUs performs approximately the same hardware functions over an extended period of time. The total number of CPU clock periods monitored in the run presented here was approximately 11.3×10^{12}.

A convenient way to look at these data is to break them into seven categories. These categories are numbered in the rightmost column in Table 11.1 headed "Ctgy." It is convenient to refer to counters within these categories by their group number and counter number. For example, the first counter in group 0 is (0,0).

Category 1 (0,0 and 0,1) shows that during 25% of all clock periods an instruction was issued, and during 55% of all clock periods an instruction was available for issuing but could not be issued because of some conflict. During the remaining 20% of all clock periods (obtained by subtracting the sum of counts in (0,0) and (0,1) from the total number of clock periods counted), no instruction was available for a potential issue. Reasons for the absence of an available instruction include 1) the operating system is active and in "monitor mode," 2) a jump instruction is in progress but the "jumped to" instruction has not yet reached the issue point, 3) the upper half of a 32-bit instruction is being passed, and 4) an instruction buffer refill is in progress.

The second category (0,2–0,4) shows that approximately 99% of all memory traffic through memory ports 0, 1, 2, and 3 was due to the user's program requesting a read or a write, 1% was due to a request to refill the instruction buffer, and less than 1% was due to I/O activity.

Category 3 (0,5–0,7) shows that among all floating-point scalar and vector operations, 50% were multiplies, 45% were adds, and 5% were reciprocals (A divide requires 1 reciprocal and 3 multiplies). These registers record the actual number of results returned by the floating-point units, not just the issues. In the case of a vector, each issue may result in as many as 64 individual operations.

The fourth category (1,0–1,7) breaks down the causes of the conflicts recorded by (0,1). In this example about one-third of the hold-issue conditions were due to S registers that were busy, and the rest were equally distributed between A-register, V-register, V-functional unit, and block memory (vector reads and writes) holds (A single issue may hold for more than one reason.) Currently the semaphore hold is due only to operating system conflicts that occur on the four processor X-MP/48 because LTSS is not a "distributed" (not itself multiprocessing) operating system. LTSS can handle only one CPU at a time, and it goes into a semaphore wait state occasionally when more than one CPU clamors for service. The New Livermore Time-Sharing System (NLTSS), an operating system under development at LLNL, is expected to address this problem.

The fifth category (2,0–2,6) gives a slightly different breakdown of memory activity. Item (2,7), vector memory references, is also counted in item (2,5). In this given case, 75% of memory traffic was due to vectors, 3% was due to other block transfers, and 22% was due to scalars.

Category 6 (3,0–3,4) breaks item (0,0) into greater detail. Essentially, instructions 000–017 are branches and special request instructions, 020–137 are arithmetic, scalar indexing, and scalar memory instructions, 140–157 and 175 are vector integer instructions, 160–174 are vector floating-point instructions, and 176–177 are vector memory instructions. Only 5% of the instructions issued were vectors.

Finally, the seventh category (3,5–3,7) counts the number of vector results due to the issues in items (3,2–3,4). A simple computation shows that the average lengths were 38 for integer and floating-point vectors and 28 for memory vectors. Thus, we see that the 5% of all instructions that were vector instructions performed roughly half again as many operations as the 95% that were scalar.

One interesting item that can be derived from these numbers is "fraction of vectorization." From the sum of (0,5–0,7) we find 26796×10^8 total floating-point operations, and from (3,6) we see that 23903×10^8 of these operations were vector results. Thus the fraction of floating-point operations vectorized was 90% during this 30 hour period. Similarly, for all operations, we find that 56001×10^8 were from vectors while 28821×10^8 were not, for an overall vectorization fraction of 66%.

Another finding of interest is that each CPU is cranking away at a rate of just under 24 MFLOPS (million floating-point operations per second), which means a rate of nearly 100 MFLOPS for the machine as a whole. In addition, each instruction issued produces, on the average, three results in four cycles, and the number of memory words moved is approximately the same as the number of other operations performed.

It should be stated that not all samples taken from other time periods show such a high rate of MFLOPS. Rates as low as 11 MFLOPS per CPU have been recorded during the prime interactive time-sharing hours of 9 a.m. to 4 p.m., and one continuous five-day sample that included system development and down time, showed only 15 MFLOPS per CPU overall.

11.4 Other Uses

In addition to the "lock-down" mode of using these counters, we have provided individual users with the capability of accumulating counts during the cycles that their particular code (or suitable subsection) is using a CPU. These counts are maintained by the system and returned to the user code on demand. Having given users this opportunity, we find that they take advantage of it. Table 11.2 is an example of a portion of the output supplied by one physics package to its users. This capability is now considered "necessary" by the administrators of some application programs.

A knowledge of the overall level of effective utilization of the X-MP has been obtained by combining total hours used by major applications with measures of their individual performance. These calculations show that the vector hardware is heavily used and allows at least twice as much real work to be completed within a given amount of time.

A summary of some of the major codes using LLNL's Cray machines for the year 1986 is given in Table 11.3.

11.5 Summary

My main message is that whatever instrumentation manufacturers provide, users will use it. Hardware that provides a look at performance without affecting it adversely is particularly valuable. Even the simple counters provided by the CRAY X-MP are useful in a variety of ways. Remember that managers, not programmers, buy computers and monitoring provides information that allows managers to make better judgements about actual usage of equipment.

Reference

1. CRAY X-MP Computer Systems Mainframe Reference Manual, HR-0097, p. 2-20.

TABLE 11.2
Performance monitor output from a physics code

I/O Routine	Minutes	Percent	Physics Routine	Minutes	Percent
XEQIO	.0367	.11	CYCLE	.0518	.15
PREGEN	.0108	.03	EU	1.5473	4.55
GEN8	.0165	.05	OP	.1137	.33
EDIT	.1623	.48	EL	.1081	.32
EDITL	.3254	.96	SO	.0704	.21
EDITS	.0395	.12	HY	1.8575	5.46
DUMP	.0072	.02	CO	.0373	2.46
DUMPZ	.1355	.40	TH	4.9738	14.62
PLOT	.8323	2.45	IC	.3195	.94
PLOTFR80	2.5565	7.52	EI	.0143	.04
TPLOT	.6429	1.89	EC	.3783	1.11
			RA	12.4371	36.56
			CY	.1003	.29
			RA	.0227	.07
			RP	.0649	.19
			XS	6.3428	18.65
TOTAL	4.7762	14.04	TOTAL	29.2399	85.96

Performance Data for Group 0

CATEGORY		/TOTAL CP'S
ISSUES	58167865040	.287501
CONFLICT	139438613961	.689192
IBUF FCH	559243550	.002764
I/O PORT	329643832	.001629
MEM REFS	61894614795	.305921
FLOAT +	26173605496	.129366
FLOAT *	29959472152	.148078
FLOAT /	2731030592	.013498

TABLE 11.3
Summary of FLOPs for major production codes at LLNL. The net rate for 1986 was 24.9±5 FLOP/second for all 10 codes.

Code Name	FLOP x 10^{12} per year	Hours Used	MFLOP Rate*	MFLOP Rate Ranking
\multicolumn{5}{c}{Production Code FLOP—FY86 CRAY XMP and CRAY 1's}
1.	1,013	6,700	42.±10	5
2.	752	3,800	55.	3
3.	729	9,200	22.±8	7
	605	2,050	82.	1
4.	580	7,000	23.	6
5.	302	1,200	70.	2
6.	251	1,550	45.±13	4
7.	201	4,650	12.	9
8.	161	5,600	8.	10
9.	121	4,800	7.	11
10.	110	2,550	12.±8	8
Totals	4,220	47,050		

*Some large time users have not reported MFLOP rates.

12

Parallel Processing a Real Code—A Case History

David Mandell and Harold Trease[1]

12.1 Introduction

Large three-dimensional, time-dependent hydrodynamics codes take an excessive amount of time to execute even on the largest supercomputers currently available, such as a CRAY X-MP/416. In order to reduce the execution time to practical values, it is desirable to multitask codes so that all of the processors can be used. A desirable goal is to provide users with overnight turnaround.

The POLLY code was originally written for a CRAY 1 [1], and in multitasking it for a CRAY X-MP, numerous problems were encountered that did not occur when smaller codes were multitasked. These problems are discussed below. The code was multitasked using the Los Alamos Multitasking Control Library [2]. In order to speed up the serial POLLY code, it was decided to rewrite this code, and the new code, called X3D, is a substantially faster serial code. X3D was autotasked using the Los Alamos Autotasking method developed by Bobrowicz [3].

By examining Amdahl's Law [4,5],

$$S = 1/(1 - P + P/NP) ,$$

[1]This work was performed under the auspices of the U. S. Department of Energy.

where S is the speedup (best serial wall clock time / parallel wall clock time), P is the fraction of serial code that is parallel, and NP is the number of physical processors, it becomes clear that in order to achieve high efficiencies, the serial portion of a code must be reduced substantially. In a real code this reduction presents a significant challenge. The first step in accomplishing this reduction is to examine the serial code in order to determine where the time is being spent. The Los Alamos utility TALLY [6] was used for this task and the timing results are presented.

In Section 12.2 the multitasking done for the POLLY code is described in the hope that the problems encountered will enable other code developers to avoid similar problems. Section 12.3 presents the autotasking method used and describes the resulting autotasked version of X3D. Four-processor TALLY results, showing points at which processors were waiting are presented. Results for the multitasked POLLY code and the autotasked X3D code are presented in Section 12.4. The work on these two codes has been an interesting learning experience and the lessons learned, as well as code design recommendations, are given in Section 12.5.

12.2 Multitasking POLLY

POLLY was a large three-dimensional, time-dependent Free-Lagrangian hydrodynamics code that had a number of features not present in earlier codes that we had multitasked. The physics portion of the code, excluding the input generation, graphics, and control sections, was about 40,000 unique lines of code. In addition, the code made extensive use of the solid-state device (SSD). The number of words written to the SSD was not known *a priori* because of the time-dependent nature of the mesh. Dynamic memory management [7] was used in all levels of the code. In smaller codes multitasking can frequently be done by using temporary arrays, but POLLY was memory bound and also took a very large amount of time to execute; thus additional memory could not be used in the multitasking. The multitasking was done by dividing the mesh into NP sections, where NP is the number of available processors. Each task worked on identical coding, but on different data.

One of the most serious problems encountered in multitasking POLLY involved the code's use of pointers. Pointers were used in low-level subroutines in a dynamic manner; that is arrays were allocated and deallocated during each time step. In the original serial code, one large array was used in some cases and pointers into different parts of the array were used. In the multitasked version, this configuration created chaos. Separate pointers were needed for each task so that arrays would not overwrite each other. Separate pointers can be easily implemented in the Los Alamos Memory Management System(MMS) [7] since this system allows for both an array name and a partition name. The task name was used as the partition name.

12.3 Autotasking X3D

Because of the extreme amount of time that it took for POLLY to execute, the code was rewritten and renamed X3D. In X3D an effort was made to keep serial sections out of the core of the code. In addition, the current version of X3D does not use the SSD. Currently, X3D has 100,000 unique lines of code and 561 subroutines. A number of real code features and requirements exist that still limit the fraction of the code that can be run in parallel. These include the need to periodically check for user interaction from the terminal, periodic graphics and restart dumps, and normal output of the results.

In order to determine where the execution time is being spent in the serial code, and thus which routines should be autotasked first, timing studies were done using the TALLY utility [6]. Figure 12.1 shows a partial list of the TALLY results. This figure shows that the main hydrodynamics routine, HYDROM, uses 62.5 percent of the execution time and the subroutine that determines the time step for the next cycle, TIMSTP, uses 32.38 percent. Therefore about 95 percent of the time is spent in these two routines and if they were made entirely parallel, Amdahl's Law (Figure 12.2) shows that the speedup would be a maximum of 3.48 on 4 processors. It is significant that the next most heavily used routine is the vector square root at only 1.48 percent. Thus it is not practical to increase the percentage of parallelism much above 95 percent because after HYDROM and TIMSTP, none of the X3D subroutines use enough time to justify autotasking them.

Autotasking is done by using a number of constructs before the Fortran statements in the code. One advantage of autotasking is that these constructs are comment statements if the code is not run through a preprocessor. Comment statements are a great advantage in a code such as X3D, which is under continuous development. In the multitasking done on the POLLY code, it was necessary to restructure large parts of the code and therefore, it was not possible to keep up-to-date with the latest code versions. Figures 12.3-12.6 show the most important autotasking constructs used in X3D.

12.4 Results

The POLLY results for four processors during dedicated system time (DST) are shown in Figure 12.7 for the Noh test problem [8]. The mesh consisted of 48,400 mass points. Only 21 time-step cycles were run in DST because of the

```
            PARTIAL TALLY RESULTS


       ROUTINE      HITS      PERCENT

       UNPACKTP      535        0.31
       HYDROM     107513       62.50
       ICONV         176        0.10
       TIMSTP      55698       32.38
       ISAMAX        503        0.29
       %SQRT        2539        1.48
```

FIGURE 12.1
Partial list of TALLY results for the serial version of the X3D code.

large execution time required for POLLY. Amdahl's Law is also shown so that progress can be judged as greater portions of the code were multitasked. The speedups are for the physics portion of the code. Initialization and final dumping and cleanup are excluded because the execution time for these took so long that it overwhelms the results if it is included.

During the initial multitasking work at Los Alamos, problems occurred in virtually every aspect of the work. These problems were in the operating system, libraries, compiler, debugger and, of course, in the code itself. The change in the speedup, for a fixed fraction of parallel code, is shown in Figure 12.7 for two different versions of the operating system, Cray Time Sharing System (CTSS), and the same version of POLLY. This CTSS bug fix resulted in a significant increase in the speedup.

The first step in multitasking or autotasking is to change from a static code compilation to a stack—reentrant—based code. This change caused a number of problems because local variables no longer exist after exiting a subroutine in stack-based code. This is not the case in static code. These local variables had to be located and changed to global variables within a common statement where it was expected that they would be needed in succeeding timesteps. In one case a buffer was defined in a subroutine using a dimension statement and then used again in a later part of the code. The array no longer existed in the stack code.

Other problems occurred because only one channel exists within CTSS to the solid-state device. In the serial code the SSD was used in such a manner in the serial code that each processor had to use the device in the multitasked code. Thus a queue, at a low level in the code, existed and processors had to wait. Significant problems existed because of the use of dynamic memory management. It was necessary to carefully sort out the pointers local to each task and those global to all tasks.

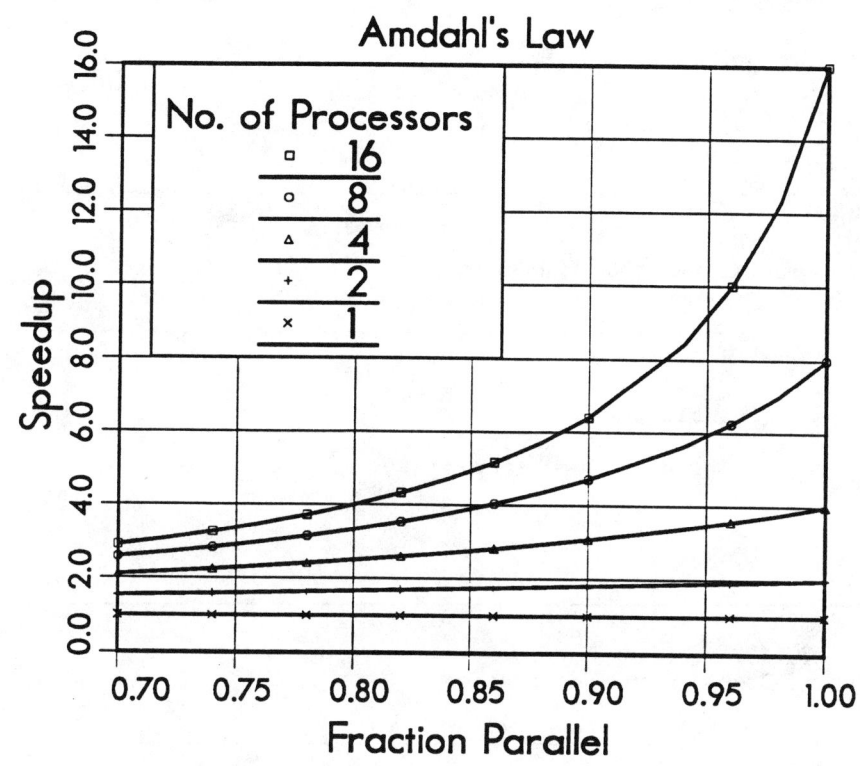

FIGURE 12.2
Amdahl's law.

```
CMLT$ MULTI

        subroutine hydrom
    *
    *
    *
```

FIGURE 12.3
Subroutine construct for autotasking.

```
CMLT$ DO MULTI
      do 1000 n=1,nblocks
         *
         *
         *
```

FIGURE 12.4
Nonvector DO loop construct for autotasking.

```
CMLT$ DO MULTI 64 2001

cdir$ shortloop
         do 2000 n=1,np(5)
            *
            *
            *
```

FIGURE 12.5
Vector DO loop construct for autotasking.

```
CMLT$ SEQ
   if (... ) ...
      *
      *
      *
CMLT$ END SEQ
      *
      *
      *
CMLT$ CRITICAL
      sum = sum + ...
      *
      *
      *
CMLT$ END CRITICAL
```

FIGURE 12.6
Sequential and critical section constructs for autotasking.

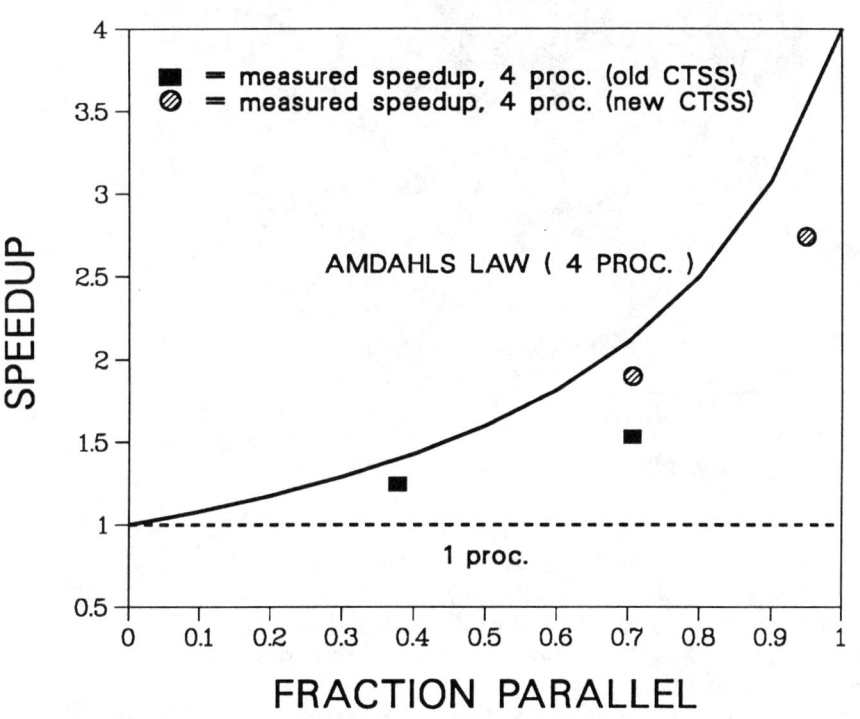

FIGURE 12.7
POLLY multitasking results.

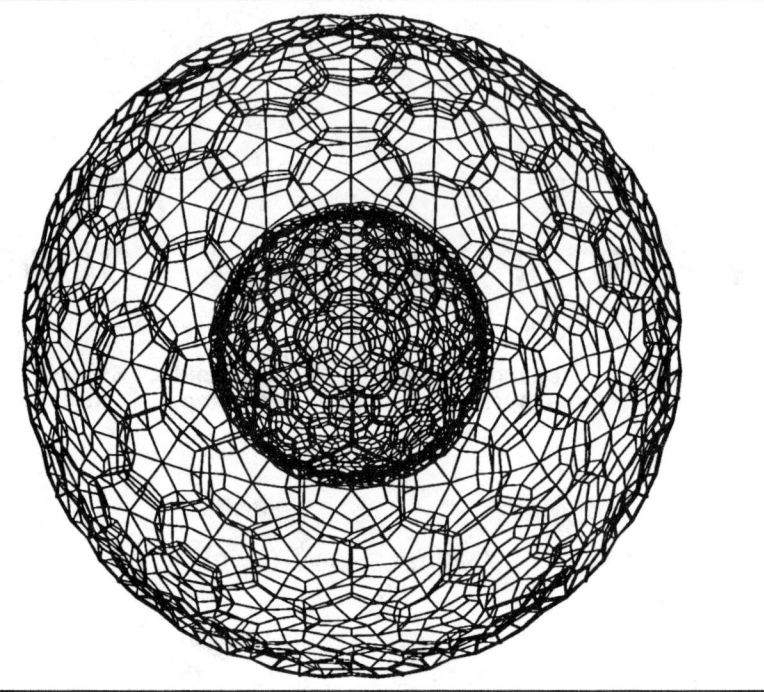

FIGURE 12.8
3-D spherical Noh problem—initial and final meshes.

Because of the above problems, numerous critical and sequential sections were necessary in the core of the physics portion of the code and the best speedup achieved was 2.82 on four processors—not an acceptable use of the resources on an X-MP/416. Because of the overall speed of POLLY, it was decided to rewrite the code.

The hydrodynamics core of X3D was designed with consideration given to autotasking the code, and thus it was much easier to autotask than POLLY. This was partially due to the fact that autotasking is inherently easier to implement than multitasking. In the case of autotasking, only 6643 mass points were defined because the SSD is not used. X3D runs fast enough that the entire Noh problem of 760 time cycles can be run during DST. The Noh problem consists of a sphere of ideal gas with an initial velocity of one inward. At time 0.6, Noh obtained an analytical solution. The density as a function of the radial position has a value of 64 and then tapers off at large radius. The initial and final meshes are shown in Figure 12.8 and the density as a function of radius is shown in Figure 12.9.

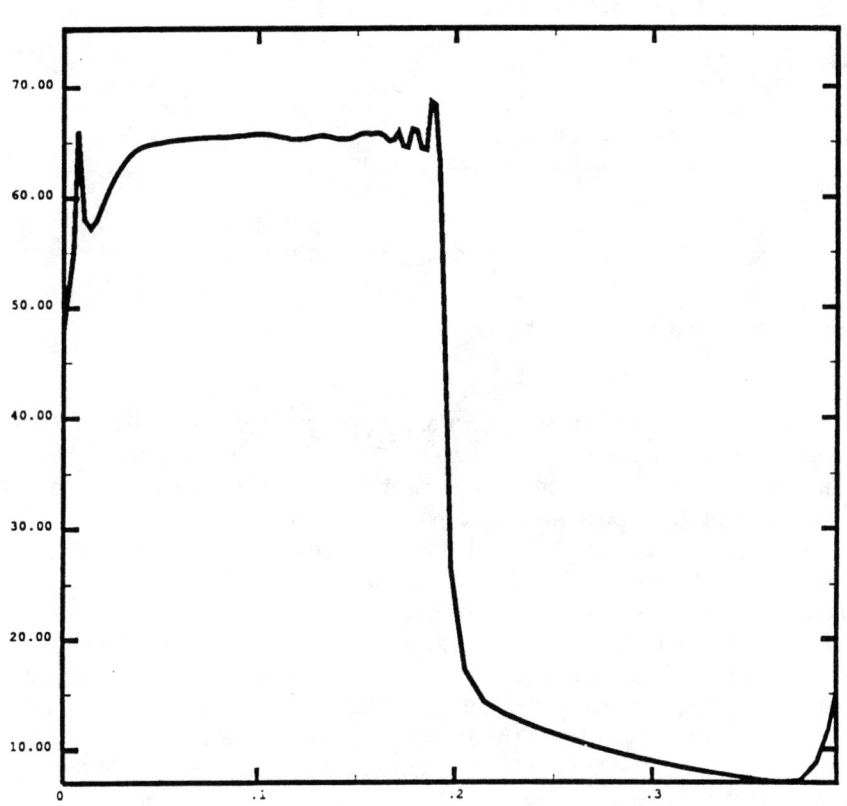

FIGURE 12.9
X3D density vs. position results for the 3-D Noh problem.

```
          PARTIAL TALLY RESULTS - 4 PROCESSORS

                % FOR EACH PROCESSOR
ROUTINE         0       1       2       3      TOTAL

MTHELP        0.00    3.46    3.48    3.47    10.41
UNPACKTP      0.16    0.04    0.03    0.00     0.23
HYDROM       12.35   12.71   12.67   12.70    50.43
AUTOTS%       0.03    0.03    0.04    0.02     0.11
AUTOFN%       0.00    0.01    0.00    0.00     0.02
AUTOLN%       0.00    0.00    0.01    0.01     0.02
TIMSTP        0.23    8.29    8.27    8.28    33.07
ISAMAX        0.03    0.03    0.03    0.02     0.11
HELOCVAL      0.07    0.00    0.00    0.00     0.08
%SQRT         0.23    0.18    0.20    0.22     0.83
```

FIGURE 12.10
Partial autotasking TALLY results.

TALLY results for four processors are shown in Figures 12.10-12.12. These results were obtained during DST because the multitasking version of TALLY is not valid for non-DST runs. These results show that a significant portion of the run time was spent with three processors waiting (10.41 percent in the MTHELP autotasking subroutine, Figure 12.10, and the waiting percentages in Figure 12.11). A more detailed timing analysis showed that most of the waiting time was in the timestep subroutine (Figure 12.12, W at statement 500B, which is the end of the DO 500 loop). Work was done to reduce the waiting time and the results are shown in Figure 12.13. The serial time, the autotasking time during DST for four processors, and the speedup are shown for three versions of X3D over a two-week period. The speedup remained almost constant at about 3, but significantly, the serial code speedup increased by 27 percent in the two-week period. A speedup of 3 was less than we were hoping for, but in terms of the total code execution time, the project has been very successful.

12.5 Lessons Learned and Recommendations

In this section we will discuss the lessons we have learned converting a code written for a serial machine, namely a CRAY 1, to a multitasked code for a CRAY X-MP/416 in the hopes that other computational physicists can avoid some of the problems we encountered. Code design recommendations are also given.

```
           PARTIAL TALLY RESULTS
           WAITS PER PROCESSOR

LOGICAL PROCESSOR    WAITS

CONNECTOR 0:          694    (  8.55%)
CONNECTOR 1:         2073    ( 25.54%)
CONNECTOR 2:         1973    ( 24.30%)
CONNECTOR 3:         2036    ( 25.08%)
```

FIGURE 12.11
Percent of time that each logicial processors was waiting.

```
         PARTIAL TALLY RESULTS - 4 PROCESSORS
                 SUBROUTINE TIMSTP

STMT NO.   ADDRS1     ADDRS2      0      1      2      3     TOTAL

           00304345   00304354   0.07   0.07   0.06   0.04   0.23
           00304355   00304364   0.04   0.03   0.05   0.02   0.14
500B W     00304365   00304374   0.65   0.83   0.71   0.80   3.00
           00304375   00304404   0.00   0.00   0.00   0.00   0.01
00019      00304405   00304414   0.00   0.01   0.00   0.00   0.01
           00304415   00304424   0.00   0.00   0.00   0.00   0.00
600B       00304425   00304434   0.00   0.00   0.00   0.00   0.00
```

FIGURE 12.12
X3D autotasking TALLY results for subroutine TIMSTP.

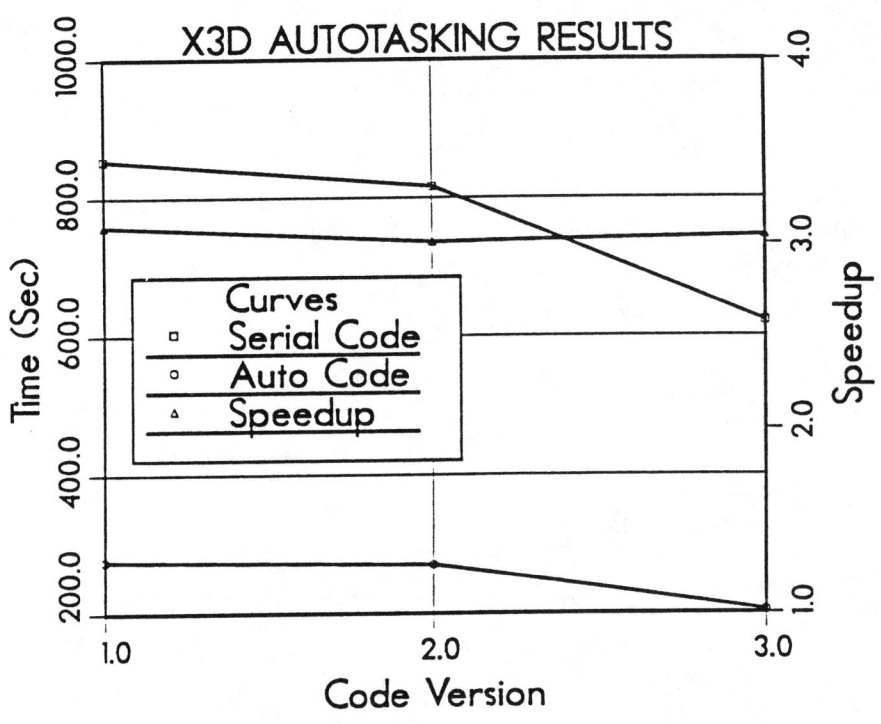

FIGURE 12.13
Speedup results for three versions of X3D.

12.5. Lessons Learned and Recommendations

As discussed above, the first step is to produce a correct serial, stack-based code. Variables that must be local have to be carefully distinguished from global variables. Dynamic memory management should be kept at the highest levels possible because memory adjustments are a serial process. If memory management must be done in multitasked parts of the code, pointers need to be defined for each task. In the Los Alamos Memory Management System, arrays can be separated into partitions so that the same array can be defined for each task and each task will have its own copy.

A desirable feature in future machines would be a separate channel to the SSD from each processor so that SSD requests will not have to enter a queue.

A problem that existed with the X3D code is that the code is under continuous development by a physics team, most of whose members have no multitasking or autotasking experience. This situation results in new code packages being added that are not optimum for subsequent autotasking. If a code is to be autotasked, then the entire code team needs to be throughly trained in the philosophy of parallel coding.

Better software tools are needed for parallel code development. Large code development requires a good dynamic debugger such as the Los Alamos Dynamic Debugging Tool (DDT) in which breakpoints can be set in all tasks, not just the root task. Better tools are needed to determine code hot-spot areas for both the serial and the parallel code. The ability to recognize and correct load balancing problems is essential. One of the hardest parts of converting serial codes to efficient parallel codes is differentiating between local and global variables. Efficient tools to do this are needed. For our codes, these tools must be able to handle pointers.

If resources are available, redesigning and rewriting the entire code is the best course of action in order to obtain an efficient parallel code. From Amdahl's Law it is clear that getting high efficiencies is extremely difficult with older codes. The serial sections must be reduced to an extremely small percentage, which is best done by redesigning the code.

References

1. H. E. Trease, Three-Dimensional Free Lagrangian Hydrodynamics in *Lecture Notes in Physics*, M. J. Fritts, W. P. Crowley and H. Trease, Eds., Springer-Verlag, New York, 1985.
2. E. Williams and F. Bobrowicz, Speedup Predictions for Large Scientific Parallel Programs on Cray X-MP-Like Architectures, *Proceedings of the 1985 International Conference on Parallel Processing*, St. Charles, Ill., (August 20-23, 1985).

3. F. Bobrowicz, Autotasking on Cray X-MP Supercomputers, in preparation.
4. G. M. Amdahl, Validity of the Single Processor Approach to Achieving Large Scale Computing Capabilities, *AFIPS Conference Proceedings*, Volume 30, 1967.
5. W. H. Ware, The Ultimate Computer, *IEEE Spectrum*, pp. 84-91, Volume 9, Number 3, 1972.
6. *TALLY*, Computer Documentation Group, Los Alamos National Laboratory Report CTSS-131, 1981.
7. W. H. Spangenberg and F. W. Bobrowicz, The Memory Management System for the Los Alamos Cray X-MP Environment, Los Alamos National Laboratory Report LA-UR-86-1254, 1986.
8. W. F. Noh, Artificial Viscosity(Q) and Artificial Heat Flux(H) Errors for Spherically Divergent Shocks, Lawrence Livermore National Laboratory Report UCRL-89623, 1983.

13

An Experience with the ANALYZER/SX Performance Tuning Tool

Koji Kinoshita

13.1 Introduction

In using supercomputers, it is ideal for users to bring out maximum performance without any effort. But, actually, hardware and software pose a lot of restrictions on executing programs with maximum performance. If no effort is made to tune programs, no benefits are obtained from supercomputers. Without an effort to tune programs, supercomputers become no more than large power eaters. Large power eaters should be required to work as hard as possible; otherwise, they become very wasteful. Therefore, a lot of effort to tune programs is necessary to make supercomputers work as effectively as possible.

13.2 Outline of the ANALYZER/SX

The ANALYZER/SX is provided by NEC Corporation as one of the tuning-support tools for the SX systems. It supports program tuning policy decisions by performing various kinds of static and dynamic analyses of programs.

In static analysis, information about various characteristics related to source program structure is provided. Such static characteristics are shown in Table 13.1.

In dynamic analysis, significant factors that determine performance are computed. Such dynamic characteristics are shown in Table 13.2. The data in Tables 13.1 and 13.2 can be used to measure the effect of vectorizing the program.

A program summary list is shown in Figure 13.1. The list represents the analysis results of the NASA KERNEL benchmark program.

The summary list gives very useful data for program tuning. It comprises information about the entire program execution and each subprogram execution. It shows the CPU time, the number of executed instructions, and the number of vector instructions executed; each is monitored by using the integrated hardware facilities without any performance degradation. It shows the average CPU time and vector operation ratio computed by software and based on information provided by hardware. It also provides the number of references by software to each subprogram.

The summary list tells which subprogram consumes a large amount of CPU time and which subprogram needs more vectorization. The costly subprogram can obtain good results through tuning. The subprogram with a low vector operation ratio might improve its vector operation ratio and shorten its CPU time by vectorization.

TABLE 13.1
Static Characteristics Analysis Function: Types of Static Analysis Lists

List name	Analyzing range	Contents of output
Cross-reference list	Each program unit	Cross-reference list on symbolic names and labels for each program unit
Program structure list	Entire program	Program configuration chart based on subprogram references
Program references list	Entire Program	Cross-reference list indicating program call relationships
Common block reference list	Entire program	Cross-reference list on common block elements and subprograms
Argument list	Entire program	Correspondence between dummy arguments and actual arguments

TABLE 13.2
Dynamic Characteristics Analysis Function: Types of Dynamic Analysis Lists

List name	Analyzing range	Contents of output
Summary list	Entire program	Overall program summary
		CPU time to execute whole program
		Total execution frequency of executable statements
		Frequency of references to each subprogram
		Execution frequency of executable statements in each subprogram
		CPU time of each subprogram
DO profile list	Program unit	Vectorizing information on DO loops subject to cost of each DO loop (the DO loops are sorted by cost in two groups: those vectorized and those not vectorized)
Source program list	Program unit	A source list with execution frequency and cost of each executable statement
Edit program list	Program unit	An edited list that presents the structure of a source program in an easy-to-view format with execution frequency and cost ratio of each executable statement

It is generally known that when the vectorizing ratio exceeds 90%, the performance is dramatically enhanced. If the most costly subprogram has been highly vectorized, the possibility of the improvement in terms of vectorization is small. However, if the vectorizing ratio of the most costly subprogram is low, the possibility of improving the performance of the program in terms of vectorization is great.

13.3 Example of Performance Analysis

If we examine the list of Figure 13.1 from the viewpoint of vectorization, we can see that the program is satisfactorily vectorized. The subprograms with low vector operation ratios such as NASKER, CPTIM, MXMTST, CHOTST, BTRTST, GMTTST, EMITST, and VPETST, do not consume much CPU time.

EXECUTION (CPU) TIME = 0 : 0 " 25 " 301 (25301 MSEC)
INSTRUCTION COUNT = 152899234
VECTOR OPERATION RATIO = 98.21%

PROGRAM	FREQUENCY	TIME (%)	AV.TIME	INSTR.	V.INSTR.	V.ELEMENT	V.OP.RATIO
NASKER	1	0(0.00)	0	2724	20	311	10.3
CPTIM	14	0(0.00)	0	2814	0	0	0.0
COPY	1420	152(0.60)	0	2371260	425120	108769200	98.2
MXMTST	1	20(0.08)	20	518986	0	0	0.0
MXM	100	489(1.93)	4	12889500	2880000	737280000	98.7
FFTTST	1	87(0.35)	87	1524886	384000	49152000	97.7
CFFTD1	201	12921(51.07)	64	9006563	2957887	757151936	99.2
CFFTD2	201	944(3.73)	4	19648963	6746687	863704448	98.5
CHOTST	1	51(9.20)	51	1341835	0	0	0.0
CHLSKY	200	629(2.49)	3	19996800	2699200	677499200	97.5
BTRTST	1	106(0.42)	106	2624008	0	0	0.0
BTRIX	600	2139(8.45)	3	41304000	25482600	713512800	97.8
GMTTST	1	0(0.00)	0	11110	2	10	0.1
GMTRY	2	801(3.17)	400	14173522	3300100	527681460	98.0
EMITST	1	69(0.28)	69	1944828	10	1000	0.1
EMIT	10	652(2.58)	65	16045470	1958660	484103100	97.2
VPETST	1	68(0.27)	68	1608765	0	0	0.0
VPENTA	400	6166(24.37)	15	7883200	4812000	615936000	99.5

FIGURE 13.1
Program summary list.

Figure 13.2 shows the effect of vectorization. The graph in Figure 13.2 represents the comparison of CPU time before vectorizing and after vectorizing. The performance of many subprograms is dramatically enhanced. The most improved subprogram, GMTRY, runs approximately 70 times faster than before vectorization. The entire program runs approximately 25 times faster than before vectorizing. However, some subprograms are not improved sufficiently. CFFTD1 runs only 1.7 times faster in spite of its high vector operation ratio of 99.2%.

The graph in Figure 13.2 does not imply that vectorization does not contribute to the performance improvement. The source program of CFFTD1 was thoroughly investigated to ascertain why CFFTD1's performance was not satisfactorily enhanced. As the result of the investigation it became apparent that some vector data were accessed with a power of 2 stride. Therefore, during the fetching of vector data from main memory to vector registers, memory bank conflicts occurred many times.

To avoid memory bank conflicts, the source program was revised. The array size of the variable in the most costly loop was modified from 128 to 129 because the main memory was constructed with 512 banks.

BTRIX and VPENTA were also investigated in the same way because they were not improved satisfactorily. The summary list in Figure 13.1 shows that the reason for the low enhancement in BTRIX is that vector lengths are small.

The reason for the low enhancement in VPENTA is memory bank conflicts.

Figure 13.3 shows the result of tuned program execution. As shown by a comparison with Figure 13.1, the subprogram CFFTD1 runs approximately 13 times faster than it did before tuning. Also, the whole program runs three times faster than before tuning. From Figure 13.4, the effect of tuning is easily appreciated.

13.4 Problem

As described in Section 13.3, some programs are not optimized by vectorizing alone, although vectorizing is an effective tuning technique. Some programs do not run according to expected performance because of factors other than vectorization. To tune programs effectively, tuning support tools must detect all the factors that prevent high performance.

One of the factors to be detected is memory bank conflict. It is caused by a power of 2 vector stride when the number of memory banks is a power of 2, as described in Section 13.3. In addition, other factors exist. These factors are, for example, busy registers and operational units, instruction issue restrictions and so on. They are known as the factors that prevent smooth instruction flow. These obstacles should be definitely recognized, and solved by vendors. Therefore, the

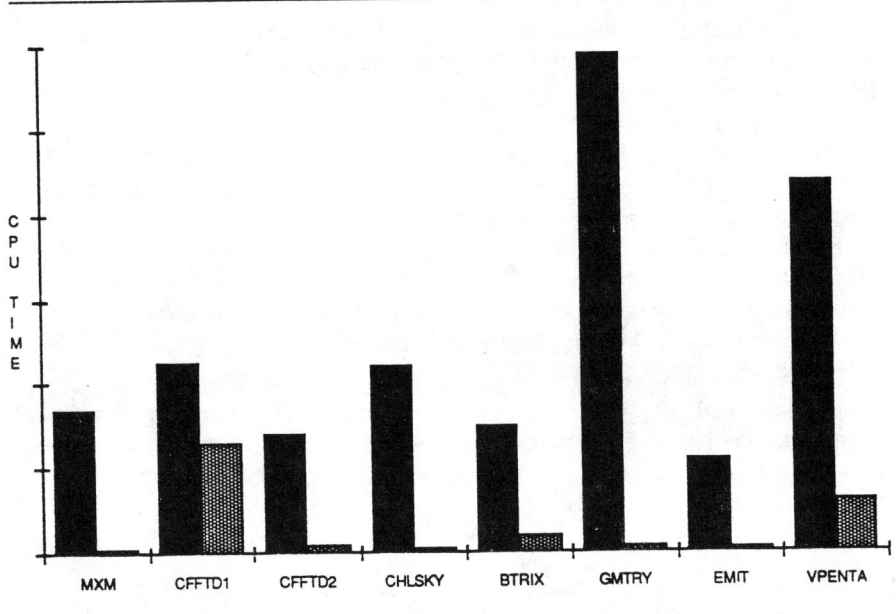

FIGURE 13.2
Effect of vectorizing.

13.4. Problem   229

EXECUTION (CPU) TIME		= 0:0" 7" 467 (7467 MSEC)					
INSTRUCTION COUNT		= 14918704					
VECTOR OPERATION RATIO		= 98.40%					

PROGRAM	FREQUENCY	TIME (%)	AV.TIME	INSTR.	V.INSTR.	V.ELEMENT	V.OP.RATIO
NASKER	1	0(0.00)	0	2724	20	311	10.3
CPTIM	14	0(0.00)	0	2814	0	0	0.0
COPY	1420	160(2.15)	0	2459260	442720	113192806	98.2
MXMTST	1	20(0.28)	20	519086	0	0	0.0
MXM	100	486(6.52)	4	12889500	2880000	737280000	98.7
FFTTST	1	85(1.15)	85	1524886	384000	49152000	97.7
CFFTD1	201	857(11.48)	4	9006563	2957887	757151936	99.2
CFFTD2	201	945(12.66)	4	19648963	6746687	863704448	98.5
CHOTST	1	51(0.69)	51	1342235	0	0	0.0
CHLSKY	200	629(8.43)	3	19996600	2669200	677499200	97.5
BTRTST	1	106(1.43)	106	2624008	0	0	0.0
BTRIX	600	2139(28.65)	3	41304000	25482600	713512800	97.8
GMTTST	1	0(0.01)	0	11110	2	10	0.1
GMTRY	2	801(10.73)	400	14173522	3300100	527681460	98.0
EMITST	1	69(0.93)	69	1944828	10	1000	0.1
EMIT	10	431(5.78)	43	4976640	1995760	490340600	99.4
VPETST	1	68(0.91)	68	1608765	0	0	0.0
VPENTA	400	613(8.21)	1	7883200	4812000	615936000	99.5

FIGURE 13.3
Result of tuning.

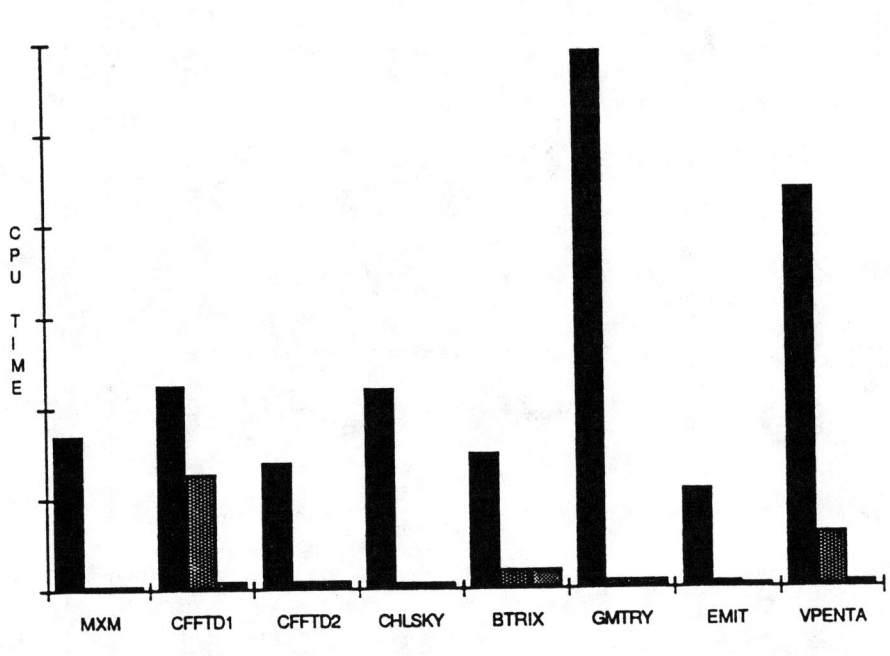

FIGURE 13.4
Effect of tuning.

factor that prevents smooth execution should be recognized in order to create a sophisticated supercomputing environment.

Moreover, if parallel processing or multiprocessing is considered, other tuning support tools must be provided. First, interprocessor blocking to shared memory must be detected. This blocking may cause serious performance degradation in some processors; CPU times may vary depending upon the processor, hour, and situation of the system, even in the same program. These variations bother many users. Therefore, a tool to measure how long the access to shared memory is blocked by other processors is necessary.

Next, interprocessor communication overhead is important. To synchronize processors or tasks, some amount of overhead cannot be helped. However, the overhead time should be minimized. A tool that measures this overhead time is very helpful in handling synchronization well.

13.5 Conclusion

NEC considers many other factors may reduce performance in parallel or multiprocessing environments. Therefore, NEC will continue to study what is needed, and to provide sophisticated tuning support tools to customers.

14

Common Memory Working Group Summary

Patricia J. Teller

14.1 Introduction

The focus of the common memory group of the Workshop on Instrumentation for Future Parallel Computer Systems was to define ways to:

- measure and tune the performance of applications running on an existing or future common memory parallel computer system, and thus make the best use of available hardware, and
- study the performance of the hardware and software components of a computer system in order to identify performance bottlenecks due to the system, as well as those inherent in the applications themselves.

To accomplish these goals, it was agreed that a computer system must provide an integrated set of hardware and software tools that enable the collection and analysis of performance data and that function in a time-sharing environment. Today's computer systems do not provide sufficient performance tools and such information is essential to application programmers, architects, and system software specialists alike. For example, performance data are needed to ascertain whether there is a good algorithm/architecture fit, if an algorithm can be modified to make better use of a machine, if the operating system and run-time facilities can be improved, and if the hardware can be modified to provide better cost/performance attributes.

14.2 Algorithm and System Tuning

The characteristics of an algorithm and of a common memory parallel computer system can make the system unsuitable for the application. For example, the load offered to the interconnection network (be it a bus, cross-point, or multistage network) can have a critical affect on performance. The cost of communication between processors, the available synchronization primitives, or operating system overheads such as the cost of context switching and the creation and destruction of instruction streams might heavily penalize some applications. It may be possible, however, to improve performance by modifying the algorithm to change the granularity of tasks, improve cache hit-ratios, decrease the page fault rate, reduce memory and network contention, decrease the amount of synchronization, and/or reduce operating system overhead. Of course, the design of the system hardware and software constrains the extent to which an algorithm can be tuned in this way.

The performance of an algorithm can also be improved by reducing the overhead due to parallelism. The primary goal of parallelizing an application to run on a parallel computer system is to decrease its execution time. To speed up the execution as much as possible, the overhead due to parallelism must be made as small as possible, i.e. the algorithm must exploit as much of the parallelism available in the computer system as it can. This overhead includes costs due to communication, contention, and synchronization.

The instrumentation required for algorithm tuning is also valuable to both the architect and system software specialist. Depending upon the intended use of the data, events can be measured for the set of processors, processes, or jobs or for a particular processor, process, or job. With such instrumentation, resource management can be monitored, thus providing data that can be used to measure the effectiveness of certain allocation policies; for instance, page replacement policies can be evaluated and various scheduling policies can be studied, e.g. preemptive vs. nonpreemptive. The performance of busy-waiting vs. context-switching can be compared, and the frequency of context switches, the performance of synchronization mechanisms, and the contention at shared system data structures (e.g. the task queue) can be measured.

14.3 Debugging

Some of the performance data sought, especially that concerning concurrency as a function of time, have another very important use. The data can be used to facilitate the debugging of parallel programs. The subject of debugging was out of the scope of this workshop but it arose many times since it is an important concern of application programmers and since much of the instrumentation needed to monitor performance can also be used to support debugging techniques.

Tracing and event monitoring during program execution are the two general strategies used to collect information in both cases. Because parallel programs are often inherently nondeterministic, minimizing the "probe effect" is an important issue for debugging as well. Unless tracing or monitoring is enabled all of the time, probe effects can change a program's behavior so that the execution is modified and, thus results may be changed and bugs may either be altered or disappear, hindering the debugging process. As with performance monitoring, prerun, runtime, and postrun techniques are applicable.

14.4 Data Collection Tradeoffs

In any case, the tools should be easy to use, the feedback timely, and the reported results accurate, comprehensive, and easily understandable. The instrumentation required to accomplish these ends, however, is not free of charge—not in terms of memory requirements, performance degradation, or expense. And, it is not clear that all of these goals can be met, especially at a reasonable cost.

During job execution, events can be sampled or continually and cumulatively recorded. Data analysis can be minimal, incremental, or rigorous. The analytical results can be studied immediately, intermittently, at the end of the job, or much later. Runtime feedback comes with minimal analysis of sampled data, and, therefore, limited memory and cost requirements. With a larger memory allotment, incremental analysis and "on-the-fly" feedback can be provided. Rigorous, accurate analysis of comprehensive data requires off-line analysis of large amounts of data and is, therefore, more expensive and may often be infeasible because of the amount of memory required. In addition, it results in untimely feedback and distorts system behavior since large amounts of data must be written out to disk. Thus, we are led back to sampling which, in addition to facilitating timely feedback, can be done at a relatively low cost without distorting the system, and has small memory requirements. cost. However, sampling may provide poor performance indicators. Considering the tradeoffs, it is not clear which method is best, but it is obvious that the choice depends on the intended use of the data.

14.5 Instrumentation Techniques

Whether data are sampled or traced, the user should not have to examine the collected data; instead the data should be analyzed, summarized, and a visualization of the performance results presented to the user. Although difficult to achieve in some cases, it would be very helpful to correlate events to the source code.

The set of events to be monitored varies with the intended use of the data; the sophistication of the tools depends on the sophistication of the user, the nature of the parallelism employed (e.g. functional vs. data decomposition), and the data structures utilized. Some instrumentation, however, has general applications. Counters were thought to be necessary for measuring many different performance indicators, for example: number of instructions executed, number of floating-point instructions executed, number of loads and stores, number of requests to shared, private, global and local memories, subroutine entries and exits, cache and translation look-aside buffer (TLB) hit rates, page fault rates, network and memory contention, nature and frequency of I/O, and processing element (PE), memory, and network utilization. In addition, since it was deemed important to be able to count the number of references to a certain memory region and to trap when a specific address is referenced, comparators are needed as well. There also was interest in the idea of being able to count the number of occurrences of a user-specified instruction type. The user is able to "color" instructions, i.e. given n counters, the user can choose n instruction types to "color" or tag. Instrumentation then is provided to recognize these instruction types (comparators) and record their occurrence (counters).

In order to tune the system to reduce the overhead of parallelism, data must be available to determine the achieved degree of parallelism and to be used as an aid in explaining how to capture whatever parallelism is being wasted. A concurrency history can provide some of these data by profiling the execution time spent by each processor (both in supervisor and user modes) at synchronization points, serial sections of code, and parallel sections of code, and by measuring critical region contention, task distribution, communications vs. computation cost, the frequency and nature of I/O, attained speedup, efficiency, and overhead due to parallelism. Processor, network, and memory utilization figures can be helpful, as can measurements of network and memory contention, task genealogies, and intertask dependency graphs. As mentioned above, profiling of this type can be displayed before, after, or during program execution.

It was generally agreed that performance analysis of a system or an executing program requires the system to have a high-resolution clock at each processor, as well as a global, system-wide clock, with little or no variance among the clocks at the processors. It does not appear that commercially available systems supply this although it does seem attainable, even on highly parallel systems. The latency of global clock accesses increases with the size of the system, but the variance between processor clocks can be kept extremely small. An inferior alternative to this would be a software clock that could be accessed via a system call or a timestamping mechanism implemented by the atomic update of a word in shared memory. Related to the topic of time, was the desire to be able to have all processors "stop on a dime." A compromise was reached: it would be satisfactory that instrumentation be provided to make the processors stop as promptly as possible, given hardware and operating system constraints—the smaller the "dime," the better.

Both of these issues, "time" and "stopping on a dime," are examples of instrumentation that range in cost and complexity from one parallel system to another. As a system becomes more parallel, instrumentation for monitoring certain events may become more complex and/or more expensive. Thus, the cost and complexity of instrumentation for parallel systems must be evaluated relative to the cost of the system. It should also be noted that systems with hundreds or thousands of processors and multistage interconnection networks pose their own additional unique problems.

14.6 Conclusions

Evaluating the performance of existing systems, both enables us to understand these systems and to tune algorithms to make better use of the available hardware. Using this information, deficiencies in hardware and software design can be identified and earmarked for improvement in future machine generations. Traditional measurements are certainly of value, for instance: operational rates (MIPS, MFLOPS), instruction mix, vector characterization, loads vs. stores, subroutine entries and exits, memory bank conflicts, and instruction execution delays. Instrumentation to collect such data is already in place on some systems of Cray, IBM, Amdahl, and NEC, for example. But with common memory parallel systems more instrumentation is essential.

Many questions remain to be answered. For example: Does the common memory parallel system facilitate instrumentation? Are dedicated processors necessary to analyze and/or collect data? How much data must be collected—do they grow linearly with the number of PEs? Can instrumentation be accomplished without introducing a probe effect? Can performance measures be correlated with source line numbers? In general, can the goals set forth be achieved?

15

Distributed Memory Working Group Summary

Daniel A. Reed[1]

> We need more LEDs! (laughter).
>
> *Distributed memory working group*

15.1 Introduction

High speed computer design continues to be driven by seemingly insatiable demands, in diverse application areas, for greater computing power. Given the clear and pressing need for greater computer system performance, there are several means of achieving this end. In the simplest approach, current computer architectures are reimplemented using faster device technologies. Although this approach will always be exploited, physical, technological, and economic limitations make it incapable of providing all the needed computational power.

---

[1] Supported in part by the National Science Foundation under grants NSF CCR86-57696, NSF CCR87-06653, and NSF ANTI TAPESTRY 1-5-30035, by the National Aeronautics and Space Administration under NASA Contract Number NAG-1-613, and by the Air Force Office of Scientific Research under grant AFOSR-F49620-86-C-0136 (URI).

Instead, *parallelism* must be exploited to obtain truly significant performance improvements.

In the spectrum of parallel processor designs, there are many demarcation points, based on the number and complexity of the processors. At one extreme there are simple, bit-serial processors. Although any one of these processors is of little value, when coupled with many others, the aggregate computing power can be large. At the other extreme, a small number of processors, built using the fastest available technology and most sophisticated architecture, can be combined. The third, intermediate approach combines a large number of microprocessors in either shared or distributed memory ensembles.

As proposed, the nodes of distributed memory systems, or *multicomputer networks*, would contain a processor with some locally addressable memory, a communication controller capable of routing messages without delaying the processor, and a small number of connections to other nodes. Because the nodes do not share memory, the cooperating tasks of a parallel algorithm must execute asynchronously on different nodes and communicate solely via message passing. Although the time to send a message has decreased substantially since the first prototypes of distributed memory systems were constructed [1], this time still is significantly longer than the time to reference a memory location. Thus, the communication latency for message passing bounds the frequency of task interaction in distributed memory systems.

As charged by the organizers of the workshop on *Instrumentation for Future Parallel Computer Systems*, the working group for distributed memory instrumentation considered tools and techniques for measuring the performance of distributed memory parallel systems. The discussion group included participants from the following sites:

Ametek Computer Research	ETA Systems
Intel Scientific Computers	Los Alamos National Laboratory
National Bureau of Standards	Oak Ridge National Laboratory
Sandia National Laboratories	University of Illinois

This report summarizes the author's impressions of the working group discussions based on a review of tapes made during the workshop. Although every attempt was made to remain faithful to the spirit of the discussions, *any errors or misrepresentations in the summary are mine*.

To put the discussions in perspective, §15.2 begins with a review of distributed memory systems, including proposed communication paradigms and commercial systems. In §15.3 we summarize the working group discussions. Finally, §15.4 offers some final comments and thoughts on the future of performance instrumentation for distributed memory systems.

15.2 Background

Although distributed memory parallel systems offer potentially enormous computational power at modest cost, like the appearance of any new computer system, they raise many design and performance issues. For example, how should the tasks of application programs be distributed across the network nodes? Or, what communication mechanisms should be used to transport messages through the network? Several transport mechanisms, including store-and-forward message switching, circuit switching, and worm-hole routing have been proposed. What hardware support is required to implement these transport mechanisms? To understand these issues and their importance to the workshop participants, we begin with a review of communication support and commercial distributed memory systems.

15.2.1 Communication Paradigms

In contrast to the design of first generation distributed memory systems, distinguished by *store-and-forward* communication networks, second generation systems have increased network performance using either *circuit-switched* networks or *worm-hole routing* networks. As Figure 15.1a shows, a store-and-forward network transfers the entire contents of a message from one node to the next before it is forwarded. The message is copied into the local memory of intermediate nodes. A worm-hole network [2,3] transfers pieces of a message as they arrive, Figure 15.1b, reducing the end-to-end latency. This network uses autonomous routing units with small, local buffers to store the message contents as they pass through intermediate nodes. This reduces communication latency by eliminating memory contention; furthermore, the routing units are special-purpose processors, and are able to route messages faster than the node processor. A circuit-switched network, Figure 15.1c, establishes a physical end-to-end connection before the data are transmitted. Both worm-hole and circuit-switched networks reduce memory contention — each message interacts only with the source and final node. This can improve both the message latency *and* the network bandwidth [4].

15.2.2 Network Topologies and Routing

All communication paradigms, regardless of their implementation, rely on a routing algorithm to select a path from the source to the destination node. Typically, these algorithms use *a priori* characteristics of the network topology to select a route. To date, the binary N-cube (or *hypercube*) [5] has been most common. As an example, Figure 15.2 shows the topology of the binary 4-cube.

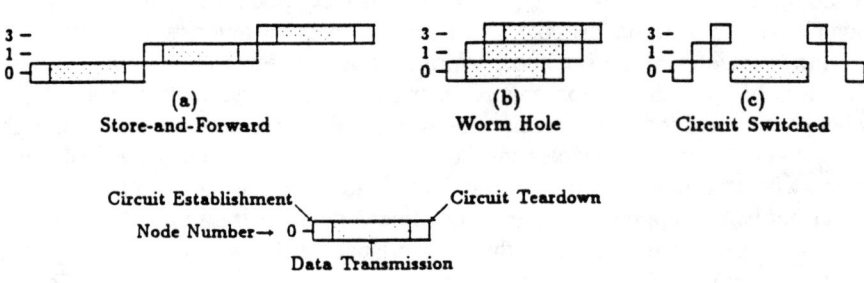

FIGURE 15.1
Components of message latency in different networks.

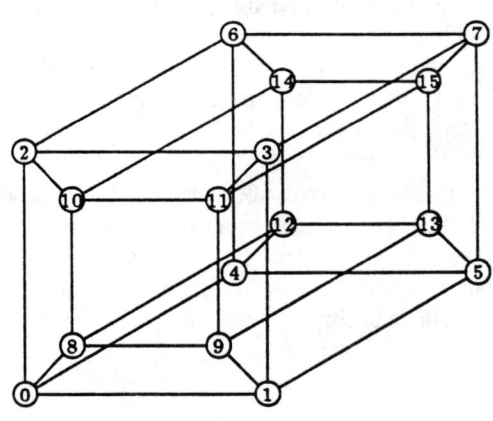

FIGURE 15.2
Topology of binary 4-cube.

The labels for adjacent nodes in a binary N-cube differ by a single digit in their binary representation. The transmission link between these two nodes is labeled with the position of the differing bit. For example, if the bit positions are numbered from zero, nodes two and ten in Figure 15.2 differ in bit position three. Thus, link number three on node two is connected to node ten, and link number three on node ten is connected to node two. Clearly, if two nodes are k hops apart, their node addresses differ in k bit positions; the links corresponding to those bit positions are the only links that will reduce the distance to the destination node. However, the links may be crossed in any order that resolves the bit differences.

Despite the many paths from a source node to a destination node, the "standard" **Ecube** routing algorithm[1] examines a single path based on the node numbers. At each routing step, **Ecube** routing considers only one of the links that will reduce the distance to the destination — the one corresponding to the leftmost bit in the difference between the source and destination node numbers.

Because the number of links connecting the nodes of a binary N-cube must increase with the dimension of the N-cube, some recent designs, notably the Ametek 2010 [8], have adopted a two-dimensional grid as the underlying network topology. Although the diameter of the two-dimensional grid is greater than that of the binary N-cube, the number of links connected to each node is fixed at four. Moreover, a worm-hole or circuit-switched communication network can mask the potentially greater communication latency due to the larger network diameter.

15.2.3 Distributed Memory Systems

Distributed memory systems have evolved rapidly, encompassing two product generations since their initial development. Although communication performance is the most significant difference between first and second generation systems, second generation systems also include more powerful processors and greater memory capacity. To understand these differences and their ramifications for performance instrumentation, we briefly review representative first and second generation systems.

Intel iPSC/1. Undoubtedly the Intel iPSC/1 hypercube [1] was the best known, first generation system. Each iPSC/1 node contained an Intel 80286 microprocessor, an Intel 80287 floating point co-processor, and 512K bytes of memory. All nodes were individually clocked. Store-and-forward internode communication was provided via eight Ethernet transceiver chips on each node. Up to seven of these transceivers connected the nodes in a binary N-cube, whence the maximum configuration of seven dimensions. The eighth transceiver connected the

---

[1] **Ecube** routing is used in the Intel iPSC/1 [1], Intel iPSC/2 [6], and Ncube/ten [7].

node to a global Ethernet, shared by all nodes and the system manager. Finally, each node contained a MULTIBUS iLBX connector to the processor bus. On the system backplane, the iLBX of each even numbered node is connected to the adjacent odd numbered node. By replacing the hypercube node boards in the odd numbered positions, hypercube variations containing additional memory or vector processors can be configured.[2]

Ncube/ten. Unlike other first generation, distributed memory systems that relied on standard microprocessors, augmented with communication support hardware, the Ncube/ten [7] contained a single-chip processor designed expressly for a distributed memory environment. Taking node design to its logical limit, each node consisted of a single processor chip and six memory chips. This compactness permitted construction of systems with up to ten dimensions: 1024 nodes on 16 boards of 64 nodes each.

Each Ncube processor contained on-chip support for IEEE standard floating-point operations and store-and-forward internode communication. The processor instruction set was augmented to support communication (e.g., there were load pointer and load counter instructions to initiate internode data transfer). The processor communication hardware included 22 bit-serial lines for communication with other nodes via asynchronous DMA transfer. These lines were paired as 11 bi-directional channels, potentially forming a ten-dimensional hypercube with one additional connection to an input-output device.

Intel iPSC/2. The second generation Intel IPSC/2 hypercube [6] incorporates evolutionary advances in technology, including an Intel 80386/80387 microprocessor pair, a 64K byte cache, and up to 16M bytes of memory on each node. As with the iPSC/1, vector processors can be added via iLBX connectors, and the maximum dimension of the N-cube is 7.

The primary difference between the iPSC/1 and iPSC/2 is the internode communication system; the iPSC/2 includes custom components to support fixed path, circuit-switched communication between nodes. This communication system eliminates most of the store-and-forward latency that existed in the iPSC/1.

Ametek 2010. The Ametek 2010 [8], containing up to 1024 nodes, includes a Motorola 68020 microprocessor, the 68881 or 68882 floating point co-processor, up to 8M bytes of memory, and a VME interface for peripheral connections, including a vector co-processor. Like the Intel iPSC/2, the Ametek 2010 contains custom components to support internode communication, although both the network topology and the communication paradigm differ from the iPSC/2. The

---

[2]This mechanism can also be used to support performance instrumentation; see §15.3.1.

2010 is based on a two-dimensional mesh and uses fixed-path, worm-hole routing. Like the iPSC/2's circuit-switched network, the 2010's worm-hole network eliminates most of the store-and-forward latency present in earlier machines.

15.3 Workshop Discussions

Because the workshop participants were drawn from distributed memory system developers, users, and researchers, the range of possible topics was very broad, and much of the discussion was only peripherally germane to performance instrumentation. Thus, this summary includes only those issues relevant to performance instrumentation:

- application software experiences,
- instrumentation scenarios and costs, and
- instrumentation mechanisms.

Although I have attempted retain to the spirit of the discussions, for clarity's sake, I have integrated and reordered comments made during several meetings. Any resulting errors or misrepresentations are my own, not those of the participants.

15.3.1 Application Software Experiences

Among the working group participants, Gary Montry (Sandia) was most experienced in developing and tuning application programs for distributed memory systems.[3] Based on his experiences debugging and tuning the performance of numerical applications for a 1024-node Ncube/ten, Montry offered the following observations.

- Most code development and testing is done on a small, 4 node system; performance analysis and application tuning began on the large system only after program correctness had been established on the small system.
- The most useful post-mortem performance information was the amount of time spent in message transmission routines and the computation time for each node.
- Because he lacked access to the Ncube/ten node operating system source code, he could not determine either the times that messages departed each node or the distribution of message buffer utilization in each node. The

---

[3]His work, with Gustafson and Brenner [9], recently received the Bell prize for best speedup on a parallel system.

two are interrelated; the Ncube/ten uses store-and-forward message passing, buffering messages in intermediate nodes. Messages in transit through a node can delay transmissions initiated at that node. If the system is operating in single user mode (i.e., only one application program), the application performance can be tuned to reduce message collisions at nodes and to overlap computation with requests for messages.

- The importance of instrumentation and tools will increase with greater user understanding and sophistication. As distributed memory systems become better understood, performance analysts will require better tools to investigate more complex interactions. In contrast, Montry noted that the radio frequency emissions of the Ncube/ten were once used, via a portable radio, for debugging and performance tuning!

15.3.2 Instrumentation Scenarios and Costs

During discussions, a consensus quickly emerged that there were several reasons for performance evaluation and instrumentation, notably

- system hardware and software design,
- purchase evaluation,
- application tuning, and
- administrative oversight,

and that the instrumentation detail and requisite performance analysis differ significantly for each of these. Reflecting the interests of the working group, subsequent discussions centered on system design and application tuning.

Instrumentation for system design depends critically on the intended system uses — consider two instrumentation scenarios. In the first, applications are developed on a "single user" distributed memory system that contains a minimalist operating system (e.g., Vertex on the Ncube/ten[4]). The second is a multiprogrammed system that supports distributed virtual memory [10], dynamic load balancing [1], and heterogeneous I/O devices.

In the first scenario, post-mortem performance summaries, based on software instrumentation of application code, and periodic capture and display of selected resource allocation states (e.g., message buffer utilizations), suffice to identify bottlenecks and tune performance. Why? All performance data can be related directly to the application program; no external factors can perturb performance. For the second scenario, virtual memory statistics, processor utilizations, communication latencies, and I/O rates must be monitored in real-time to provide adaptive control. The acquisition of high volume, time-dependent performance

---

[4] Vertex occupies only 5K bytes in each node.

data suggests hardware support to minimize the performance perturbation for instrumentation and data capture. Not surprisingly, the instrumentation costs for these two scenarios are strikingly different. More importantly, the acceptable cost depends on the environment.

Paul Pierce (Intel Scientific Computers) observed that the demand for performance instrumentation and its associated support was greatest among researchers, not production users. For the researcher, performance analysis and experimentation are intellectual exercises. Detailed performance instrumentation is necessary to completely characterize system behavior, and high costs, by both monetary and performance measures, are often acceptable. For the production user, instrumentation is valuable if it permits performance tuning, but not if it reduces performance or greatly increases the system purchase price.

The participant from ETA Systems observed that, at ETA, less than one percent of system cost was related to performance instrumentation and that it was not possible to force system redesigns to accommodate performance instrumentation. In response, Pierce noted that one percent of a large ETA system was significant, but one percent of most distributed memory systems was very little instrumentation. Pierce also explained that Intel was unable to include a wide counter in each node of the iPSC/2 — the cost in extra chips was too high. James Ramsey (Ametek Computer Research) noted that including instrumentation in hardware system designs can perturb the designs and their expected performance, particularly if the hardware has been optimized for performance.

In other discussions, Reed (Illinois) and Montry (Sandia) were asked what increase in latency would be acceptable if the communication software were instrumented to record message transmissions. Both responded that, if communication latency were 300 microseconds, 50 microseconds was an acceptable penalty for instrumentation.

Finally, Montry (Sandia) suggested that the hardware routing (i.e., circuit-switching in the iPSC/2 and worm-hole routing in the Ametek 2010) in second generation, distributed memory systems makes performance analysis more difficult. Because routing is now managed in hardware, it is no longer possible to instrument the store-and-forward routing software to determine the pattern of message transmission conflicts and their associated delays. Hardware improvements have eliminated instrumentation points.

15.3.3 Hardware Instrumentation Mechanisms

All participants agreed that hardware support for performance data capture was crucial, and several principles quickly emerged.

- A trace of events, ordered and time-stamped via a *global clock*, is needed to understand system dynamics.

- It should be possible to add events to the trace by writing to a "magic" memory location; no system software calls should be necessary.
- Event data transmission and storage costs are significant.
- Storage for event traces should not be accessible by application programs, otherwise it will be used by application program developers.

During the discussions, Paul Close and Paul Pierce (Intel Scientific Computers) and Robert Carpenter (National Bureau of Standards) described two hardware mechanisms to realize these goals; see [11] for a survey of instrumentation approaches. Both mechanisms require software support to generate events; they differ primarily in their approaches to event time-stamping and storage.

National Bureau of Standards. Carpenter's design currently is being implemented for an Intel iPSC/1.[5] As discussed in §15.2.3.1, each node of the iPSC/1 contains a Multibus iLBX connector; Intel uses this connector to support vector co-processors and expanded memory. In Carpenter's design, the iLBX physically connects the node to a 512K byte memory that is logically accessible by writing to a "magic" memory location in the 80286 microprocessor's I/O address space. Each write to the magic memory location records event data and a 40-bit clock value in the 512K byte event memory.[6] Each node writes to a separate event memory (i.e., a 512K byte event memory exists for each node), and the clocks of all event memories are synchronized. Finally, all event memories are connected via a global interrupt; one processor can force all other processors to record their current state.

Because the data bandwidth to the iPSC/1 system manager is limited, the event memory is dual ported — after the performance experiment completes, the nodes can read the event data and compute performance statistics in parallel.

Intel. The approach described by Close and Pierce relies on an external clock and collection of performance events at a central site.[7] The backplane of the Intel iPSC/2 has been extended to provide 4-5 data bits from each node at a single interface. Just as in the National Bureau of Standards design, these bits are logically accessible on each node by writing to a "magic" memory location. Events whose data are longer than 5 bits require multiple writes, or the additional data must be recorded in the nodes.

A hardware monitor connected to the event data interface can time stamp and record the events. Because the events are collected at a single location, a

---

[5] However, the techniques also are applicable to the iPSC/2 and Ametek 2010.

[6] This is an additional 512K byte memory for each node. It is *not* the 512K byte node memory.

[7] In collaboration with Intel, an implementation of this approach is in progress at the University of Illinois.

single clock suffices to provide a global time stamp. The data width (4-5 bits) is a compromise of complexity and utility. A wider data width would increase the maximum event data rate but add greatly to backplane complexity and cost.

15.4 Conclusions

Despite the breadth of topics and diversity of instrumentation goals, the members of the distributed memory instrumentation group found themselves in agreement in many areas. First, better software tools are needed to capture static performance summaries (e.g., application execution profiles and counts of system calls) and dynamic performance (e.g., time varying message buffer utilizations). Second, hardware support is needed for capturing event traces *with global time-stamps*. Third, the acceptable complexity and cost of performance instrumentation depends on the intended use; different groups will "pay" more for instrumentation than others.

Acknowledgments

The workshop organizers at Los Alamos graciously provided both tapes and transcripts of the discussions. Without their help, the preparation of this summary would not have been possible. At Illinois, Dirk Grunwald provided invaluable editorial assistance.

References

1. D. A. Reed and R. M. Fujimoto, *Multicomputer Networks: Message-Based Parallel Processing*, The MIT Press, 1987.
2. W. J. Dally and C. L. Seitz, The Torus Routing Chip, *Journal of Distributed Computing* 1, 3 (1986).
3. W. J. Dally and C. L. Seitz, , Deadlock-Free Message Routing in Multiprocessor Interconnection Networks, *IEEE Transactions on Computers* C–36, 5 (May 1987), pp. 547–553.
4. D. C. Grunwald and D. A. Reed, Networks for Parallel Processors: Measurements and Prognostications, in *Proceedings of the Third Conference on Hypercube Concurrent Computers and Applications, Volume I*, (Pasadena, CA, January 1988), Association For Computing Machinery, pp. 610–619.
5. Y. Saad and M. H. Schultz, Topological Properties of Hypercubes, *IEEE Transactions on Computers* C–37, 7 (July 1988), pp. 867–872.

6. R. Arlauskas, iPSC/2 System: A Second Generation Hypercube, in *Proceedings of the Third Conference on Hypercube Concurrent Computers and Applications, Volume I*, (Pasadena,CA, January 1988), Association For Computing Machinery, pp. 38–42.

7. J. P. Hayes, T. Mudge, Q. F. Stout, S. Colley and J. A. Palmer, A Microprocessor-Based Hypercube Supercomputer, *IEEE Micro* 6, 5 (October 1986), pp. 6–17.

8. C. L. Seitz, W. C. Athas, C. M. Flaig, A. J. Martin, J. Seizovic, C. S. Steele and W.-K. Su, The Architecture and Programming of the Ametek Series 2010 Multicomputer, in *Proceedings of the Third Conference on Hypercube Concurrent Computers and Applications, Volume I*, (Pasadena, CA, January 1988), Association For Computing Machinery, pp. 33–36.

9. J. L. Gustafson, G. R. Montry and R. E. Benner, Development of Parallel Methods for a 1024-Processor Hypercube, *SIAM Journal on Scientific and Statistical Computing* 9, 4 (July 1988), pp. 609–638.

10. K. Li and P. Hudak, Memory Coherence in Shared Virtual Memory Systems, in *Proceedings of the Fifth ACM Symposium on Principles of Distributed Computing*, (August 1986), Association For Computing Machinery, pp. 229–239.

11. R. J. Carpenter, Performance Measurement Instrumentation for Multiprocessor Systems, in *High Performance Computer Systems*, North-Holland, 1987, pp. 81–92.

16

Dataflow Working Group Summary

James R. McGraw[1]

16.1 Introduction

This paper summarizes approximately four hours of discussion held at the Workshop on Instrumentation for Future Parallel Computing Systems. The general topic of the discussion centered on performance evaluation techniques and measurement tools appropriate for dataflow computers. Key contributors to this discussion included: Wim Bohm (University of Manchester), Kei Hiraki (Electrotechnical Laboratory), Bob Hiromoto (Los Alamos National Laboratory-LANL), David Jefferson (UCLA), Olaf Lubeck (LANL), Karl Ottenstein (LANL), Greg Papadopoulos (MIT), Margaret Simmons (LANL), and myself. In this paper, I have tried to extract as much of the discussion as possible and organize it in a form that is clearer for readers to follow.

The paper contains four major sections. The first section gives some very brief background information on dataflow computing to provide a framework for the topics that follow. The second section examines several major implications of the dataflow architecture approach on the issue of performance measurement and evaluation. The third section identifies the primary measurement objectives the

---

[1] This work was supported in part by the Applied Mathematical Sciences subprogram of the Office of Energy Research, U.S. Department of Energy and by Lawrence Livermore National Laboratory under contract W-7405-Eng-48.

discussion group listed as being important to study. The fourth section presents tools the group highlighted as possible techniques for getting to the important measurements.

16.2 Background

Most of the discussion centered on dataflow machines in the style of Arvind's machine [1] and the Manchester Dataflow machine [2]. In these machines, high-level language programs are translated into dataflow graphs. In these graphs, each node represents a functional operation and each arc represents the transmission of a result from the producing operation to the consuming operation. In this scheme, each node can be viewed as an independent entity that is scheduled for execution at run-time as soon as all of its inputs are available. The results of the program's execution are assured of being determinate (independent of the specific node execution pattern of any one run) so long as two conditions are met: (1) all of the nodes are functional, and (2) the order of node execution obeys the partial ordering specified by the graph. In these machines each node has at most two inputs (to simplify the identification of nodes ready for execution), but it can have an arbitrary number of outputs.

For purposes of discussion here, I will use a very simple dataflow machine model shown in Figure 16.1. This machine contains a large number of processing elements (PEs) connected by some routing network. Also attached to the routing network is a special box called a structure store. Each processing element has five primary components. The switch manages the routing of tokens (data values that travel along graph arcs) to and from each processing element. The token queue buffers the arrival of these tokens from the Arithmetic Logical Units (ALUs) and other PEs. The matching store holds tokens that have arrived for a graph node but must wait for their input partner prior to the node's execution. Once matching tokens are found, they pick up information about the nature of the operation and the destination locations of results in the instruction store. (It is the instruction store that holds a program's dataflow graph.) The node is then executed in any one of a number of ALUs within the ALU box and the results are sent to the appropriate PEs. The structure store is a special device (which can actually be distributed and interleaved) for holding large data objects such as arrays. It creates objects, stores values in them, replies to requests about current values, and manages the allocation and deallocation of space. All of the operations on these objects must be functional to retain the dataflow execution paradigm.

Dataflow machines can handle the dynamics of program execution (e.g., two parallel calls to the same function graph with different parameters) in a variety of ways. For the dataflow model emphasized in the discussions, the most common approach is token labeling. Each function call generates a unique

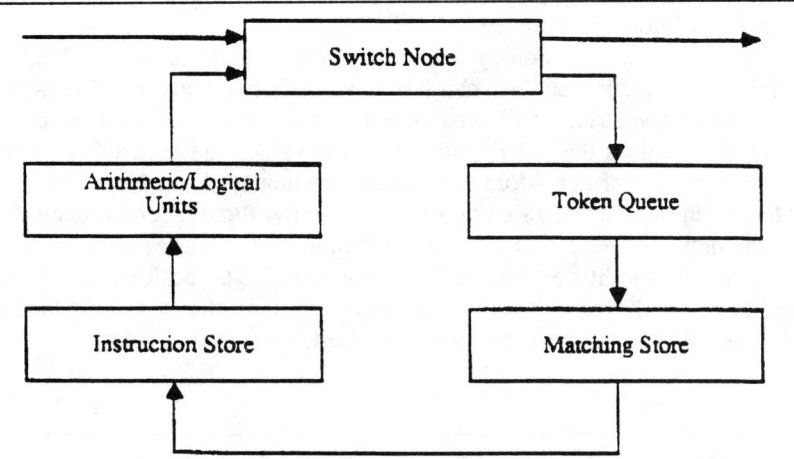

A. Basic Processing Element Structure

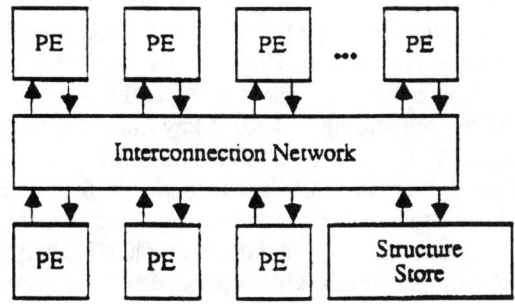

B. Overall Machine Structure

FIGURE 16.1
Simplified dataflow machine structure.

"label" attached to each of the input parameters of a specific call. Output data tokens from each function's operation then inherit the same label as their input tokens carried. In this way, separate data sets can simultaneously share the same static graph without interference.

One last bit of terminology needs to be defined before we can begin the discussions. Dataflow machines can have two different "flavors" of data structures: strict or non-strict. Strict data structures require the full data structure to have all of its values defined before any of the values can be read by an operation node. Nonstrict data structures permit reading of defined portions of the structure even though not all components are ready. From a concurrency standpoint, the nonstrict version obviously creates more possibilities for concurrency because the availability of data may be recognized. The positive side to strict structures is that they may be easier to implement in machines. (At the language level, nonstrict and strict structures carry additional pros and cons.)

16.3 Implications of Dataflow Approach for Measurement

Before jumping into the issue of what kinds of measurements and performance evaluation techniques seem reasonable for dataflow systems, I want to highlight some of the important discussions our group went through regarding the implications this approach has for the problem in general. Hardware scheduling of operations for execution and the lack of reliance on any timing of individual tokens complicates measurement. They force a heavier emphasis on algorithm selection and also on options for partitioning and mapping. Also, the relatively chaotic nature of the scheduling and some key limited resources create potential deadlock problems. This section elaborates on these issues in a bit more detail.

As described earlier, the PE's are responsible for determining when each operation can be scheduled for execution. Furthermore, this decision is made independently for each node in a dataflow graph. The only sequencing control imposed by the program graph is data dependency. If node B depends on the result from node A, then we know that B will execute at some unspecified time after A. Hence, if there are huge amounts of concurrency in a graph (something we desire), the actual order of execution could vary dramatically from one run to the next. Since the order of execution influences almost every performance measurement we could possibly make, that creates some serious "uncertainty" elements into every measure we make. In a very real sense, the same mechanism we hope will allow high system utilization (hardware scheduling of operations) is exactly the same mechanism that may make it harder to take measurements. In our discussions, the conjecture (or maybe it is a hope) is that the actual variances we will see in most cases will be relatively minor ($\sim 10\%$).

An extreme case of this problem deserves special discussion. The variation in order of execution could be sufficiently severe to create program deadlock due to limited availability of resources. As an example, consider many different parallel functions that each need large amounts of temporary array storage to produce their final results. By all starting at nearly the same time, each function may only get part of its space needs met before storage runs out. It is too early to determine how difficult this problem will be for real programs, but one conjecture advanced is that non-strict data structures are likely to make matters worse. The increased amount of parallelism caused by relaxed forms of data synchronization seem to naturally require larger amounts of storage. Hence, we note it as a serious problem worthy of attention.

Likewise, timing measurements within this type of system can be a problem, particularly if they try to use the normal token transmission system. In the dataflow model we hope there will be so many different operations available for execution, that the delayed arrival of any one particular token will be inconsequential. The system has no guaranteed arrival time for any token. Therefore, if you have any timing operators in the system sending times via normal token traffic, they can be rough approximations at best. The only timing data that can be absolutely accurate would be timing information that is not triggered by specific token input. For example, the structure store could output data that showed its storage occupancy level for any specific point in time. However, if that datum value is transmitted to some function in the program, then the timing on its arrival may be arbitrarily later.

Given these constraints, the two primary tools remaining under user and compiler control are algorithm selection and partitioning/mapping. For purposes of our discussion, we assumed that all of our measurement and analysis efforts were with respect to a specific algorithm selection by the programmer. We believe this is the only reasonable assumption, but it is important to recognize that the choice of algorithm is critical to the rest of the process. Partitioning and mapping are critical because these activities determine (at compile time) where each node of a graph will execute at run-time. A dataflow graph can be spread across a machine in a huge number of ways. For small problems, each PE may be able to hold a full copy of the program graph, thus allowing the dynamics of the program graph to do more at run-time. However, if a node cannot hold the whole graph, then the static decision of which graph section goes where becomes a major contributor to the load balancing process.

16.4 Key Items that Need to Be Measured

Given the basic structure of dataflow machines and the general implications this structure has on performance and measurement, our discussion group identified five primary areas that were almost certain to require measurements. These five areas were: algorithm quality measures, theoretical versus achieved speeds, processor utilization, network communication load, and storage occupancy. This section tries to elaborate on our rationale behind the selection of these areas as being most critical.

The first area, the quality of the algorithm (and its translation into graphs), should be obvious. In any system the machine is limited by the algorithm it is given to execute. We highlighted this point heavily because of its added importance in the dataflow world. With less control over the actual run-time scheduling and resource allocation system, we need to understand the possibilities for execution that much more. Because the static portion of the partitioning and mapping process (which PE's can execute which nodes) can be under compiler and user advice control, this will be one of the biggest factors in determining the overall performance of the program. Any measures of the static program graphs that can consistently relate to the performance of the system at run-time will be enormously beneficial.

In terms of assessing the "goodness" of a particular program execution, our group continually came back to the comparison between the best theoretical execution time for the program and its actual time. For relatively small programs (or more accurately, large programs with small data sets), we can compute the theoretical limit via simulation. In fact, most of the existing dataflow systems already use such a tool routinely. At the present time, we have too little experience to determine what are likely to be good and bad ratios for various systems, but we do believe that this measure is likely to be a cornerstone of analysis.

On the topic of processor utilization, an interesting debate arose about what should be the focal point. Probably the closest view to conventional evaluation of parallel systems would be to focus on the utilization of the ALUs within each PE. If those ALUs are running at full capacity then we must be doing extremely well. However, the other view advocated focused on the usage of a PE as the critical factor; all of the elements of a PE function toward the completion of the computation. For example, the matching store is the scheduling algorithm for the code. In this context, a PE could be working to its limit, without having all of its ALUs running all of the time. In this sense, the previous definition of utilization may be totally unreachable. We went so far as to carry through some interesting test cases that seemed to support this latter definition as the appropriate measure. However, in fairness to the group, I would have to say that this issue seems far from settled. For me, the interesting point is that within the dataflow community even such a simple issue of processor utilization does not yet have a clearcut definition on which all could agree.

One area that seems to be quite similar to the cases of shared and distributed memory systems is that of network traffic. Just as in those systems, we need to know when the network is the limiting factor in the execution of a program. We saw no particular issue in this area that was unique to dataflow, but we wanted to make sure that this area of measurement was recognized as a critical factor in our analysis.

The last general area of importance for measuring and analysis in dataflow systems is that of storage occupancy. A common criticism of dataflow systems (and the constraint on functional nodes) is that this style tends to demand excessive amounts of memory beyond that required by more conventional language approaches. Recent progress in compile and run-time optimizations leads us to believe that we can reduce this excess significantly. However, beyond this issue is still a very basic storage occupancy problem. Two specific areas of storage were repeatedly identified as being critical: structure store and matching store. For scientific programs, the conjecture was that the former is far more likely to be the critical resource. In either case, the problem appears to be quite real and quite difficult to address. In general, scientific programs can require limitless amounts of resources and scientists want to solve the largest possible programs available. In this sense, they will want to run near the limiting capacity of any parallel machine. Because the exact timing of various node executions can change the intermediate amounts of storage capacity required, it is possible that the same program could sometimes run to completion and other times deadlock for lack of resources. To better control these situations, we need to know what the usage levels are during execution for these critical resources. We cannot afford to run at the ragged edges of a machine's capacity.

Probably the most difficult aspect of the measurement question that we found (and left unanswered) was the need to be able to relate each of these measures back to the source code in some meaningful way and also to relate them to each other. As an example, through monitoring processor utilization we discover that partway through a program we find a significant stretch of low usage, where we saw no such low in the program. We need to know what code is being executed during this slow time. Similarly, if we see some apparent hot spot traffic to one PE, is this due to some requirement in the program definition or some coincidence of scheduling to different functions to the same node? Likewise, does this high traffic hotspot correspond to the time when the processor utilization was low or not? This issue looks very difficult!

16.5 Suggested Techniques for Performance Analysis and Measurement

The group discussion identified a variety of tools and techniques that appear to be useful for studying performance analysis and improving program execution. It is important to note, however, that due to the relative immaturity of this area of computing, we believe these are only a starting point of ideas. Many more tools (and probably better ones) are likely to be needed. Three of the tools address analysis performed on the program graph prior to any execution. This can be an important area of analysis because so much of the control of program execution is lost to the machine. The three tools are: theoretical concurrency curves, annotations for these curves, and quality of code analysis. Three other tools deal with codes in execution: adding barriers, special timing nodes, and "radioactive" tokens. I will present each of these six ideas briefly.

Like all other parallel systems, dataflow systems can only exploit the parallelism presented in an algorithm. A concurrency curve plots the maximum amount of parallelism (assuming infinite processors) against time, for a particular program with all of its inputs. Clearly, if this curve shows too little concurrency, the programmer must try a new algorithm. This curve also indicates the theoretically fastest time in which the program could complete. As such, it provides an important standard by which we can compare actual achieved speeds. We consider the concurrency curve to be an absolutely vital tool for performing any analysis on dataflow machines.

Having this curve to study opens the door for a wide variety of analysis related to this curve. For example, just seeing the curve yields no information about how two different functions are able to overlap their execution. We need to be able to relate the content of the curve back to the actual program. For example, it may be useful to color-code each of the different functions in the program and color the area under the curve to represent the execution nodes of each function. Maybe this coloring mechanism could be somehow tied to the labeling scheme used during execution to keep different function invocations separate. Likewise, it may be possible to code the curve to show how the various operations are planning to be partitioned among the PEs. Different colors could represent different PE's to see how the load may be balanced over time.

Another important aspect of performance evaluation is understanding the "quality of code" a machine is attempting to execute. Obviously, part of this issue goes back to the selection of algorithm mentioned previously. However, even if the algorithm is "good," its translation may be weak. Although we were unable to identify many specific code quality measures, it seems like an important area of further study. The one simple measure we do have experience with in scientific codes is the MIPS/MFLOPS ratio. The argument is floating-point operations in some sense represent the necessary work and the remaining operations represent the overhead. The lower the ratio, the better a compiler does translation. Clearly, this is not a concrete argument, because some codes do not require any floating-point operations. However, the concept of careful code analysis does play a critical role in evaluation. We have all seen too many examples of linear speedups, where speedup is maintained by having lots of dubious overhead work keeping otherwise idle processors busy. As an aside, we see this issue as being common to all kinds of parallel processors, not just dataflow systems.

16.5. Suggested Techniques for Performance Analysis and Measurement 259

Moving on to run-time tools for performance measurement and evaluation, we seemed to come back repeatedly to the option of adding artificial "barriers" to dataflow codes to get a handle on activity. Given the often chaotic ordering of executable nodes in a dataflow graph, we believe the ability to add barriers to dataflow graphs will add an important measure of control and understanding. Artificial barriers can be used to delay the initiation of parallel activity that need not be executed quite so quickly. It could also be used as a controlled breakpoint allowing programmers to better understand the "state" of execution at specific points in time. We did find it ironic that while most other types of parallel systems are trying desperately to remove barriers from programs to get good performance, we were actually proposing it as an option for helping in certain cases.

Another suggestion we identified for possibly helping in performance evaluation is a special type of identity/timing node. This node would have one input and two outputs. The input is passed through as an identity operation. The second output is the result of reading some global or local time clock. If two of these were to "surround" a function, we could get some indication of the time taken to execute that function. Likewise you could compare the starts or stops of two different functions. As mentioned earlier, the drawback to this kind of tool is its lack of precision. The timing data from these special node firings may be skewed and meaningless, except at the coarsest of levels.

In general, we identified many kinds of timing data we would like to have in the system to help control resource allocation, but recognized that because of possible traffic delays, the data might be useless by the time it was acted upon. For example, let's assume that we could get the token queue to indicate when the concurrency load is getting too much for the machine to handle. Sending out a token to the manager responsible for dealing out new "token colors" could solve the problem. However, if this token gets caught up in the heavy traffic, its delayed arrival may request the manager to slow down after the problem has worked itself out.

The last idea we discussed for helping with measurements seems to be the most novel, but least well developed. The idea is more of a descriptive concept. Consider being able to selectively make certain tokens radioactive. Such a token travelling across the network would light up its path as it moved. Radioactive tokens going into operation nodes would distribute their radioactivity among the outputs of that operation. Coupled with appropriate visualization tools, it occurred to us that this could provide a wealth of information regarding how the machine was actually executing portions of a program. The color intensity in the readout could indicate the number of tokens, with the radioactive trace, that had passed this point within some specified time period. By highlighting all the inputs to a particular function, you could observe the degree of its parallel execution on the machine. By highlighting all accesses to a particular array, you could see the degree of data parallelism exploited. If we extend this idea to multiple distinct colors of radioactivity we can again try to compare different kinds of activity within the network at the same time.

16.6 Summary

Rather than trying to summarize specific points, I would like to highlight general observations. First, it was clear to me that unlike the areas of shared-memory and distributed-memory systems, dataflow systems are still very much in their infancy. Too few have been built and exercised heavily to really make conclusive statements about what things are needed for effective machine evaluation and performance measurement. What was reflected in our discussions, was more hypothesizing about what we might need. Second, by the very nature of dataflow systems taking over more responsibility for scheduling work in hardware, it means less predictability and understanding on the part of system users. That loss of control over scheduling is what we hope will gain us speed in execution, but it may make it harder to understand the reason when that scheduling fails to perform as we expect. Likewise, the lack of emphasis on timing (other than extreme efforts to balance the processing power within a PE's elements and efforts to balance network transfer speeds) makes meaningful timing measures more difficult. Timing measures in this context seem to be of less value than those in shared or distributed memory systems.

On the up side, dataflow systems do appear to be more amenable to analysis of code and graphs prior to program execution. It seems plausible we will be able to study specific programs with tools that will allow us to examine and exploit possibilities for concurrency. Unlike other types of parallel machines, we seem to be worried about how to control too much concurrency from creating resource deadlocks or intense traffic patterns than finding enough concurrency to get good performance. Obviously the status is premature, but it may be far easier for compilers and programmers to orderly in excess concurrency than to determine what is needed to get more out of a system. Finally, in the direction of new ideas for the future, we think that more graphically-oriented and color-oriented display tools could add a whole new dimension to approaches for performance measurement and analysis in dataflow systems.

References

1. Arvind and D. E. Culler, Dataflow Architectures, *Annual Review of Computer Science I*, 1986, pp. 225-253.
2. J. R. Gurd, C.C. Kirkham, and I. Watson, The Manchester Prototype Dataflow Computer, *Communications of the ACM* 28, 1, January 1985, pp. 34-52.

OCT 0 2 1989